Defensive Killing

Defensive Killing

Helen Frowe

OXFORD
UNIVERSITY PRESS

OXFORD
UNIVERSITY PRESS

Great Clarendon Street, Oxford, OX2 6DP,
United Kingdom

Oxford University Press is a department of the University of Oxford.
It furthers the University's objective of excellence in research, scholarship,
and education by publishing worldwide. Oxford is a registered trade mark of
Oxford University Press in the UK and in certain other countries

First Edition published in 2014

Impression: 1

Published in the United States of America by Oxford University Press
198 Madison Avenue, New York, NY 10016, United States of America

British Library Cataloguing in Publication Data
Data available

Library of Congress Control Number: 2014944418

ISBN 978–0–19–960985–7

Printed and bound by
CPI Group (UK) Ltd, Croydon, CRO 4YY

For Alan, Andrew, Brad, Jimmy, and Jeff

Acknowledgements

Many people have helped me to clarify and develop the ideas in this book. I owe thanks to Yitzhak Benbaji, Jules Coleman, John Cottingham, Andrew Cullison, Jonathan Ichikawa, Steve Kershnar, Harry Lesser, Lionel MacPherson, Gerhard Øverland, Daniel Schwartz, Danny Statman, and Noam Zohar. I owe special thanks for written comments and/or many helpful conversations to David Rodin, Jon Quong, Frances Kamm (especially for letting me borrow her class of Harvard undergraduates for an evening), Jimmy Lenman, Brad Hooker, Adam Hosein, Andrew Williams, Gerald Lang, Massimo Renzo, Victor Tadros, Jeff McMahan, Saba Bazargan, Andréas Lind, John Oberdiek, Peter Vallentyne, Ian Frowe, Michael Neu, Suzanne Uniacke, Guy Sela, James Pattison, David R. Mapel, and Tyler Doggett (this list is probably not exhaustive). Conversations with Victor Tadros (often whilst waiting for planes, trains, or automobiles, but occasionally in rather nicer places) have been especially helpful. As always, I owe super-special thanks to Seth Lazar for his thoughtful comments and encouragement.

I am very grateful to the Leverhulme Trust, which awarded me an Early Career Fellowship during my time at Sheffield that enabled me to do much of the work contained within these pages, and to the University of Kent for a period of sabbatical in 2013. Thanks also to the Knut and Alice Wallenberg Foundation, which has been funding me during the final stages of this work. I'm particularly grateful to my wonderful new colleagues in the Stockholm philosophy department for their enthusiastic support of my obsession with war and killing. Gustaf Arrhenius, Torbjörn Tännsjö, Krister Bykvist, and Staffan Carlshamre all deserve a special mention.

Bits of this book have been presented in various forms at the following conferences, workshops, and department seminars: Nordic Network in Political Ethics; Summer School at Aarhus University; the APA (Pacific Division); The Joint Sessions of the Aristotelian Society and Mind Association; the Society for Applied Philosophy annual conferences; the British Postgraduate Philosophy Association conferences; Philosophy Days Conference (Gothenburg); Harvard University; Boston University; Belgrade University; SUNY Fredonia; York University; Oxford University; Lancaster University; the Open University; Sheffield University; the University of Kent; Brighton University; Glasgow University; MANCEPT; Institute for Advanced Studies, Hebrew University of Jerusalem; Westmont College, Santa Barbara; University of California at San

Diego; Workshop on Self-Defence, Bowling Green State University; Centre for Ethics, Law and Public Affairs, Warwick University; Workshop on the *Ends of Harm*, Rogoznica; UK Association for Legal and Political Philosophy Annual Conference, Cambridge University; Oxford Workshop for Political Philosophy, University of Arizona; Nottingham University; and Stockholm University. I am very grateful to the audiences for their comments. The lovely people at the Centre for Ethics, Law and Public Affairs at Warwick University also organized a workshop on a draft of the manuscript—thanks to Massimo Renzo for arranging this, to the SAP for sponsoring it, and to James Pattison, Vittorio Bufacchi, Victor Tadros, and Jonathan Parry for their comments. Thanks also to all those who attended.

Writing this book has been made immeasurably easier by the support of my friends and family. In particular, Andréas Lind not only discussed, read, and commented on large sections of the text, but also provided a steady stream of tea, wine, and canapés to see me through the difficult stages. He's also put up with my frequent and often prolonged absences without complaint. My dad Ian read and commented on various chunks of the book when it was in Ph.D. form. My mum Julia bore the burdens of visiting me in Boston, New Jersey, and California surprisingly well ('Martha's Vineyard? Well, if I must...'). Clare Crowson, Fiona Whittle, and Emma Crowson have, as always, provided welcome distractions from the world of death and destruction that I usually inhabit, not to mention unfailing support throughout the trickier times of life.

As made evident by the list above, I have been lucky enough to benefit from the support and advice of many excellent philosophers (and good friends) during the course of writing this book, which started out as a Ph.D. thesis. But I would not have pursued philosophy at all had Alan Thomas not gently ushered me towards an MA degree many years ago. His friendship and wisdom have been invaluable ever since. Brad Hooker and Andrew Williams were the best doctoral supervisors I could have hoped for—an unbeatable combination of American enthusiasm and Welsh pedantry. I am eternally grateful for their patience and encouragement. Both have continued to cheerfully offer their support long past my days as a graduate student at Reading. I was equally lucky at Sheffield to have Jimmy Lenman as my official department mentor—an administrative task that seemed to entail lots of nice home-cooked dinners and long walks in the countryside. Jimmy now knows more about just war theory than he ever thought necessary or desirable, and hardly ever complains that I haven't read enough of his papers on metaethics. The time I spent at Rutgers with Jeff McMahan has had a profound influence on both the direction of my philosophical interests and my understanding of how to do philosophy. Jeff has been more generous with his time and support than I could ever have expected. I hope these five wonderful people will not mind sharing a dedication (I suspect that writing them a book each would be beyond me).

Helen Frowe

Cambridge, May 2014

Contents

Introduction: Aims and Methods 1

Part I. Self-Defence 19

1. Threats and Bystanders 21
   - 1.1 The Orthodox View 22
   - 1.2 The Problem of Obstructors 25
   - 1.3 Culpable Bystanders? 26
   - 1.4 A New Taxonomy 31
   - 1.5 'Threat' as a Non-moralized Notion 40
   - 1.6 Direct and Indirect Threats 43
   - 1.7 Summary 45
2. Killing Innocent Threats 46
   - 2.1 Thomson's Account of Self-Defence 47
   - 2.2 The Moral Equivalence Thesis 48
   - 2.3 Ways of Killing 51
   - 2.4 Quong's Account of Permissible Defence 54
   - 2.5 Direct Threats 63
   - 2.6 Summary 70
3. Moral Responsibility and Liability to Defensive Harm 72
   - 3.1 Agential Responsibility and Moral Responsibility 74
   - 3.2 Moral Responsibility 75
   - 3.3 Mistakes and Reasonable Opportunities 80
   - 3.4 Summary 86
4. Liability and Necessity 88
   - 4.1 Accounts of Liability 88
   - 4.2 Internalism and Externalism, and the Importance of Liability 91
   - 4.3 Moral Luck 94
   - 4.4 Ineffective Force 97
   - 4.5 Insufficient Force 99
   - 4.6 The Pluralist Account 102
   - 4.7 Against Punitive Justifications for Harming 106
   - 4.8 Honour-Based Justifications for Harming 109
   - 4.9 Prohibitions on Counter-Defence 115
   - 4.10 Honour and Necessity 116

4.11 Liability and Proportionality 118
4.12 Summary 119

Part II. War 121

5. War and Self-Defence 123
5.1 Just Cause and *ad bellum* Proportionality 124
5.2 Responsibility for Mediated Harms 129
5.3 The Revised Defence Account 135
5.4 Political Interests and Reductivism 139
5.5 Proportionality and a Reasonable Prospect of Success 147
5.6 An Essentially Political Requirement? 156
5.7 Summary 160

6. Non-combatant Liability 162
6.1 The Principle of Non-combatant Immunity 164
6.2 Intervening Agency 166
6.3 McMahan's Account of Non-combatant Liability 172
6.4 Ignorance 181
6.5 Risks of Threatening, and Risks That One's Threat Is Unjust 184
6.6 Summary 186

7. Non-combatant Immunity 188
7.1 Broad Liability and Narrow Liability 189
7.2 The Identification Problem 195
7.3 The Isolation Problem 196
7.4 Summary 197

8. Implications and Objections 198
8.1 Terrorism 198
8.2 The Red Cross Objection 202
8.3 The Unlimited Casualties Objection 207
8.4 Taxation 209
8.5 Summary 213

Bibliography 215
Index 219

Introduction: Aims and Methods

Self-Defence

It is generally impermissible for people to inflict non-consensual harm on others. One exception to this general prohibition is the use of defensive force. Most people believe that it is at least sometimes morally permissible for a person to engage in self-defence—that is, to use force against another person or persons in order to protect herself from harm. Most people also believe that it would be permissible to use force to protect some other innocent person from harm (we usually call this 'other-defence'). But while most people agree that the use of defensive force can be permissible, there is considerably less consensus about when and why such force may be employed.

The 'when' is difficult because, although most people subscribe to the notion that defensive force must be necessary and proportionate, it's not obvious what *counts* as necessary or proportionate force. The 'why' is no less controversial, because it determines the range of people whom it's permissible to harm in self-defence. If, for example, we think that the reason why we may harm an attacker is that she deserves to be harmed, it seems that the scope of permissible defence is limited to culpable attackers (such as those who threaten from greed, malice, or jealousy). And whilst many attackers *are* culpable, some have only a lesser degree of moral responsibility, perhaps because they threaten as a result of a mistaken belief that doing so is necessary to save their own life. Still more attackers are wholly innocent. Examples of innocent threats include a person who threatens as a result of an illness that causes paranoid delusions, a person who suffers uncontrollable seizures that cause him to dangerously flail his arms around, and a foetus whose presence threatens its mother's life.

But, if we jettison the idea that only the culpable are legitimate targets of defence, we risk spreading our net too wide. Most people want to retain a prohibition on killing 'innocent bystanders' in the course of saving our own lives. For example, it seems clearly impermissible for me to lethally use your body to shield myself from an attacker even if this is the only way in which I can save my own life—that is, even if killing you is both necessary and proportionate. If killing bystanders is indeed wrong, the correct account of why we may use defensive force should explain this wrongness.

In this book, I aim to tackle some of the philosophical problems that arise in the context of permissible defence. I should stress that this is a moral enquiry: I am not seeking to establish rules by which we might legislate the use of defensive force (although it is of course a good thing if our legislation is philosophically informed and philosophically sound). I begin by considering the use of defensive force between individuals. I consider the different roles that people can play with respect to threats to our lives, and develop a view that permits us to use force against innocent threats whilst prohibiting the harmful use of bystanders.

I also pay considerable attention to what I call indirect threats—that is, people who are not going to inflict harm upon anyone, but who nonetheless contribute to threats. My interest here is twofold. First, as I argue, a complete and plausible account of the ethics of self-defence needs to distinguish between the different sorts of threat that a person can pose. Second, the later part of my inquiry concerns the ethics of killing in war, and many of the threats posed in war are indirect threats.

War is typically thought of as another exception to our usual prohibitions on the use of force. But over the last two decades, traditional just war theory—a very state-based, collectivist approach to war—has been significantly undermined by a revisionist position known as reductive individualism.[1] Reductive individualists hold that it is a mistake to think of war as a morally distinctive enterprise, governed by rules that are irreducible to the moral rules of ordinary life. Rather, the rules that govern harming in war are the rules that govern harming between individuals. Defensive war is not, on this view, *another* exception to our prohibition on the use of force, in addition to the exception that permits individual defence. Rather, war is the *very same* exception as individual defence. If this is correct—and I think that it is—our accounts of individual defence have much work to do. They will determine not only the permissibility of defensive killing in domestic life, but the permissibility of much of the harming that occurs between the members of states or other groups who find themselves on the opposing sides of a war. In this book, I'm especially interested in what this might mean for the permissibility of harming non-combatants who contribute to their country's unjust war.

The Method, and Some Methodological Assumptions

In first part of the book I develop and defend an account of when and why we are permitted to use force to save our own lives. In the second part, I apply this

[1] See, especially, Jeff McMahan, *Killing in War* (Oxford: OUP, 2009).

account to certain aspects of harming in war. The argument throughout is primarily developed by considering a variety of thought-experiments designed to help us identify the necessary and sufficient conditions for permissible defence. The philosophical analysis I employ is informed by both intuitive responses to these cases and a desire to develop a coherent, principled framework that explains these responses. The cases deal almost exclusively with defence against lethal harms. I focus on whether Victim may kill or harm a person in order to avoid being killed himself. But the argument is intended to apply, *mutatis mutandis*, to defence against non-lethal harms as well. I assume a non-consequentialist perspective throughout the book. I do not offer an explicit defence of the merits of this perspective compared to those of its rivals. Rather, I hope that the account I develop will, by its coherence and attractiveness, serve as evidence of the resources and benefits of the non-consequentialist view.

The account I develop does not aim at uncovering a single principle that can capture and explain all instances of permissible defence. The situations in which we might need to defend ourselves, and the types of threat that people might pose to us, are, I think, too complex to lend themselves to this sort of neat resolution. My central aim is to identify the range of considerations that are relevant to our judgements concerning permissible defence, and develop an account that gives us some insight into why these considerations matter and how they interact with each other. I hope that the result is sufficiently fruitful and robust to make this endeavour worthwhile.

The hero of our tale is Victim, who suffers a frankly implausible number of attacks and mishaps in order that we might notice the salient features of cases in which a person can prevent harm to him or herself only by killing someone else. Unless otherwise stipulated, the threat of harm that Victim faces can be assumed to be an *unjust threat*. An unjust threat is a threat of a harm that Victim has a right not to suffer. Amongst other things, this means that Victim is not *morally liable* to the harm that he faces.

On my account of liability, a person is morally liable to a harm if she lacks a right against having that harm inflicted upon her *because she has forfeited her usual rights by behaving in a particular way*. Forfeiture is but one way that a person can come to lack rights. On my account, forfeiture requires voluntary behaviour. It is possible to lose one's rights through involuntary behaviour (or wholly independently of one's behaviour), but such losses are not examples of forfeiture. For example, a person with advanced dementia can lose her right to drive, but this is not because she has forfeited her usual right to drive by behaving in a particular way. Rather, the loss is entirely involuntary, arising as it does from a medical condition that is beyond the agent's control.

As I shall argue, liability to a defensive harm cannot be entirely involuntary. Rather, only those who are morally responsible for an unjust threat can be liable to defensive harm—that is, only these people can forfeit their usual rights against defensive harm. When someone is liable to a defensive harm, she is not wronged by the infliction of that harm. And, ordinarily, she may not harmfully defend herself against that harm. But, as will become clear, that a person is liable to a defensive harm does not entail that it is all-things-considered permissible to harm her. It might be, for example, that an attacker is liable to be harmed, but has positioned herself in such a way that harming her would cause disproportionate collateral harm to other people who have rights not to be killed. In such a case, it would be all-things-considered impermissible to harm the attacker, even though she herself is liable to be harmed. This distinction between liability and overall permissibility is important in both self-defence and war.

The second part of the book takes our findings about interpersonal defence and uses them to illuminate certain aspects of killing in war. In so doing, I adhere to the reductivist view described above that the moral rules that govern harming within war are, ultimately, the same rules that govern permissible harming between individuals outside of war. My aim here is partly to defend and partly to develop this reductivist view of war.

The cases I discuss throughout the book are both simple and fantastic. They are simple so that we can more easily isolate the variables that influence our intuitions about whether a person may use force in a given case, and more easily compare and contrast the cases with each other. They are fantastic so that we can cover a wide range of situations and thus more thoroughly test our intuitions and principles.

Some people might wonder why, with all the available real-life examples of killing, especially killing in war, philosophers often make up these simple and fantastic cases. Wouldn't it be more realistic (and perhaps more exciting) to illustrate our arguments by drawing on the array of examples provided by legal and military history? I suspect that this sort of question is partly motivated by a desire for philosophy to be 'relevant' or 'practical' in a sense easily recognizable by both other philosophers and those working in related fields, and partly motivated by a worry that whatever we say about these artificial cases, no matter how interesting, just won't transfer to actual cases of killing in real life. The cases are *too* simple and fantastic to offer such guidance.

As I understand philosophy—even moral or political philosophy—its practicality does not lie solely in its ability to churn out answers to particular real-life cases. This is not to say that philosophy cannot produce such answers—it can and it does, and this is no bad thing. On the contrary: it is good that philosophers adopt a variety of means and ends, and there are certainly enough of us around to be able to do this without detriment to our subject. But philosophy's practicality can sometimes lie in its ability to clarify our ideas and our thinking before we get to the level of real life, and this is often best achieved by being one or two steps removed from real-life cases. Stripping away the detail can enable us to identify general principles that can be obscured by the intricacies of historical cases.

This is especially so in war. For example, imagine that one is investigating whether there is a moral presumption against firebombing—a notoriously indiscriminate method of warfare. The most natural real-life example to use to illustrate this question is of course the firebombing of Dresden by the Allies during the Second World War. But once we invoke a historical example like Dresden, we cannot help but import our existing judgements about the wider context of that example—about the justness of the Allied war against Germany, the evils of the Nazi regime, perhaps the collective guilt of the German people, and so on. Rather than helping us clarify the morality of firebombing, our focus inevitably shifts to the overall justification of the Allied war, and to whether firebombing was justified *in that particular case*. This is indeed an important question, but it is not the question that we were seeking to answer. We wanted to know whether there is a moral presumption against firebombing *in general* in virtue of its intrinsic features. We need not assume that this presumption can never be overridden, but we do need to answer this general question before we can begin to address more particular questions. We cannot forgo the abstract groundwork if we want to provide illuminating answers to real-life cases.

The second concern about the applicability of our findings is perhaps best elaborated as the thought that, whilst it might be all very well to pronounce on what a person ought to do when we stipulate certain facts, those acting in self-defence in real life are acting without such stipulation, in conditions of fear and uncertainty. This concern, of course, is only exacerbated in war. Thus, we might think, the claims we make about the artificial cases can't help us in real life. But I think this inference is mistaken. When we are deciding how to act, we must, of course, proceed on the basis of the evidence available to us—on what we take the facts to be. But we nonetheless need things to *aim* at when in conditions of partial ignorance. Our deliberations should be guided by the principles or rules that will obtain if our beliefs about the facts turn out to be correct. It's these principles or rules that we seek to establish in moral enquiry. We don't need to know whether it's true that a person will be killed if he doesn't defend himself in order to know whether, *if it is true* that he will be killed if he doesn't defend himself, it is permissible for him to do so.

We should also remember that moral theory is not legal theory, even when it deals with topics such as self-defence that clearly raise legal questions. Whilst we do want our legal systems to be guided by our best moral theories, the question 'What may I do?' is not the same as 'What will I be prosecuted for?', or even 'What should I be prosecuted for?' Nor is it the same as 'What should I be blamed for?' These are all important questions, but they are not the questions that I am addressing here. However, this point notwithstanding, it is surely desirable to legislate on the basis of what we would want people to do were they thinking clearly and in possession of the facts. The same is, I think, broadly true of a moral account of permissible killing. We can have mechanisms in place to deal with cases in which people may be acting under difficult conditions or with limited knowledge, and we can distinguish between permissibility and blame. But we need not and should not place these considerations at the centre of either our moral or legal theories.

The Argument

Part I: Self-Defence

The account defended here holds that it is permissible for an innocent person (Victim) to kill another innocent person who will otherwise kill him. It does this whilst retaining the widely held and desirable prohibition on killing bystanders in the course of saving one's own life. However, a central tenet of the account is that many characters who are traditionally classed as bystanders are in fact threats, and that it can sometimes be permissible to kill these characters in the course of saving one's own life.

In Chapter 1, then, I begin with existing accounts of the distinction between a threat and a bystander. This distinction plays a key role in Michael Otsuka's influential account of why it is impermissible to kill innocent threats.[2] Otsuka's Moral Equivalence Thesis holds that it is impermissible to kill bystanders, and that there is no morally significant difference between killing a bystander and killing an innocent threat. Thus, killing innocent threats must also be impermissible.

Judith Thomson's argument in favour of a permission to kill innocent threats also relies upon a distinction between threats and bystanders.[3] Thomson argues that, unlike bystanders, even innocent threats are on course to violate Victim's

[2] Michael Otsuka, 'Killing the Innocent in Self-Defense', *Philosophy and Public Affairs*, Vol. 23, No. 1 (1994), 74–94.

[3] Judith Jarvis Thomson, 'Self-Defense', *Philosophy and Public Affairs*, Vol. 20, No. 4 (1991), 283–310.

rights, and that this explains why innocent threats (but not bystanders) can be permissibly killed.

I show that both Otsuka and Thomson have faulty conceptions of what it is to be a bystander. Both include as bystanders characters who contribute to the threat to Victim's life. Because Otsuka and Thomson believe that it would be impermissible for Victim to kill these characters to save his own life, they mistakenly infer that this means these characters are bystanders. But, as I argue, it is not only bystanders whom it is impermissible to kill. There are some types of threat whom it is also impermissible to kill. So, we should not infer from the impermissibility of killing a person that she is a bystander.

I argue for a non-moralized account of what it is to be a threat or a bystander. By non-moralized, I mean that on my account the facts that determine whether a person is a threat or a bystander are not moral facts about whether one may kill her to save one's own life. I distinguish between four characters: onlookers, bystanders, indirect threats, and direct threats. A person is an *onlooker* if she meets two conditions: (i) she does not contribute to a threat to Victim, and (ii) neither the intentional harming of her, nor an action that harms her as a side-effect, will avert or mitigate the threat to Victim. Given this definition, we can see why onlookers are not interesting to accounts of permissible defence—they don't threaten, and actions that harm them serve no purpose in averting the threat to Victim. I therefore say little about onlookers here.

I define a *bystander* as a person who does not contribute to a threat to Victim, the intentional harming of whom *would* avert or mitigate the threat to Victim. I define an *indirect lethal threat* as a person who contributes to the threat to Victim's life, but who is not going to kill Victim. This category includes indirect lethal causes—a person whose movements, presence, or actions are causally upstream of a direct threat to Victim's life. A *direct lethal threat* is a person who is going to kill Victim. I include as direct threats those who (will) kill Victim through the use of a tool, where Victim's death is causally downstream of the threat's actions, movements, or presence, and there is no intervening agency between the threat's actions, movement, or presence and Victim's death.

With this new taxonomy in place, Chapter 2 shows how the mistaken conception of bystanders undoes both Thomson's argument in favour of a permission to kill innocent threats and Otsuka's claim that killing innocent threats is morally akin to killing bystanders.

Thomson claims to endorse a causal account of what it is to be a bystander, describing a bystander as someone who is causally uninvolved in the threat to Victim's life. She includes in this category people who obstruct Victim's escape from something else that threatens him, for example by blocking a bridge that

Victim needs to cross. But this turns out to be implausible. I think that Thomson would want to endorse a permission for Victim to kill a person who *maliciously* blocks his escape route from some lethal threat—it seems very plausible that such a culpable obstructor would be a legitimate target of defence. This is worrying enough for Thomson: if she sanctions such a killing, she is, by her own lights, endorsing the killing of a bystander. Cases like this show why her account of what it is to be a bystander is incorrect. But even more problematic is that if Thomson grants a permission to kill such a person—irrespective of what we call her—she cannot restrict this permission to only those who culpably obstruct. If such a person can be killed, it must be because she is going to violate some right of Victim's. But Thomson's account of self-defence does not distinguish between the culpable and the innocent when it comes to rights violation. A permission to kill a culpable obstructor must therefore extend to permit the killing of innocent obstructors as well, something that strikes most people (including Thomson) as impermissible. Thomson's account of the permission to kill innocent threats is therefore also incorrect.

Otsuka rejects Thomson's account of the wrongness of killing bystanders. He argues that it is their lack of lethal agency that makes it impermissible to kill bystanders. But innocent threats also lack lethal agency. There is therefore no moral difference between the killing of a bystander and the killing of an innocent threat. But Otsuka is mistaken to think that the impermissibility of killing bystanders stems from their lack of lethal agency. Drawing on the discussion in Chapter 1, where I argue for a narrower account of bystanders, we can see that the wrongness of killing bystanders come from the fact that bystanders are not lethal. They do not contribute to the threat to Victim's life. This means that bystander killings are necessarily *exploitative*. Killing a bystander will always be aimed at making use of her in some way (for example, by employing her as a human shield). But this wrongness can hardly be found in the killing of an innocent threat. Such a killing is eliminative, not exploitative, since it aims at removing the threat that she poses, not deriving a benefit from her presence. Otsuka's argument that the killing of an innocent threat can be morally assimilated to the killing of a bystander is therefore mistaken.

Jonathan Quong has independently developed a similar critique of Otsuka's view, drawing attention to these differences between types of killing.[4] Quong then draws upon these differences to defend an account of permissible killing based upon the idea of agent-relative permissions. I show that Quong's account, which also relies heavily upon ownership of resources, fails to ground a plausible

[4] Jonathan Quong, 'Killing in Self-Defense', *Ethics*, Vol. 119, No. 3 (2009), 507–37.

account of self-defence. Quong's view is overly permissive, and generates different permissions in morally similar cases.

My account holds that three considerations can justify harming an innocent person in self-defence. The first is that harming her is the lesser evil—that is, harming her inflicts significantly less morally weighted harm than Victim will otherwise suffer. The second is that she is going to inadvertently and non-defensively harm another innocent person—that is, she poses one kind of innocent direct threat. The fact that someone is going to non-defensively harm an innocent person is morally significant even if the threatening person is also morally innocent and threatens only inadvertently. On my account, as in Victor Tadros's recent work, these two considerations combine in the case of self-defence against an innocent direct threat to make inflicting even lethal harm permissible as a means of saving Victim's life.[5] An innocent person has a duty to bear significant, but not lethal, cost to prevent herself from inadvertently non-defensively killing Victim. And, as Tadros argues, the infliction of the remaining, morally weighted harm that exceeds what the innocent threat has a duty to bear can be justified as a lesser evil. The innocent threat suffers significantly less morally weighted harm if she is killed than Victim will suffer if she kills him.

The third justification for harming an innocent person is that she has intentionally turned herself into either a direct unjust threat, or an indirect cause of a direct unjust threat. The latter is the only circumstance in which my view permits Victim to kill an innocent indirect threat to save his own life. A person who knowingly threatens Victim can still count as an innocent threat on my view, provided that she threatens as the result of very good evidence that she lacks a reasonable opportunity to do otherwise. This could include very good evidence that the person whom she threatens is going to non-defensively and unjustly kill her. But, I think that when a person is mistaken about the reasonableness of her opportunity to avoid posing an unjust threat—if, for example, it turns out that the person was not going to kill her after all—she has a duty to bear even lethal costs to stop that threat from eventuating in lethal harm. In these cases, Victim can inflict lethal harm even without a lesser-evil justification and even if the person threatens only indirectly, provided that she is a cause of the direct threat to his life. I defend this view in Chapter 3.

A lesser-evil justification could, in some circumstances, make it permissible to exploitatively harm a bystander. If I can save the lives of a thousand people by lethally pushing a bystander in front of a runaway trolley, it might be permissible to do so. And, if pushing a bystander in front of a trolley would save Victim's life

[5] Victor Tadros, *The Ends of Harm* (Oxford: OUP, 2010).

but cost the bystander a broken arm, this would probably be permissible too. But lesser evil is more demanding than mere proportionality. It would not be permissible to usefully break the bystander's arm merely to save Victim a broken leg. The disparity between the harm averted and the harm inflicted must be very great indeed to justify harming a bystander. In cases where Victim will avert even very serious harm only to himself (or one other innocent person), my account will not permit him to inflict more than a moderate cost upon a bystander.

Lesser-evil justifications can also permit harming innocent indirect threats. Since, unlike with bystanders, killing an indirect threat does not exploit her, there need not be such great disparity between the harm averted and the harm inflicted for a lesser-evil justification to obtain. For example, I am permitted to divert a runaway trolley away from where it will kill five people to where it will kill one on the basis of lesser-evil considerations. But there should still be significant disparity. My account thus prohibits Victim's harming an innocent indirect threat in the course of avoiding a similar or even somewhat greater morally weighted harm to himself, except from in the very limited circumstance described above where the person is a cause of the threat to Victim's life.

Whilst it is nearly always impermissible to kill innocent indirect threats merely to save one's own life, my account holds that it can often be permissible to kill *morally responsible* indirect lethal threats to save one's own life. When a person is morally responsible for the fact that she indirectly threatens an unjust harm—when, for example, she deliberately impedes Victim's only escape route—that person renders herself liable to defensive force.

Chapter 3 develops an account of what it is to be morally responsible for posing a threat. I argue that there need not be any malicious or even harmful intent on the part of an agent in order for her to be morally responsible for posing a threat. Rather, I suggest that a person is morally responsible for posing a threat if she intentionally fails to avail herself of a reasonable opportunity to avoid posing that threat. When the threat she poses is unjust—when it threatens harm to a person who has a right not to suffer that harm—such moral responsibility renders the agent liable to defensive force.

What we need to know, then, is what counts as an *intentional failure* to take a reasonable opportunity to avoid posing an unjust threat, and what counts as a *reasonable opportunity* to avoid posing an unjust threat. I suggest that an agent counts as intentionally failing to take a reasonable opportunity to avoid posing an unjust threat if she correctly believes that a given course of action will expose Victim to an unjust harm, that she has alternative courses of action available to her that are not too costly to her and will not so endanger Victim, and she chooses not to take an alternative course of action. I argue that whether an opportunity to avoid posing an unjust threat is too costly for an agent is sensitive to several considerations, including the cost to the agent of taking the opportunity, the prospective unjust harm to Victim if she does not take the opportunity, the sort of threat that the agent poses, and whether the agent will be allowing herself to threaten or causing herself to threaten. I suggest that the last of these considerations is grounded in the wider moral significance of the doing and allowing distinction.

I argue that the threshold at which an opportunity becomes unreasonable is set lowest in the case of indirect threats who will be allowing themselves to threaten. People posing these types of threats must bear some non-trivial cost to avoid endangering Victim, but they need not bear high costs to do so. This means that lesser-evil justifications cannot permit Victim to use lethal force against a person posing this sort of threat to save his own life. When a person need bear only a moderate cost to avoid posing a threat, using lethal force against her inflicts a significant amount of morally weighted harm. There is thus insufficient disparity between the morally weighted harm she suffers and the harm that Victim averts to himself to make it permissible for Victim to kill her to save his own life. The threshold at which an opportunity becomes unreasonable is set highest with respect to people who will be causing themselves to directly threaten or to indirectly cause a direct threat. People who will pose these types of threat ought to bear even lethal harm rather than kill Victim.

This chapter also considers the responsibility, and liability, of those who make mistakes about whether they have a reasonable opportunity to avoid posing an unjust threat. I argue that if a person has a reasonable belief that an opportunity to avoid posing a threat is too costly for her to be required to take it, her failure to take it doesn't count as an *intentional* failure. This precludes her being morally responsible for posing a threat. But, again, the standard by which we judge whether her belief that the opportunity is too costly is reasonable varies depending on the sort of threat that she will be posing. If she will be intentionally turning herself into a lethal threat to Victim, the bar for a reasonable belief that can preclude liability is set very high. I argue that the same is true when one intentionally contributes to an endeavour that aims at inflicting harm. I shouldn't drive the car for a drive-by shooting unless I have very strong evidence that refusing to do so would result in my bearing more cost than I could be required to bear for the victim's sake. It is in these sorts of cases that, I argue, Victim may use lethal force against an innocent indirect threat in order to prevent her causing him to suffer an unjust harm.

Chapter 4 explores the relationship between liability and necessity. Internalists argue that liability to defensive harm has an internal necessity condition, such that a person cannot be liable to a defensive harm unless it is the least harmful means of averting a threat. This position is usually contrasted with the view that liability is wholly backwards-looking. On this sort of account, a person is liable to defensive harm in virtue of facts about what she has done—about whether, for example, she is morally responsible for an unjust threat. The necessity of harming her can be a constraint on the all-things-considered permissibility of harming her, but it is a constraint that is external to her liability. The threatening person has still forfeited her right against being harmed, irrespective of whether harming her is necessary.

Whether a person is liable to a harm has implications for whether she may defend herself against the infliction of that harm. Prima facie, it looks like internalists permit even a culpable threat to defend herself against the infliction of unnecessary defensive harm, since internalism holds that nobody is liable to unnecessary defensive harm. In contrast, purely backwards-looking externalist accounts deny that a threat may defend herself against unnecessary harm, since she lacks rights against suffering such harm.

I argue that purely backwards-looking accounts cannot succeed as accounts of liability to defensive harm. A harm can count as defensive only if it is a means of averting a threat. It need not be the least harmful means of doing so, but it must be *a* means of doing so. Because backwards-looking accounts of liability sever the link between harming and averting a threat, they justify the infliction of harms that are not even defensive. I argue that such accounts must be rejected. In light of this argument, we can see that a recent attempt by Jonathan Quong and Joanna Firth to undermine internalism fails. Quong and Firth explore insufficiency cases (where the victim can inflict some defensive harm but not enough to avert or mitigate the threat) and impossibility cases (where the victim has no opportunity or ability to fight back). I show that Quong and Firth have misunderstood what internalists say about such cases and explain why their own pluralist view produces largely unconvincing results.

But, I also argue that the insufficiency cases that Quong and Firth discuss are important for theorists of permissible defence because they draw our attention to what looks like the permissible harming of a culpable threat, even when the harming isn't obviously defensive. If, as seems likely, this justification for harming is grounded in the threat's culpability, it will likely have force in other cases involving culpable threats in which Victim can effectively defend himself by harming the threat. This could have implications for a threat's right of counter-defence.

I argue that what justifies harming in insufficiency cases is the defence of the victim's honour. Following Daniel Statman, I argue that a culpable aggressor poses two threats to her victim: the primary threat (such as the threatened physical harm), and a parasitic threat to the victim's honour. In harming a culpable aggressor, a victim can succeed in defending her honour even if she does not mitigate the physical threat. I argue that honour-based justifications for harming do better at capturing our intuitions about these cases than punishment-based accounts.

Having rejected purely backwards-looking accounts of liability, I argue that the only genuine rival to the internalist account is what I call the *proportionate means account*. The account is externalist, because it holds that a person can be liable to more than the least harmful means of averting a threat. But it is not purely backwards-looking, since it holds that a person can be liable to harm on grounds of defence only if that harm is a proportionate means of averting a threat. I argue that combined with an honour-based justification for harming, both internalism and the proportionate means account can cope well with a range of cases involving unnecessary defence. However, in Chapter 6, I argue that we should prefer the proportionate means account to internalism, since it better explains the purposes for which a person may be killed. Specifically, it explains when and why it is permissible to kill one aggressor to avert a threat posed by another.

Part II: War

Although many writers use ideas from self-defence in order to illustrate aspects of war, some think the comparison mere analogy, lacking genuine explanatory power of the sort that can ground the moral principles that govern killing in war. In Chapter 5, I defend a reductive individualist account of war. This account is reductivist because it holds that the rules that govern killing in war are reducible to the rules governing interpersonal killing in ordinary life. Indeed, for a reductivist, war *is* part of ordinary life, insofar as it is governed by the same moral principles that govern all our activities. Reductivists reject the view that there is something morally special about collective political violence, such that those engaged in political violence enjoy special moral permissions. The account is individualist because it holds that individuals are the proper focus of moral theory and evaluation, rather than collectives such as corporations or states.

I concentrate here on recent arguments that reductive individualism cannot make sense of the rules of *jus ad bellum*, or justice prior to war. The first part of the chapter considers the Conditional Force Argument, which has been most fully articulated by David Rodin. This objection holds that reductivist accounts of war cannot permit a state to wage a defensive war against purely political aggression. Political aggression is aggression that directly threatens only 'lesser', political interests—for example, the sovereignty of another state—and that will become violent, threatening 'vital' interests, only if it is resisted. If it is disproportionate for individuals to endanger lives to defend their lesser, political interests, it must also be (by the reductivist's lights) impermissible for states to resist political aggression if they foresee that this will endanger lives. Only if states themselves warrant lethal defence, independent of their members, could lethal force be a proportionate response to threats to sovereignty. But this is to attribute to the state precisely the sort of special permissions to do violence that the reductivist wants to deny them.

The Conditional Force Argument relies in part upon the claim that we are morally responsible for mediated harms—that is, harms that we do not intend or facilitate, but that we predict we will cause others to wrongfully inflict. It is the fact they know that the aggressor state will respond with violence that is said to make the victim state's defence disproportionate. I argue for a revised version of what I call the Defence Account of mediated harms, according to which foreseen but unintended mediated harms are relevant to the permissibility of an agent's defence, but are heavily discounted in her proportionality calculation. I suggest that the cost an agent ought to bear rather than trigger merely foreseen mediated harms to others is limited to that which she ought to bear in order to rescue others from harm. This limits the role that mediated harms can play in making defence—including defensive war—disproportionate.

I also reject the claim that lesser interests cannot warrant lethal defence in their own right. I argue that Rodin is mistaken to think that the distinction between vital interests and lesser interests tracks, respectively, those goods that warrant lethal defence and those that do not. Rather, it tracks those goods that warrant lethal defence without aggregation and those that warrant lethal defence only when sufficiently aggregated. Since political aggression threatens harm to many individuals, and since their interests aggregate, it can be proportionate to use lethal force to avert political aggression. Moreover, it can be proportionate to risk lethal collateral harm to innocent people in the course of averting harm to the lesser interests of a sufficient number of other people.

This chapter also examines the relationship between the *ad bellum* proportionality requirement and the requirement that war have a reasonable prospect of success. I argue that Jeff McMahan and Tom Hurka are mistaken to claim that we can incorporate this requirement into the proportionality requirement. Contra Hurka, wars that have no prospect of success are not disproportionate but rather, like all harms that cannot achieve their goal, unnecessary. Such wars are unjust because they fail the *ad bellum* condition of last resort, not because they are disproportionate. Whereas McMahan and Hurka think that proportionality calculations are sensitive to the probability of a use of force's achieving the desired end, I argue that proportionality calculations must proceed on the assumption that the force to be employed will be successful. Harms that do not succeed do not achieve a good—and this means not that they are disproportionate but that they too are unnecessary.

With this in mind, I argue that the reasonable prospect of success requirement asks us to consider how likely it is that a use of force will be a means of achieving a proportionate end. Thus, whilst the requirement makes reference to proportionality, it is a distinct *ad bellum* condition. I argue that the requirement is motivated by concerns about collateral harm to innocent people. It is therefore primarily a lesser-evil standard, and lesser-evil justifications (unlike proportionality) are sensitive to probability. I then defend this collateral harm-based account against Suzanne Uniacke's claim that reductivism cannot capture the essentially political dimension of the success requirement.

There are, of course, further *ad bellum* requirements, and indeed there is much more to be said about the conditions I discuss here. I do not take myself to give anything like a comprehensive reductivist account of *jus ad bellum*. Rather, my aim is to show that reductivist views are worth taking seriously as accounts of war and can withstand the sorts of objections that have sometimes been thought to decisively undermine them.

Reductive individualism is a revisionary approach to just war theory. Jeff McMahan has forcefully and prolifically argued that adopting this position requires us to rethink our view of the moral status of combatants, since reductivism shows us that unjust combatants cannot be the moral equals of just combatants. I argue in Chapter 6 that reductivism requires a similar revision of our view of the moral status of non-combatants. My argument focuses on the liability of non-combatants in Western democracies who contribute to their country's unjust war. This does not mean that the implications of my argument are limited to non-combatants in such countries, nor to non-combatants who contribute to interstate conflicts. Some of the claims that I make will obtain in other, non-democratic countries. Others will not. If, for example, the citizens of a country fighting an unjust war are exclusively subjected to overwhelming state propaganda that their war is just, this might undermine their moral responsibility for contributing to the war. But many just war theorists believe that even when non-combatants have largely unrestricted access to a range of sources of information, and even when those non-combatants have doubts about the justness of their country's war or firmly believe it to be unjust, they are still not liable to be harmed even if the war *is* unjust and they voluntarily contribute to it. But if what I have said about the liability to defensive harm of those posing indirect threats is correct, then the scope of liable targets in wartime is potentially much wider than these more orthodox accounts of the ethics of war allow.

I set out an argument that it is not only combatants who bear moral and causal responsibility for the harms perpetrated in war. A range of non-combatants—including taxpayers, munitions workers, scientists, and anyone supplying their country's armed forces with either military or welfare goods, including food—contribute to the threat posed by their country. If that threat is unjust, there is a prima facie case for holding those contributors liable to defensive killing by the combatants on the just side of the war.

Several contemporary writers have recognized this prima facie case, but have tried to argue that it *is* only prima facie. David Rodin has argued that, even though non-combatants do contribute to their country's war, these contributions are too causally remote to render the non-combatants liable to defensive killing.[6] Jeff McMahan argues that a number of factors combine to preclude holding non-combatants liable to lethal defence, including the necessity of killing them, the effectiveness of killing them, and the proportionality of killing them. Cécile Fabre also argues that non-combatants do not contribute enough, as individuals, to render themselves liable to defensive killing.[7] Killing them would be disproportionate to the threat that they, individually, pose.

Fabre further claims that non-combatants are not morally responsible for the indirect threats they pose, which on my account would preclude their being rendered liable by those threats. Her argument rests on the idea that non-combatants are non-culpably ignorant about the justness of the threats they pose. Drawing on my claims in Chapter 3, I argue that when one knows that one is causing oneself to pose a threat, one cannot evade liability to defensive harm simply on the basis that one is unsure about whether the threat that one poses is just.

I argue that all these attempts to show that non-combatants are not liable to be killed fail. This conclusion should be unsurprising for those who hold a reductive individualist view of the ethics of war, since the claim that non-combatants are liable to harm best reflects our thinking about the liability of those who contribute to unjust lethal threats to individuals in domestic contexts. If non-combatants have reasonable opportunities to avoid posing indirect lethal threats of unjust harm, and they intentionally fail to take those opportunities, they are liable to defensive killing.

But, as I argue throughout the book, there is a difference between a person's being liable to harm and it's being all-things-considered permissible to harm her.

[6] David Rodin, 'The Moral Inequality of Soldiers: Why *jus in bello* Asymmetry is Half Right', in D. Rodin and H. Shue (eds.), *Just and Unjust Warriors* (Oxford: OUP, 2008).

[7] McMahan, *Killing in War*, 225, and Cécile Fabre, 'Guns, Food and Liability to Attack in War', *Ethics*, Vol. 120 (October 2009), 36–63.

In Chapter 7, I explore the circumstances under which a non-combatant who is morally liable to harm might nonetheless enjoy moral immunity from harm, such that intentionally harming her would be impermissible. One consideration that might generate such immunity is the necessity of killing a person. I begin by considering two rival accounts of the purposes for which an otherwise liable person may be harmed: the narrow and broad accounts of liability. The narrow account holds that a person is liable only to harms that avert a threat for which she is responsible. The broad account holds that once a person is liable to defensive harm, she is liable to be harmed to avert any proportionate threat. I argue that the narrow account is correct as an account of liability, but that it can nonetheless be all-things-considered permissible to harm a person to avert a threat for which she is not responsible. I then argue that once we take into account the macro-threats of war, even the narrow account of liability does not preclude liability in the case of many non-combatants. Killing a person could be necessary for averting those threats even if it is not necessary to avert more specific macro-threats for which she is responsible.

Rather, any immunity from attack that is enjoyed by non-combatants comes from the difficulty of identifying liable non-combatants and the difficulty of attacking liable non-combatants without causing impermissible amounts of collateral harm. These difficulties provide considerable protection for non-combatants. But we ought not to mistake these contingent sources of immunity for a morally significant feature of non-combatants themselves.

In Chapter 8, I elaborate on some implications of my view and anticipate some objections to it. I begin by defending my account against Noam Zohar's claim that views like mine unwittingly endorse acts of terrorism. I also consider the objection that my view sanctions the targeting of neutral medical personnel. I argue that this is indeed a possible upshot of my view, but that this is not an objection, since medical personnel can be morally responsible for contributing to unjust threats. I then address Frances Kamm's concern that my view allows a just combatant to kill any number of liable non-combatants to save his own life. Finally, I consider whether paying one's taxes can be a ground of liability to defensive harm.

PART I

Self-Defence

1

Threats and Bystanders

Individuals are not usually morally permitted to non-consensually harm other people. But most people think that there are some exceptions to this prohibition. The most obvious example of such an exception is the use of force in self-defence. Most people think that it is permissible for an individual to use force if doing so is necessary to defend her against some proportionate harm. Not everyone grants the existence of such a permission—strict pacifists argue that it is always wrong to use force. But most people are not pacifists. In this book, I explore the circumstances under which it is morally permissible to use defensive force.

An innocent threat is typically defined as someone who poses a threat over which she has no control. A foetus whose growth inside a woman's body threatens the woman's life is an example of an innocent threat. A schizophrenic who threatens as a result of uncontrollable paranoid (but temporary) delusions is another example. Whether or not one is permitted to kill an innocent threat to save one's own life is one of the most controversial questions in the ethics of self-defence.

Michael Otsuka argues against such a permission. Part of his argument relies upon what I will call the Moral Equivalence Thesis (MET).[1] This thesis holds that those who innocently threaten are morally equivalent to bystanders. Since most people agree that it is impermissible to kill a bystander in the course of saving one's own life, it looks like it must be similarly impermissible to kill a person who innocently poses a threat.

If we are to resist this conclusion, we must identify some morally significant difference between the killing of an innocent threat and the killing of a bystander. I will argue that much of the difficulty in locating this difference arises from confusion about what it is to be a bystander and what it is to be a threat. In particular, existing accounts of self-defence either ignore or misidentify people whom

[1] Michael Otsuka presents this argument in 'Killing the Innocent in Self-Defense', *Philosophy and Public Affairs*, Vol. 23, No. 1 (1994), 74–94, which offers the most comprehensive and influential rejection of a permission to kill innocent threats. Jeff McMahan cites Otsuka's view as underpinning his own in *The Ethics of Killing: Problems at the Margins of Life* (New York: OUP, 2002), 407–9.

I will call *obstructors*. An obstructor is someone who is not going to kill Victim, but who contributes to the threat to his life by blocking an escape route of which Victim needs to avail himself. Such characters are widely assumed to be bystanders whom it is impermissible to kill. Because of this assumption, advocates of a permission to kill innocent threats have sought to offer some principled basis for distinguishing threats from obstructors, thinking that this must form part of the essential distinction between threats and bystanders.

In this chapter, I argue that it is a mistake to think that obstructors are bystanders. I defend a novel account of the distinction between bystanders and threats. A bystander is a person whose actions, movements, or presence do not endanger Victim. Her presence does not reduce the number of courses of defensive action morally available to Victim. However, harm directed at this person would nonetheless serve to avert or mitigate the threat to Victim: she offers by her presence additional opportunities for averting a threat, compared to those that Victim would have in her absence. I distinguish between indirect threats and direct threats. An indirect threat is a person who endangers Victim, but who is not going to kill Victim. Her actions, movements, or presence would reduce the number of courses of defensive action morally available to Victim, if Victim were not permitted or able to harm that person. A direct threat is a person who is going to kill Victim, if Victim (or a third party) does not act to prevent this.

I argue that this non-moralized account of the distinction between threats and bystanders is to be preferred to alternative accounts. An upshot of the account is that obstructors are not bystanders, but threats. This insight helps us to get the robust distinction between innocent threats and bystanders necessary for resisting the Moral Equivalence Thesis.

1.1 The Orthodox View

1.1.1 *Threats and Bystanders*

As a working definition, we can describe a lethal threat as someone who endangers your life. An *innocent* lethal threat is depicted in *Ray Gun*:

> *Ray Gun*: Falling Person is blown by the wind down a well at the bottom of which Victim is trapped. Falling Person will crush Victim to death unless Victim vaporizes her with his ray gun. If he does not vaporize her, Victim will cushion Falling Person's landing, saving her life.[2]

[2] Based on Robert Nozick's case in *Anarchy, State and Utopia* (New York: Basic Books, 1974), 34.

Falling Person is innocent because, in Michael Otsuka's words, she 'is not responsible for her endangering presence or movements because they are not voluntary, intentional or welcomed by her, and are the product of circumstances completely beyond her control'.[3]

A bystander is generally defined as someone who does not endanger your life. Judith Thomson, for example, says that a bystander is usually someone who is not causally involved in the threat to Victim's life. However, Thomson allows that we might describe someone as a bystander if they have *some* causal role in a threat, provided that it is only a minimal role.[4] The conventional view, then, is that bystanders are, as the term suggests, simply 'standing by' as something else threatens you. Worker in *Trolley* is a typical example of a bystander as found in the self-defence literature:

> *Trolley*: Victim is stuck on a trolley track, with a runaway trolley heading towards him. Victim can save his life only by diverting the trolley down a sidetrack. However, the trolley will then kill Worker, who is lying unconscious on the sidetrack.

There is a widespread consensus that it is wrong to kill bystanders in the course of saving one's own life. But there is significant disagreement about whether Victim may kill an innocent threat such as Falling Person in order to save his own life. This is true even though both sides of the debate agree that Victim is himself morally innocent, by which I mean that Victim has done nothing to forfeit his usual right not to be killed.[5] Since Victim has a right not to be killed, the threat that Falling Person poses to Victim is a threat of unjust harm.

There are various possible explanations of the wrongness of killing bystanders. Two will be central to our discussion here. The first, from Thomson, holds that Victim is permitted to use defensive force against only those people who will otherwise violate his (sufficiently important) rights. Bystanders are not on course to violate people's rights, and this is why killing bystanders is wrong.

Otsuka suggests, contra Thomson, that killing a bystander is wrong because the bystander lacks moral responsibility for what threatens Victim's life. As I will discuss in Chapter 2, it is this similarity between bystanders and innocent threats such as Falling Person that leads Otsuka to claim that killing either is impermissible.

These two positions have framed the debate about the permissibility of killing innocent threats. Given that both sides of the debate make use of the notion

3 Otsuka, 'Killing the Innocent in Self-Defense', 75.

4 Judith Thomson, 'Self-Defense', *Philosophy and Public Affairs*, Vol. 20, No. 4 (1991), 283–310, at 298.

5 In all the cases that follow, Victim is assumed to be morally innocent in this respect.

of a bystander, we ought to be clear about precisely what a bystander is. As I will argue, neither Thomson's nor Otsuka's account succeeds in this respect.

1.1.2 Obstructors

Pedestrian in *Bridge* is an obstructor:

> *Bridge*: Victim is fleeing Murderer, who wants to kill him. Victim's only escape route is across a narrow bridge that has space for only one person at a time. Pedestrian is out for a walk on the bridge, and cannot get off in time to allow Victim to escape Murderer. Only by knocking Pedestrian off the bridge, killing her, can Victim cross the bridge in time to save his own life.[6]

Obstructors are usually described as a sort of bystander. Thomson, for example, says that if Victim were to force his way across the bridge, this would be to '"ride roughshod" over a bystander'.[7] David Rodin talks of 'killing a bystander who was innocently obstructing your escape from an aggressor'.[8] Most people think it impermissible for Victim to knock Pedestrian off the bridge in order to save his own life. Thomson, for example, says that it is, 'plain that [Victim] may not proceed'.[9]

I agree that Victim may not kill Pedestrian in *Bridge*. However, I will suggest that most authors' reasoning proceeds not, as we might expect, from the fact that Pedestrian is a bystander to the conclusion that it would be impermissible to kill her. Rather, it proceeds from the belief that it would be impermissible to kill Pedestrian to the conclusion that she is *therefore* a bystander. This way of reasoning is faulty, and it arises because people have been tempted to allow a person's moral innocence to play a tacit role in determining whether or not she is a bystander. But, as I shall argue, we can and ought to establish whether a person is a threat or a bystander independently of her moral innocence or responsibility. As Jeff McMahan has pointed out, the origin of the term 'innocent' is that of material innocence.[10] The materially innocent are those who are *not noncentes*: not causing

[6] A classic real-life example of an obstructor is the frightened passenger on the sinking *Herald of Free Enterprise* in 1987. As water rose inside the ship, those trapped inside began to escape via a ladder to the deck. One passenger became so terrified that he refused to move up the ladder, blocking the escape of those still inside. Eventually the other passengers threw him off the ladder back into the water where (we assume) he drowned.

[7] Thomson, 'Self-Defense', 290.

[8] David Rodin, *War and Self-Defense* (New York: OUP, 2002), 81.

[9] Thomson, 'Self-Defense', 290.

[10] See Jeff McMahan, 'The Ethics of Killing in War', *Ethics*, Vol. 114 (July 2004), 693–733, at 695, for a discussion of the relationship between these two sorts of innocence.

harm. But a person can be causing harm whilst remaining innocent in the (now more familiar) moral sense of the 'innocent'. For example, Falling Person is materially non-innocent because she is on course to kill Victim. But she is morally innocent—and we call her an innocent threat—because she lacks agency over this fact. In section 1.2, I argue that adopting an account of the distinction between threats and bystanders that does not rely on thoughts about moral status enables us to properly accommodate obstructors in a way that alternative accounts cannot.

1.2 The Problem of Obstructors

Here is Thomson's account of what it is to be (and to not be) a bystander:

> First, if Y is in no way causally involved in the situation that consists in X's being at risk of death, then Y is clearly a bystander to it. And second, if Y is causally involved in it, and not minimally so—as, for example, when it is Y himself or herself who is about to kill X—then Y is clearly not a bystander to it.[11]

This looks like a purely causal account of the threat/bystander distinction—it makes no explicit reference to a bystander's moral innocence. But, nonetheless, I think that an assumption of moral innocence underpins Thomson's idea of a bystander. Imagine a case similar to *Bridge*, but with one important difference:

> *Malicious Bridge*: Victim is fleeing Murderer, who wants to kill him. Victim's only escape route is across a narrow bridge that can hold only one person at a time. Pedestrian is out for a walk on the bridge. Pedestrian could easily get off the bridge in time to allow Victim to escape Murderer. But she dislikes Victim and decides to stay where she is, realizing that this will impede Victim's escape. Only by knocking Pedestrian off the bridge, killing her, can Victim save his own life.

I think it plain that in *this* case, Victim may proceed. He may knock Pedestrian off the bridge in order to save his own life. And, I suspect, Thomson would agree with me. Pedestrian intentionally tries to help Murderer wrongfully bring about Victim's death. But how can Thomson allow for different permissions in these two cases?

According to the orthodox view, Pedestrian is a mere bystander who plays no part in the threat to Victim's life. Now that she *intends* to block Victim's escape, however, Pedestrian seems to be a legitimate target of defensive force. But

[11] Thomson, 'Self-Defense', 298–9.

intending her role in the threat to Victim's life does not alter the role itself. Her part in Victim's death is the same in both cases: it is only her responsibility for playing that part that changes.

It seems to me that this difference in responsibility is sufficient to change Pedestrian from an illegitimate target of force into a legitimate target of force. She takes on, in legal terms, the role of an accomplice. But given the identical causal role that Pedestrian plays in both cases, it is problematic to hold that she stops being a bystander—allegedly a role about causal facts—simply because she is no longer morally innocent.

There are two ways in which we might try to account for the shift in Pedestrian's status from an illegitimate target to a legitimate target. The first is to maintain that Pedestrian is a bystander even in *Malicious Bridge*, but that there can be such things as morally responsible or culpable bystanders who, unlike innocent bystanders, are legitimate targets of force. This could explain why, when she deliberately obstructs Victim, Pedestrian can be permissibly killed. The second option is to deny that Pedestrian is a bystander in either case. Rather, she threatens Victim in both *Bridge* and *Malicious Bridge*. This option allows us to sustain the idea of bystander immunity—a permission to kill Malicious Pedestrian will not be a permission to kill a bystander. But it also narrows the category of bystander so as to exclude obstructors. I will explore and reject the first of these options before arguing for the second.[12]

1.3 Culpable Bystanders?

Jeff McMahan agrees that in *Malicious Bridge*, Malicious Pedestrian is a legitimate target of force. But McMahan also insists that Malicious Pedestrian is a bystander.

> [I]t would be plausible to regard her as liable [to be killed], *even though she would still be a bystander*—for status as a bystander is a matter of one's causal position, not of one's responsibility. She would then be no more a threat than she is in [the original case], but she would be to some degree morally responsible for the threat one faced from the Culpable Threat, which her presence would impede one's ability to escape from ... what matters is not whether one poses a wrongful threat through one's own action but whether one is morally responsible for a wrongful threat.[13]

[12] We might say that there are three options. We could argue that Pedestrian changes from a bystander to a threat on grounds of culpability. This seems to me rather hopeless. It makes it hard to understand why, for example, we would have a category of innocent threat at all, if being a threat is about being culpable.

[13] Jeff McMahan, *Killing in War* (New York: OUP, 2009), 172.

There is something troubling about McMahan's assertion that Victim may kill Pedestrian not because Pedestrian poses a threat, but because Pedestrian is, to some degree, *morally responsible for the threat that Victim faces from Murderer.* How can this be? How can her intentional presence on the bridge make Pedestrian morally responsible for Murderer's pursuit of Victim? I do not think that it can: it isn't *that* for which she is responsible and that grounds a permission to kill her. Rather, by intentionally staying where she, she is responsible for the fact that she further endangers Victim by blocking his only escape route. If Pedestrian and Murderer had colluded in this attack on Victim from the outset, and blocking the bridge is Pedestrian's designated role in the plot, we might *then* assign her some responsibility for the threat that Murderer poses to Victim. But this isn't a necessary feature of the case—in my version above, Pedestrian isn't part of the earlier plan that culminated in Murderer's attack, but simply takes the opportunity to block Victim's escape. This seems to me sufficient to make her a legitimate target of defensive force. But her causal role is identical to that of a wholly innocent person who simply cannot get off the bridge in time.

So, the responsible bystander option strikes me as implausible. And there are other reasons not to adopt it. If we take the option of arguing for a category of responsible bystanders of the sort that McMahan seems to have in mind, we must reject the view that bystanders are not causally involved in what threatens Victim's life. After all, not just *any* wrongdoing will render a person a morally responsible bystander whom Victim can permissibly kill. Victim may not kill Pedestrian because, for example, she is cheating on her husband or fiddling her tax returns. Moral responsibility for these wrongs will not do. Rather, Pedestrian must be morally responsible for a *relevant* wrong. As McMahan says, it is her responsibility regarding a wrongful threat to Victim's life that matters. But I don't see how Pedestrian can be morally responsible regarding a wrongful threat to Victim's life unless she makes some contribution to that threat, where it is moral responsibility *for this contributing role* that makes her relevantly responsible. What could delineate the scope of moral responsibility relevant to the purposes of Victim's defence other than causal relevance to the threat to Victim's life? If Victim is permitted to kill Pedestrian to save his own life, she must be morally responsible for being causally instrumental in the threat to Victim's life.

So, arguing for a category of responsible bystanders undermines the idea that bystanders do not play a causal role in what threatens Victim. Of course, McMahan might argue that Pedestrian has only a minimal causal role, and say (as Thomson does) that such involvement does not preclude one's being a bystander. But, as I suggested above, if we think about the legal and moral status of an accomplice to murder, the 'minimal role' approach seems a rather implausible view of a person who is deliberately blocking Victim's escape route from a lethal threat. Moreover, if Malicious Pedestrian's causal role is only very slight, it is hard to see how killing her could meet McMahan's own understanding of the proportionality condition of self-defence. In his discussion of the attacking of non-combatants in war, McMahan argues that when the contribution of a non-combatant to an unjust threat is very slight, any attack aimed at her would violate the proportionality requirement.[14] If killing Malicious Pedestrian is permissible (or as McMahan puts it, she is liable to be killed), killing her cannot be disproportionate, and thus her contribution cannot be a minimal one. But counting as bystanders people with roles in Victim's death of the sort sufficient to render it proportionate to kill them threatens to collapse the distinction between a threat and a bystander altogether.

In addition, if we take McMahan's view that we are permitted to kill at least some bystanders in self-defence, we undermine the idea that bystanders are off limits. Indeed, if being a bystander entails neither material innocence nor moral innocence—bystanders can play a causal role in a threat, and be morally responsible for that role—describing a person as a bystander will have no implications at all for how we are allowed to treat her. Even if we could maintain a conceptual distinction between threats and bystanders under the pressures described above, we would lose any normative benefit that the distinction brings.

I think that we can see why arguing for the idea of morally responsible bystanders is mistaken by thinking more about the idea of material innocence that I mentioned above. I suggest that, properly understood, the idea of a responsible bystander is not only unattractive, but conceptually incoherent. The innocence of a bystander does not consist in the fact that they are not to be blamed for what they are doing or where they are, as with an innocent threat. They are innocent because they are not doing (nor have they done) anything with respect to the threat to Victim for which blame would be *appropriate*. A bystander is a person who does not make Victim worse off by her actions, movements, or presence. She does not reduce the courses of action that are available to Victim as he tries to save his life. There is thus nothing with respect to the threat to Victim *for which* a bystander can be morally responsible.[15] And it is this that tells us why a

[14] For more on this, see Chapter 6.

[15] It might be objected that someone who makes a laughably inept attempt at murder is materially innocent yet blameworthy. This looks like a counter-example to my claim, since it shows a non-threatening character who is nonetheless culpable. However, my claim is that there is nothing *with respect to the threat to Victim* for which a bystander can be culpable. A person who makes a wholly ineffectual attempt at murder is not culpable with respect to the threat to Victim, because there *is* no threat to Victim. Such a person can of course be culpable with respect to other things (such as making Victim believe that there is a threat to his life, or causing Victim to pose a defensive threat). See Chapter 4 for more on this.

character like Pedestrian is not really a bystander at all. As we have seen, what she is doing is precisely the sort of thing for which she *can* be morally responsible if she does it deliberately. Malicious Pedestrian is culpable for her role in the threat to Victim's life. And, moreover, that role is sufficient to make killing her a proportionate response.

Compare Pedestrian with Signalman in the following case:

> *Tracks*: Victim is stuck on the trolley tracks as a runaway trolley heads towards him. Signalman is standing down the line by the side of the tracks. Only by shooting Signalman, causing him to fall in front of the trolley, can Victim save his own life.

This case depicts someone who really is uninvolved in the threat to Victim's life. Victim would be killed even in Signalman's absence. Whilst Signalman's presence offers Victim an additional course of action for saving his life than Victim would have in Signalman's absence—given that Signalman is there, Victim can use his body to block the trolley—he does not, by his presence, reduce Victim's options for saving his life. Moreover, there is no sense in which Signalman could be relevantly culpable with respect to what he does, because nothing he does is instrumental in the threat to Victim's life. Signalman is materially innocent, and thus there is no part of his behaviour for which blame could be appropriate. He is a genuine bystander.

However, whilst *all* those who can be morally responsible with respect to their position are threats, it is not *only* those people who can be threats. There are some types of threat that are just not the sort of thing for which one can be responsible. For example, the threat posed by a foetus to its mother in a dangerous pregnancy seems to fall into this category. We can properly call the foetus a threat, but it is necessarily an innocent threat.

Someone might resist my claim that there is something conceptually incoherent about the idea of a morally responsible bystander by hypothesizing a case like *Drowning Child*.

> *Drowning Child*: Walker passes a lake on her morning stroll. Child is drowning in the lake. Walker observes Child's predicament, and does nothing to help Child, even though she could easily save her. Child drowns.

Walker is morally responsible for her failure to save Child. But she does not make Child worse off by her presence, for in her absence Child would have drowned anyway. Thus, on my account, it looks like Walker is a bystander, and a culpable one at that.

Compare *Drowning Child* with *Racist Ray Gun*:

Racist Ray Gun: Falling Person is helplessly falling towards Victim. She will crush Victim to death unless Victim vaporizes her with his ray gun. As she falls, Falling Person hurls racist abuse at Victim.

Falling Person is culpable with respect to her hurling of the abuse. And she is clearly a threat to Victim. Put these things together, and it looks as if we have a culpable threat. But this way of reasoning is of course confused, and there is a similar confusion involved in labelling Walker a culpable bystander. As I argued above, it's only relevant moral responsibility that matters: responsibility with respect to what endangers Victim.[16]

We might reply that in this case Walker's culpability is *constituted* by the fact that she is *standing by*. And surely this means that it *is* her role as a bystander for which she is culpable. But this too is a mistake. We can see this because Walker would not cease to be a bystander in the event that she saved Child. It is perfectly sensible to speak of a person's being rescued by a bystander, since it is consistent with being a bystander that one make a person better off for one's presence. So while Walker *is* culpable, because she fails in her duty to save Child, she is not culpable qua bystander, any more than Racist Falling Person is culpable qua threat.

My contention, then, is that the distinction between threats and bystanders has nothing to do with whether or not one is innocent with respect to one's position. Since Malicious Pedestrian is instrumental in the threat to Victim's life, she is not a bystander. And since her position is the same between *Bridge* and *Malicious Bridge*, innocent Pedestrian in *Bridge* is not a bystander either. Both characters are best understood as posing a threat to Victim. This result requires us to devise a new account of threats and bystanders.

[16] Whitely Kaufman, for example, makes exactly this sort of mistake in 'Torture and the "Distributive Justice" Theory of Self-Defense: An Assessment', *Ethics and International Affairs*, Vol. 22, No. 1 (Spring 2008), 93–115, and again in *Justified Killing: The Paradox of Self-Defence* (London: Rowman and Littlefield, 2009), 26. Kaufman suggests a variation on *Dudley and Stephens* to give an example of what he calls a 'culpable bystander'. In the original case, two shipwrecked sailors (Dudley and Stephens) killed Parker, the cabin boy, in order to eat him to ward off starvation. Kaufman says: 'suppose the cabin boy in *Dudley* had earlier tried to kill one of the sailors, but had failed and now was too weak to cause trouble any longer. The remaining sailors cannot kill him on "self-defense" grounds, however culpable he may be, because he is not now an attacker but merely a bystander" (98). Kaufman does almost exactly what I describe in *Racist Ray Gun*: he takes event x, for which the cabin boy is culpable, and conflates it with event y, to which the cabin boy is a bystander. He then pronounces the cabin boy a culpable bystander whom it is impermissible to kill. But the reason why the sailors cannot kill the cabin boy is that he plays no causal role in the threat currently facing the sailors: he is simply a bystander to that threat, and it thus makes no sense to talk of his culpability (or lack thereof) with respect to that threat. He is no more a 'culpable bystander' than he would be if he had hurled racist abuse at the sailors the previous week, or stolen a loaf of bread before setting out to sea.

1.4 A New Taxonomy

I will distinguish between four types of character: onlookers, bystanders, indirect threats, and direct threats.

Onlooker: A person whose movements, actions, or presence do not contribute, and have not contributed, to the threat to Victim. Harm directed at this person would not serve to avert or mitigate the threat to Victim, and no action that would harm the person as a side-effect can avert or mitigate the threat to Victim.

An example of an onlooker is Nosy Parker in *Poison*:

Poison: Villain is poisoning an unconscious Victim. Nosy Parker watches from behind a very high fence that she cannot scale. The dose is deadly and there is no antidote. Nothing can be done to save Victim or mitigate his suffering.

Nosy Parker is an onlooker because she has not contributed to the threat to Victim and no harm directed at her could improve Victim's situation. As with bystanders, it makes no sense to distinguish between morally responsible and innocent onlookers, since there is nothing an onlooker does with respect to the threat to Victim for which she could be responsible or innocent. But whilst bystanders are often interesting to theorists of self-defence (we want to know whether, when, and why they may be harmed), onlookers are outside the scope of even potential permissible harming—at least for the purposes of defence—since they play no role in the threat to Victim *and* harming them can serve no purpose in eliminating the threat.

Bystander: A person whose movements, actions, or presence do not contribute, and have not contributed, to the threat to Victim. Harm directed at this person would serve to avert or mitigate the threat to Victim.

To see the difference between an onlooker and a bystander, compare *Poison* with *Tracks*:

Tracks: Victim is stuck on the trolley tracks as a runaway trolley heads towards him. Signalman is standing down the line by the side of the tracks. Only by shooting Signalman, causing him to fall in front of the trolley, can Victim save his own life.

A bystander, in contrast to an onlooker, is someone the harming of whom could make Victim better off, even though she does not herself contribute to the threat to Victim. So, Signalman in *Tracks* is a bystander because, whilst his presence makes no contribution to the threat to Victim's life, harming him could save Victim's life.

I want to further distinguish between direct and indirect threats.

Indirect lethal threat: A person whose movements, actions, or presence contribute, or have contributed, to the threat to Victim's life, but who will not kill Victim. Contributing to the threat can include helping to bring the threat about, or obstructing a valuable escape route of which Victim could avail himself.

Pedestrian in *Bridge* is an example of an indirect lethal threat.

Direct lethal threat: A person whose movements, actions, or presence will kill Victim unless someone acts to prevent this. A person counts as a direct threat to Victim if she kills him through the use of a tool, if there is no intervening agency between her actions, movements, or presence and Victim's death.

Falling Person in *Ray Gun* is a direct lethal threat. There can, of course, also be cases in which there is more than one direct threat to Victim. This is most obvious when Victim faces multiple, independent attacks. But it can also be true if a person is employed as a tool by someone else, as in *Paralysis*:

Paralysis: Villain uses snake venom to paralyse Friend. He then uses Friend's rigid body to beat Victim to death.

Both Villain and Friend count as direct threats on my account. There is no intervening agency between Villain's beating of Victim and Victim's being killed. Villain kills Victim, just as he would if he had used a bullet or baseball bat instead of a rigid human object. But just as bullets and baseball bats kill their victims, so too does Friend kill Victim.

1.4.1 *Obstructors as Indirect Threats*

The most controversial distinction in this taxonomy will likely be that between a bystander and an indirect threat. The controversy arises primarily because of the obstructor cases I have been discussing: on my account, obstructors count as indirect threats, not bystanders (and the category of obstructors will be more inclusive than generally assumed).

One way in which we can establish whether a person is an obstructor is by asking the following question: if Victim were not permitted, or not able, to harm this person, would this person's actions, movements, or presence reduce the valuable courses of defensive action morally available to Victim, compared to the number of valuable courses of action that would be morally available in her absence?[17] For example, if Victim is not permitted or able to harm Pedestrian in *Bridge*, her presence reduces Victim's morally permissible options for saving his life compared to the options he would have in Pedestrian's absence. If he may not harm her, her presence means that he may not cross the bridge, whereas in her absence he would be so permitted. By 'valuable courses of defensive action', I mean courses of action that are among the least costly means of averting or mitigating the threat to Victim.

But if Victim is not permitted or able to kill Signalman in *Tracks*, Signalman's actions, movements, or presence will not reduce the courses of defensive action morally available to Victim, compared to what they would be in Signalman's absence. If Victim may not harm Signalman, using his body to block the trolley is not a morally available option. The same would be true in Signalman's absence, since then it would not be an option at all.

This test also shows that some people who are not usually identified even as obstructors are in fact threats. Consider again the case I gave earlier as a paradigmatic example of a bystander:

> *Trolley*: Victim is stuck on a train track, with a runaway trolley heading towards him. Victim can save his life only by diverting the trolley down an alternative track. However, the trolley will then kill Worker, who is lying unconscious on the other track.

This case illustrates the classic 'bystander' of the sort that Otsuka uses to argue for the moral equivalence of threats and bystanders.[18] Thomson argues that killing Worker would be 'making a bystander be a substitute victim'.[19] But I do not think that Worker is a bystander at all. If Victim were not permitted to harm Worker, Worker's presence on the tracks will reduce Victim's morally available courses of defensive action, since it will rule out diverting the trolley. Just as in *Bridge*, Worker blocks an escape route of which Victim can avail himself only if he harms Worker. The only difference is that whereas in *Bridge*, Victim needs to get himself down the blocked route, in *Trolley* he needs to send the trolley down the blocked route.

Again, we can further support the claim that Worker is not a bystander by thinking about whether she could be morally responsible for what she does. Consider *Deliberate Trolley*:

[17] We can ask the same question, *mutatis mutandis*, about a third party contemplating rescuing Victim, but for simplicity's sake I'll just focus on Victim.

[18] Otsuka, 'Killing the Innocent in Self-Defense', 85.

[19] Thomson, 'Self-Defense', 290.

Deliberate Trolley: Worker sees the trolley approaching Victim. Knowing that Trolley Driver will not steer down the sidetrack if Worker is on the sidetrack, Worker intentionally remains on the sidetrack even though she could easily get off, because she wants Victim to be killed by the trolley. Victim can shoot and kill Worker, in which case Trolley Driver will steer down the sidetrack, saving Victim's life.

We are supposed to think that Worker in *Trolley* is a bystander. And, Worker's position in *Deliberate Trolley* is the same as in *Trolley*. When she intends to be on the tracks, however, Worker seems to pose a culpable threat to Victim. She is deliberately trying to stop Trolley Driver from saving Victim's life. But the fact that Worker intends to contribute to the threat to Victim's life is not what makes it the case that she contributes to that threat. Like Pedestrian, Worker's role in Victim's death is the same whether she plays it innocently or responsibly.

Passer-By in Richard Norman's *Discovery* case is also obstructor, and thus a threat:

Discovery: Victim is hiding from Murderer, who wants to kill him. Passer-By is about to unwittingly stumble upon Victim, whereupon her startled cry will alert Murderer to Victim's hiding place. Only by quietly killing Passer-By before she sees him can Victim save his life from Murderer.[20]

I take hiding (along with running away) to be a type of defensive action. If Victim is not permitted or able to harm Passer-By, her actions will decrease the number of defensive actions available to him, since hiding will no longer be a way of saving his life. And, we can easily imagine a variation of *Discovery* in which Passer-By deliberately gives Victim away. In this case, she would play the same causal role in Victim's death, but with malicious intent, hoping to reveal Victim's hiding place to Murderer. However, she's not going to kill Victim, and thus she counts as an indirect threat on my account.

The test I've suggested for identifying obstructors asks us to consider what would happen if Victim were not permitted or not able to harm a given person. So far, I've focused on Victim's not being permitted to harm that person. But there might be cases in which Victim is not able to harm a person, irrespective of whether or not he is permitted to do so. Depending on the case, this can affect whether or not a person poses a threat.

[20] Richard Norman, *Ethics, Killing and War* (Cambridge: CUP, 1995), 126.

Heavy Bridge: Pedestrian is unconscious on the bridge. She is so heavy that Victim cannot move her out of the way.

Helpless Trolley: A runaway trolley is heading towards Victim. Worker is standing on a nearby sidetrack. Victim has no way of diverting the trolley down the sidetrack.

In *Heavy Bridge*, Pedestrian obstructs Victim's escape and poses a threat to him. Since he's not able to harmfully move her, her presence reduces the number of courses of valuable defensive action available to Victim, compared to her absence. But in *Helpless Trolley*, since Victim cannot divert the trolley down the sidetrack irrespective of whether or not Worker is present, Worker does not, by his presence, reduce the number of courses of defensive action available to Victim.

These cases depict situations in which Victim has only one possible escape route. But what if there is more than one way in which Victim can avoid or avert a threat?

Multiple Bridges: Victim is fleeing Murderer, who wants to kill him. There are two bridges across the ravine. Pedestrian is occupying one of the bridges. Crossing either bridge will equally enable Victim to escape Murderer.

If Victim is not permitted to harm Pedestrian, her presence reduces the courses of defensive action available to Victim. But it doesn't seem that she reduces the number of valuable courses of action, since Victim has another, equally effective and equally costly, way of evading Murderer. Cases like this help us to see why the cost to Victim of taking an escape route matters for whether or not a person poses an indirect threat. In a case where Victim has multiple (equally effective and costly) ways of escaping a threat, Pedestrian's presence doesn't seem to matter—the bridge she occupies isn't a valuable way of escaping Murderer. But imagine that the second bridge is very old and rickety, and Victim is likely to incur some serious injury if he attempts to use it, or may fail to get across the ravine at all. In these cases, Pedestrian's presence does matter: if Victim is not permitted to harm her, the number of valuable courses of defensive action avail to him is reduced, since crossing the bridge that she occupies is the least costly (and perhaps most effective) way of escaping Murderer. In this case, Pedestrian indirectly threatens Victim.[21]

[21] Thanks to Nicola Kemp for pressing me on this point. Many thanks to Victor Tadros for helping me deal with it.

1.4.2 *More Indirect Threats*

So, thinking about these questions will distinguish obstructors from bystanders. But it will not capture all those people who, intuitively, count as indirect threats. For example, it won't capture Mafia Boss:

> *Mafia*: Mafia Boss hires Hit Man to kill Victim. Harming Mafia Boss will not serve to avert or mitigate the threat to Victim—Mafia Boss has paid Hit Man in advance, and Victim cannot make use of Mafia Boss's body to avert the threat or shield himself against it, nor will any potential course of defensive action against Hit Man harm Mafia Boss as a side-effect.

Under these circumstances, if Victim is not permitted or able to kill Mafia Boss, Mafia Boss's movements, actions, or presence do not reduce the courses of defensive action morally available to Victim. Since there is anyway no course of action that harms Mafia Boss that can stop Hit Man's attack, Mafia Boss's presence doesn't make him worse off. But, given his clear contribution to the threat facing Victim, I should think that we want to include Mafia Boss as an indirect threat. He's not going to kill Victim, but his role in the threat to Victim's life is the sort of role for which one could be culpable, since Mafia Boss *is* culpable with respect to that role. I'll call this sort of indirect threat an indirect cause.[22] An indirect cause is someone whose actions, movements, or presence are causally upstream of the direct threat to Victim. All direct threats—those who will inflict harm upon Victim—are causes, but not all causes are direct threats. Mafia Boss, for example, is not a direct threat—Hit Man, not Mafia Boss, kills Victim—but his actions are instrumental in bringing about the direct threat.

Any account of contributing to a threat that includes Mafia Boss is probably going to be quite broad. This means it will capture lots of people whom we don't usually think of as posing a threat. For example, it will also cover those making more remote causal contributions, as in *Baseball*:

> *Baseball*: Bob makes baseball bats for a living. The vast majority of his bats are used for playing sport. But Bob knows that there is a small chance that someone will use one of his bats to kill someone. One day, Customer buys one of Bob's bats. A week later, Customer uses the bat to try to kill Victim.[23]

[22] The label isn't ideal, since Pedestrian is also causally relevant to Victim's death, but as I'll use it, it refers only to those whose actions are upstream of the *direct* threat to Victim—the thing that will kill (or harm) Victim.

[23] I think I owe this particular case to Gustaf Arrhenius.

Bob's actions have, in an obvious sense, materially contributed to the threat to Victim's life. But we do not think that Bob is liable to be killed by Victim—that Victim could, for example, permissibly employ Bob as a human shield against Customer's attack.

Clearly, then, given the broad scope of my account of what it is to pose a threat, the category of permissible targets of defensive force is not going to correspond to the category of 'threat'. In Chapter 2, I argue that there is a morally significant distinction between killing direct threats and killing bystanders that answers the challenge posed by the Moral Equivalence Thesis. I then argue that there's also a morally significant distinction between direct threats and indirect threats, such that it can be permissible to kill innocent direct threats but not, in general, innocent indirect threats. Absent a lesser-evil justification for harming them, indirect threats are permissible targets of force only when they are morally responsible for posing a threat. In Chapter 3, I defend an account of moral responsibility for posing a threat, which requires, amongst other things, that a person realize that her actions endanger Victim, and that she has a reasonable opportunity to avoid so endangering Victim. Given this account of responsibility, only a subset of those who are indirect threats will be permissible targets of defensive force.

1.4.3 *Shields of Threats*

One of the most persuasive parts of Otsuka's argument for the impermissibility of killing innocent threats comes from his comparison of the following three trolley cases:

(1) An innocent person is lying alongside the path of a runaway trolley. Unless Victim hurls at the trolley a bomb that will destroy the trolley but will also kill the innocent person, the trolley will kill him.
(2) An innocent person is trapped *inside* the trolley. Unless Victim throws a bomb, destroying both the trolley and the innocent person, he will be killed.
(3) There is no trolley, but merely a falling person. Unless Victim vaporizes the person, she will fall on him and kill him.[24]

It is, says Otsuka, clearly impermissible to hurl the bomb and kill the innocent person in the first case. Moving the location of the innocent person in the second case should not make any moral difference, and thus hurling the bomb must be similarly impermissible. In the third case, the removal of the trolley should make no difference (it was, after all, the presence of the person that made throwing the bomb impermissible in the second case). And the third case is the case of the

[24] Otsuka, 'Killing the Innocent in Self-Defense', 85.

innocent threat, whom it looks like it must be impermissible to vaporize, given the impermissibility of killing the innocent people in (1) and (2).

This argument does not rely upon the claim that in killing the person in the third case, Victim uses her as a means. Rather, it is intended to put pressure on the threat/bystander distinction in a way that makes it hard to argue that killing in (3) is permissible, if killing in (1) and (2) is not. Most people who defend a permission to kill innocent threats would, I think, try to draw the line between the cases in this way. We might argue that in (2) it is the trolley that is going to kill you, not the person trapped inside it. Thus, in both (1) and (2) the innocent person is a bystander, whereas the innocent person in (3) is a threat. But Otsuka gives us good reason not to characterize (2) in this way, arguing that it will lead to 'intuitively bizarre' cases in which it would be, 'impermissible to kill a falling person if it were only the mass of the enormous ski boots attached to her feet that would kill you'.[25]

On my account, all three of the characters depicted in Otsuka's trolley cases count as threats, not bystanders. The person by the side of the tracks in (1) is an indirect threat: if Victim is not permitted to harm her, her presence reduces the morally available courses of action available to him. But I agree with Otsuka that it is impermissible to kill such a person if they innocently threaten.

The person who is trapped inside the trolley as it hurtles towards Victim in (2) is usually referred to in the literature as a 'shield' of a threat. There are two distinct ways in which a person might play the role of a shield.

Shootout: Gunman is shooting at Victim. As Victim begins to return fire in self-defence, Gunman positions himself behind Bartender. Bartender now obstructs Victim's line of fire.

Grenade: A runaway trolley is heading towards Victim, and will kill Victim unless he destroys it with his grenade. Guard is tied to the front of the trolley, and will be killed if Victim uses the grenade.

Most accounts of threats and bystanders do not distinguish between Bartender and Guard, and will identify both as bystanders. I think this analysis wrong on both counts. On my account, both Bartender and Guard count as threats to Victim. If Victim is not permitted to harm either, their presence reduces the courses of defensive action available to him. However, Bartender and Guard do not pose the same sort of threat. Bartender, as an Obstructing Shield, indirectly threatens Victim. Victim is certainly made worse off by her presence, but she is not going to kill him. It is Gunman who will kill Victim, not Bartender.

[25] Otsuka, 'Killing the Innocent in Self-Defense', 86.

Guard, in contrast, is what I will call an Attached Shield, and counts as a direct threat. I cannot see any difference between this case, and a case in which Falling Person hurtles towards Victim in a heavy box or, as Otsuka imagines, wearing heavy ski boots. It would be an odd moral theory that treats Falling Person as a threat when it is *her* weight that will kill Victim, but not when it is the weight of her ski boots that will kill him. When the threatening object will kill Victim qua object—when is it the physical mass that threatens Victim's life—being part of that threatening mass is morally relevant. Since Guard contributes to the trolley's mass, he contributes to the threat.

We might object that the trolley would suffice to kill Victim, without Guard's additional mass. If the contribution of Guard's mass doesn't make a difference to the trolley's capacity to kill Victim, how can it be relevant? But, as Gerald Lang argues, when it comes to objects that kill qua object, e.g. by crushing Victim to death, we are often unable to point to any particular part of the object and identify it as *the* threat.[26] Lang points out that individual components of a lethal object will often not be lethal in themselves. It's not as if a single cog of the trolley is independently lethal. But if we deny that any component of a given object *X* can be described as lethal whilst affirming that *X* consists of nothing more than its parts, we would seem to be committed to the idea that *X* is not lethal after all.

> But dependence on this 'ground-up' approach would do us out of a reason for destroying *X*. This consideration compels us, I believe, to regard the overall threat in terms of the combined presence of the original threat itself—whether that is, for example, a tank or a trolley—and the Innocent Shield attached to it. Properly analysed, they form a *composite* object which constitutes the lethal threat to the Victim.[27]

Lang's analysis seems to me to be correct. We do not ask whether each component of the whole poses a threat independently of the whole, nor claim that the 'real' threat is, for example, only the trolley's wheels since the wheels alone are heavy enough to kill Victim. It is, as Lang says, the object as a whole that can be properly called a threat. We should regard the person tied to the trolley as part of the object that will kill Victim, and thus as a direct threat.[28]

But this analysis seems appropriate only when the threat an object poses comes from its mass. For example, if Gunman were to grab hold of Bartender rather than merely position himself behind her, she would be physically attached to him.

[26] Gerald Lang, 'The Limits of Self-Defence', unpublished manuscript (2007), 21.

[27] Lang, 'The Limits of Self-Defence', 21–2.

[28] Frances Kamm also argues that a person who is 'on a physical threat coming at a nonthreatening person' counts as a threat whom Victim may permissibly kill (*Creation and Abortion* (Oxford: OUP, 1993), 47). I suspect that by 'physical threat', Kamm has in mind the sort of 'killing qua object' that I describe below.

But physical attachment to a threatening object isn't morally relevant when it isn't the physical mass of the object that is the source of the danger. It's not Gunman's body that's going to kill Victim, but the bullets that he's firing at him. Thus, her physical attachment to Gunman's body does not make Bartender a direct threat in this case.

So, the relevant distinction in Otsuka's trolley cases is not that between people lying beside the tracks or inside the trolley, and a person who falls alone, where the former are bystanders and the latter a threat. Rather, a person lying beside the tracks is an indirect threat, and the people inside the trolley or falling alone are direct threats. As I shall argue, it is impermissible to kill an innocent person lying at the side of the tracks, as in (1). But it is permissible to kill both the person inside the trolley in (2) and the person who falls alone in (3), since both count as innocent direct threats: they will kill Victim if Victim does not kill them.

1.5 'Threat' as a Non-moralized Notion

The account of the distinction between threats and bystanders defended here is a *non-moralized* account, by which I mean that it establishes whether someone is a bystander without relying on a judgement about whether Victim is permitted to kill her, or whether she is morally responsible for her position. I do not argue that, for example, Victim is not permitted to kill Worker, and that Worker therefore reduces the options available to Victim. That would be a moralized account, since it makes the moral judgement about what Victim is permitted to do part of how we identify a threat. On my account, the claim is rather that *if* Victim were not permitted to kill Worker, this would reduce the courses of action that are (morally) available to Victim. But this is not itself a moral claim: we can establish whether this is true without making a moral judgement about whether or not Victim is in fact permitted to kill Worker. The same goes when Victim is not able to harm Worker in *Helpless Trolley*: it's a change in the non-moral facts (the lack of a lever that can divert the trolley down the sidetrack) that affects whether Worker is a threat, not a shift in what Victim is permitted to do.

The test concerning moral responsibility is not moralized either. I'm not arguing that, for example, Pedestrian is a threat in virtue of the fact that she's morally responsible for her position. That would allow moral facts to determine whether someone is a threat, which is what I'm trying to avoid. Rather, the claim is that she is a threat because her position is the sort of position for which one *could be* morally responsible, and that rules her out from the class of bystander.

Some writers argue that 'threat' is an essentially moralized notion, and that the sort of account I'm trying to offer cannot succeed. For example, Suzanne Uniacke suggests that a threat is someone who disturbs the normative status quo, and not merely someone whose 'existence, presence, or conduct thwarts my interests'.[29] Uniacke argues that if two shipwrecked people simultaneously grab hold of a piece of driftwood that can support only one of them, both are endangered, but neither threatens the other.

> Normative considerations can be relevant to determining the status quo against which another person's existence, presence, or conduct is a threat. For instance, I have a legitimate claim to parts of my living body, my property, my position in a queue, etc.; so someone competing with me for these things is a threat to me and not I to him.[30]

So, Uniacke holds that since neither of the shipwrecked people has a legitimate claim on the driftwood, neither can be said to threaten the other. But she also holds that,

> the considerations which determine the *status quo* are not necessarily strongly normative (the police sharp-shooter is a threat to the hijacker holding hostages); and they can be a matter of luck (those who get to the lifeboat first are threatened by those arriving later [who will overload the boat], and not vice versa).[31]

This position strikes me as odd. If posing a threat is about competing for something over which someone else has a legitimate claim, thus disturbing some kind of normative baseline, it's hard to see how the police shooter can be said to threaten the hijacker (assuming that it is permissible for him to shoot the hijacker, and that therefore whatever claims the hijacker has over his body, they do not include a claim that the police officer not shoot him). The officer does not disturb the normative baseline, any more than the victim of an attack disturbs such a baseline in trying to defend herself. If both the police officer and the person acting in self-defence pose threats, which they clearly do, this is because of their causal relationship to the relevant agent, not because they are competing for things over which others have legitimate claims.

Given that it is thus possible for a person to pose a threat even if she is not competing for something over which another person has a legitimate claim, as is the case with the police officer, it's unclear why the two people competing for the driftwood do not mutually threaten each other. Of course, the police officer threatens a person who *is* threatening things to which others have legitimate claims. This gives the case an asymmetry that is lacking in the shipwreck case. But it is an asymmetry between unjustly threatening and justifiably threatening, rather than between

[29] Suzanne Uniacke, *Permissible Killing: The Self-Defence Justification of Homicide* (Cambridge: CUP, 1994), 69.

[30] Uniacke, *Permissible Killing*, 69.

[31] Uniacke, *Permissible Killing*, 69.

threatening and not threatening. Similarly, in a case where two people 'endanger' each other, but neither party is threatening something to which the other has a legitimate claim, we ought to describe both parties as justifiably threatening, rather than declaring that they do not threaten each other at all.

Noam Zohar also rejects the idea of a non-moralized account of the difference between a threat and a bystander, claiming that '[w]hether or not a person is perceived as a (prospective) cause of my death depends on how the situation is judged and therefore cannot—on pain of circularity—serve as a basis for formulating such a judgement.'[32] Pointing to cases like *Bridge*, Zohar argues that causation can't be relevant to self-defence because there can be cases in which a person's causal role remains constant, and yet her normative status changes (much as I have argued above). Zohar claims that '[c]ausal attributions are, in H. L. A. Hart's phrase, "ascriptive," not descriptive: rather than reporting an "objective" sequence of events, they ascribe responsibility to an agent.'[33]

> Realizing all this, one could yet adhere to the standard of 'causal involvement' enhanced now by moral significance. The 'innocent obstructor' would be distinguished from the 'villainous obstructor': only the latter can be legitimately seen as causally involved in the threat to my life. But this would be, of course, totally at odds with Thomson's intent. The whole point in adopting the causality criterion was to find an objective way of distinguishing between those 'innocent threats' whom one could legitimately eliminate in self-defense and others (equally innocent)—'bystanders' who were to be immune. The point in the above analysis was to show, on the contrary, that no recourse can be had to a 'neutral factuality'. Rather, on all accounts, it is the moral guilt of the aggressor that defines him or her as such, regardless of the technicalities of the situation.[34]

I think Zohar's conclusion is infected with the same problem as undermines Thomson's account. Because it seems implausible to think that one could kill an innocent obstructor, Zohar concludes that we must say that whether or not someone is an aggressor depends on his moral guilt. Similarly, Thomson reasons from the fact that one ought not to kill innocent obstructors to the conclusion that obstructors are bystanders. Both seemingly assume that if one thinks causation relevant to self-defence, one must think that (a) one cannot distinguish, morally, between different sorts of causal role, and (b) causation is *all* that is relevant to what Victim may do to save his life. But both these assumptions are false.

On the view that Zohar is attacking—Thomson's—no distinction is drawn between different sorts of threat, and Thomson's formal definition of what it is

[32] Noam Zohar, 'Collective War and Individualist Ethics: Against the Conscription of "Self-Defense"', *Political Theory*, Vol. 21, No. 4 (1993), 606–22, at 612.

[33] Zohar, 'Collective War and Individualist Ethics', 612.

[34] Zohar, 'Collective War and Individualist Ethics', 613.

to be a bystander is inconsistent with the people (such as Pedestrian) whom she herself identifies as bystanders. But this is no reason to think that a better, more nuanced causal account could not play the role of distinguishing threats from bystanders in a way that accounts for our intuition that culpable obstructors are legitimate targets, but bystanders are not. Indeed, as I have argued, we should very much hope that causation can help us to draw such a distinction, since looking to moral guilt or innocence cannot do the work required in establishing this distinction, even if it might help us answer questions about the moral status of a particular threat.

So, I don't think we need to accept that 'threat' is an essentially moralized notion, and that causal accounts of the threat/bystander distinction are doomed to failure. But we should not take the mere description of a person as a threat to determine how one may treat them. After all, it hardly follows from identifying the policeman as a threat to the hijacker that the hijacker may shoot the policeman, or from the fact that a person is posing a permissible defensive threat that she may be killed by her attacker. As I will argue, more must be said about the sort of threat that a person poses before we determine her normative status.

1.6 Direct and Indirect Threats

I should make it clear that I am not denying that there are differences between Falling Person, who is on course to crush Victim to death, and a person who blocks an alternative trolley track or who reveals Victim's hiding place, enabling someone else to kill him. My contention is that these differences are not those between a threat and a bystander, but rather those between a direct threat and an indirect threat. As I argue in Chapters 2 and 3, this difference has implications for what Victim is permitted to do in the course of saving his life.

I have suggested that anyone whose actions, movements, or presence contribute, or have contributed, to a threat to Victim's life counts as a lethal threat. A *direct* lethal threat is someone who does this because she is going to kill Victim. This includes characters who kill Victim by way of a tool or weapon. Absent intervening agency, I take such characters to be direct threats. If, when she hits the bottom of the well, Falling Person will land on a button that will detonate a bomb that kills Victim, she still counts as a direct threat on my account. An *indirect* lethal threat is someone who is not going to kill Victim, but whose actions, movements, or presence nevertheless endanger Victim's life.

The test we used above for identifying obstructors doesn't capture direct threats, because when the person in question is the thing that's going to kill Victim, the comparison between Victim's defensive options in the person's absence versus his defensive options in their presence doesn't make sense. Falling Person's absence would not reduce or increase the number of defensive actions available to Victim. Rather, in her absence, there would be no need for defensive action at all. (And in many cases, this question—whether, in a person's absence, defensive action would be necessary—will help us to identify whether someone is a direct threat.) Whilst the distinction between threats and bystanders emerges as pretty robust on my account, there will be some grey areas concerning the distinction between direct and indirect threats.

Given this, it might look like all my account does is move the bump in the carpet: we get a sharp distinction between threats and bystanders, but at the cost of shifting all the difficult cases in to the category of 'threat'. But I don't think this undermines the account, for at least two reasons. First, my taxonomy is more plausible. The reason why there might be grey cases between direct and indirect threats is because causation is messy—whether or not a person counts as killing you will sometimes be unclear. But my account at least reflects that these people *are* all causally relevant to what threatens Victim—they all endanger him—in a way that gets lost on alternative accounts that mistakenly focus on whether Victim is permitted to harm a person in order to determine whether that person poses a threat or not. It's unlikely that any account will sharply distinguish between all the categories I outline, but my account gets a sharp distinction in the most important place—between threats and bystanders.

Second, my account is preferable not just because it better reflects the causal structure of the cases, but because it shows what's wrong with the Moral Equivalence Thesis. The MET appeals because the first premise—that it's impermissible to kill a bystander to save one's own life—is so intuitively attractive. But I submit that the force of this intuition comes largely from the way that Otsuka conflates killing people such as Worker with killing people by using them as human shields. The clear moral objection to using a person as a human shield makes Otsuka's claim that killing bystanders is always wrong seem plausible. If we assume that all bystander killings are as repugnant as this, and we accept the claim that Worker is a bystander, then of course we will accept the first premise of the MET that killing bystanders is impermissible.

But if we ignore human shields and ask whether, for example, Victim may knock someone off a bridge to save his own life, the answer is much less clear, precisely because of the argument I have made here—it matters whether or not the person is deliberately blocking the bridge. And thus we must either say that the first premise of the MET is false, since it looks like we may kill some bystanders (the strategy I rejected above), or we must revise our account of threats and bystanders in the way that I've suggested, so that those people no longer count as bystanders.

But once we do that, the MET loses much of its intuitive appeal. The first premise of a revised version of the MET would have to be something like 'it's wrong to lethally use an innocent person's body as a human shield against something else that threatens you'. And whilst everyone would probably agree with *that*, the contrast between that sort of killing and killing Falling Person in order to prevent her from killing you is so stark that the crucial second premise—that there's no morally significant difference between the two killings—just becomes much less plausible. As I argue in Chapter 2, there *are* morally significant differences between these sorts of killings, and thus the MET is false.

1.7 Summary

I have proposed a new account of what it is to be a bystander or a threat, according to which many people who are usually classed as bystanders count as threats. I argued that it is a mistake to take the permissibility of killing a person to determine whether she is a threat or a bystander. Bystanders are not those people who are innocent with respect to their role in the threat to Victim, or those people whom Victim is not permitted to kill in the course of saving his own life. Rather, bystanders are not causally involved in the threat to Victim at all. It thus makes no sense to ask about their innocence or responsibility with respect to what threatens Victim.

I suggested two tests that can establish whether a person is a bystander. The first asks us to consider whether, if Victim were not permitted or able to harm the person, their presence would reduce the number of valuable courses of defensive action that are morally available to Victim, compared to what would be available in their absence. The second asks whether we can make sense of the person's being morally responsible for their position with respect to Victim. Neither test is necessary, but either is sufficient, for showing that a person is not a bystander.

I proposed a distinction between indirect threats and direct threats. I suggested that whilst an indirect (lethal) threat contributes to the threat to Victim, she is not going to kill him. Such contributions can sometimes take the form of being an indirect cause of Victim's death, as in the case of Mafia Boss, who hires Hit Man to kill Victim. A direct (lethal) threat is someone who is going to kill Victim. I argue in Chapter 2 that the fact that a direct threat will kill Victim is morally significant, irrespective of whether she threatens innocently or responsibly.

2

Killing Innocent Threats

Now that we are in possession of a non-moralized account of the distinction between threats and bystanders, we are in a position to tackle the question of whether, and why, it is permissible to kill innocent threats. In this chapter, I show how my account of threats and bystanders substantially undermines both Thomson's account in favour of a permission to kill innocent threats, and Otsuka's account against such a permission.

I argue that Otsuka is mistaken to think that the impermissibility of killing bystanders rests on their lack of harmful agency. The relevant feature of bystanders is that they are not harmful. I argue that their non-harmful status entails that the harming of a bystander will always aim at making use of the bystander. Consequently, harming a bystander without her consent to avoid anything other than a much greater harm to another innocent person always treats her as a means.[1] This is why it is impermissible to harm bystanders in the course of defending oneself. In contrast, harming a person who poses a threat—innocent or otherwise—does not treat that person as a mere means. The claim that killing an innocent threat is morally equivalent to killing a bystander is therefore false.

I then develop the distinction between direct threats and indirect threats posited in Chapter 1. A direct threat is someone who is going to inflict harm upon someone else. An indirect threat is someone who is not going to inflict harm upon anyone, but who nonetheless contributes to the fact that someone else is in danger, perhaps by blocking an escape route that the person could use. I argue that the fact that a direct threat is going to harmfully interfere with an innocent person's body is morally significant, even if the threat lacks moral responsibility for the interference. Since averting such interference requires only non-exploitative, eliminative force, it is permissible for a morally innocent person to use proportionate force to prevent such harmful interference.

[1] In what follows, I assume that Victim is not harming a bystander in order to avoid a much greater harm to himself or some other innocent person. Harming a bystander under those circumstances could be justified on lesser-evil grounds.

However, when a person will not interfere with an innocent person's body, as in the case of an indirect threat, it is permissible for an innocent person to defensively use force against her only if there is some other justification for doing so. I suggest that moral responsibility for endangering an innocent person can serve as such a justification. Thus, on my account, indirect threats are permissible targets of force only if they are morally responsible for their contribution to the threat to Victim.

2.1 Thomson's Account of Self-Defence

In developing her account of permissible defence, Thomson begins by observing that neither culpable threats nor innocent threats have a right to kill Victim. They lack, in Hohfeldian terms, a privilege of killing Victim. If one has a privilege to do something, this amounts to the claim that one is under no duty not to do it. Correspondingly, should one lack a privilege to do something, this entails that one *does* have a duty not to do it. Since, as Thomson argues, Falling Person lacks a privilege of killing Victim, she has a duty not to kill Victim. She fails in this duty, and violates Victim's right, just in case she does, in fact, kill Victim. Victim may lethally defend himself against this impending violation of his right.[2]

Unlike most commentators, then, Thomson denies that one needs agency in order to violate a right. It doesn't matter that Falling Person is not acting when she kills Victim. All that matters is that Falling Person will kill Victim and that Victim has a right that she not kill him.

Various people have objected to this position, focusing on the objectivity of Thomson's conception of rights violations and giving rise to a debate about whether one needs agency to violate a right.[3] But, as I'll show, we can set that debate aside. By drawing on the discussion in Chapter 1, we can see that Thomson's account fails on its own terms, irrespective of whether one accepts her conception of rights.

Thomson argues that Victim is permitted to kill Falling Person only if, and because, Falling Person will violate Victim's right not to be killed if she lands on

[2] Judith Jarvis Thomson, 'Self-Defense', *Philosophy and Public Affairs*, Vol. 20, No. 4 (1991), 283–310.

[3] I think these objections to Thomson do, for the most part, fail, and tend to stem from confusion about Thomson's particular meaning of what it is to violate a right, and rather uncharitable interpretations of her view. See e.g. Noam Zohar, 'Innocence and Complex Threats: Upholding the War Ethic and the Condemnation of Terrorism', *Ethics*, Vol. 114 (2004), 734–51, and David Rodin, *War and Self-Defence*, 85–7. For a defence of Thomson's view, see Yitzhak Benbaji, 'Culpable Bystanders, Innocent Threats and the Ethics of Self-Defense', *Canadian Journal of Philosophy*, Vol. 35, No. 4 (2005).

him. Since, on Thomson's view of rights, Falling Person will violate Victim's right, she lacks her own right not to be killed by Victim. Victim will therefore violate none of Falling Person's rights in killing her.

A bystander, in contrast, will not violate Victim's right not to be killed. So, the bystander retains her own right not to be killed, and Victim would violate this right if he killed the bystander to save his own life. It is this difference that demarcates the scope of permissible targets on Thomson's account. Thomson stresses that rights violation is essential to permissible defence: that, 'it—or something that does a comparable job—is necessary, for it just is not sufficient to justify your killing a person that that person will otherwise kill you.'[4] Only those who will lethally (or very harmfully) violate your rights are permissible targets of lethal defensive force.

Consider *Bridge* again. Thomson is adamant that Pedestrian is a bystander, causally uninvolved in Victim's death. She will not violate Victim's right not to be killed, and thus Victim may not kill her. But what will Thomson say about the *Malicious Bridge* case from Chapter 1, in which Pedestrian culpably obstructs Victim's escape? If Pedestrian is not instrumental in Victim's death, she certainly cannot be culpably instrumental, and she thus cannot be a legitimate target of force. But, as I argued in Chapter 1, a person who maliciously blocks Victim's escape from a lethal threat certainly seems to be a legitimate target of force. The problem for Thomson is that if she permits Victim to kill Pedestrian when she culpably obstructs his escape, she has no way of restricting this permission to *culpable* obstructors. On Thomson's account, Victim may use force only against those who will violate his (sufficiently important) rights. If Victim may use force against Pedestrian when she maliciously obstructs him, she must be about to violate some right of his. But, since Thomson does not require agency to violate a right, it looks like innocent Pedestrian, who helplessly obstructs the bridge in the original case, can also violate this right. If Victim is permitted to use force against a culpable obstructor, Thomson's account will permit him to use force against an innocent obstructor as well. Given this, I think we are forced to reject Thomson's account of permissible defence, and with it her argument in favour of a permission to kill innocent threats.

2.2 The Moral Equivalence Thesis

The best articulation of the case against killing innocent threats comes from Michael Otsuka, and is echoed by both Jeff McMahan and David Rodin.[5] Otsuka's argument consists of two parts. The first undermines Thomson's argument in

[4] Thomson, 'Self-Defense', 303.

[5] Otsuka makes this case in 'Killing the Innocent in Self-Defence', *Philosophy and Public Affairs*, Vol. 23, No. 1 (1994), 74–94. McMahan's endorsement is in *The Ethics of Killing: Problems*

favour of a permission to kill innocent threats. The second presents a positive argument against killing innocent threats, based upon the Moral Equivalence Thesis that I described in Chapter 1. Since I am not in the position of trying to defend Thomson, we can safely bypass the first part of Otsuka's argument and focus upon the positive argument he offers for the impermissibility of killing innocent threats.

There is general consensus about the wrongness of killing bystanders in the course of saving one's own life. Otsuka's argument makes use of this general consensus, and looks like this:

(1) It is impermissible to kill a bystander to prevent oneself from being killed.
(2) The killing of an innocent threat and the killing of an innocent bystander are, other things being equal, on a par as far as permissibility is concerned.
(3) Therefore, it is impermissible to kill an innocent threat to prevent oneself from being killed.[6]

There are two strategies that one might employ to support the claim that the killing of an innocent threat is morally akin to the killing of a bystander, as required by premise (2). The first is to argue that bystanders are morally equivalent to innocent threats. That is, we could argue that there is no moral difference between the *targets* of the killings. The assumption would then be that if killing one is impermissible, killing the other must be similarly impermissible. The second strategy examines the moral status of the *killings*, rather than the moral status of the targets. If the way in which one kills a bystander is what makes the killing wrong, and this is also the way in which one kills an innocent threat, then it looks like killing innocent threats must also be wrong. Otsuka's argument employs both these strategies. We will begin with his argument for the moral symmetry of threats and bystanders.

Otsuka argues that, 'the moral property that explains why we may not kill a bystander is her lack of responsible lethal agency, and not the absence of her body from the sequence of events that results in death.'[7] The reason why it is impermissible to kill bystanders is not that bystanders are causally irrelevant to the threat to Victim's life. It is that bystanders lack moral responsibility for the threat to Victim's life. But, Otsuka points out, this feature is shared by innocent threats like

at the Margins of Life (New York: OUP, 2002), 407–9. For an argument that McMahan's attempted improvement of Otsuka's view fails, see Frowe, 'Equating Innocent Threats and Bystanders', *Journal of Applied Philosophy*, Vol. 25, No. 4 (2008), 283–4. Rodin's similar argument is in *War and Self-Defense*, 79–89.

[6] Otsuka, 'Killing the Innocent in Self-Defense', 76.

[7] Otsuka, 'Killing the Innocent in Self-Defense', 84.

Falling Person. She too lacks moral responsibility for what threatens Victim, even though she *is* what threatens Victim. The threat that Falling Person poses does not proceed from her agency. If it is true that the reason why we cannot permissibly kill bystanders is their lack of lethal agency, and if it is true that innocent threats also lack lethal agency, it follows that we cannot permissibly kill innocent threats.

This strategy is unpromising as an independent explanation of the impermissibility of killing bystanders because it will not generalize. Consider the following two cases:

Diversion: A runaway trolley is lethally heading towards five people. Only by diverting the trolley down the alternative track can the five be saved. However, the trolley will then kill an innocent person who is lying on the alternative track.

Barrier: A runaway trolley is lethally heading towards five people. Only by pushing an innocent person in front of the trolley, using his body as a barrier, can you save the five. The innocent person will be killed when the trolley hits him.

Nearly everyone agrees that whilst you may divert the trolley to where it will kill one person in *Diversion*, you may not push an innocent person onto the tracks so that his body presents a barrier to the trolley, as in *Barrier*. But if the reason why you cannot push the innocent person in front of the trolley is a reason about *him*—about his innocence or lack of responsibility—then this would make diverting the trolley impermissible as well. After all, the two people are both innocent.

While we cannot identify any moral difference between the targets of the killings in *Diversion* and *Barrier*, we can identify differences between the way in which killing them saves the lives of the five. And, it seems, these differences alter what it is permissible for you to do. What this shows us is that it matters not merely *that* a person is killed, but also *how* that person is killed. Focusing on the moral status of the person one kills, therefore, cannot provide a general principle for identifying permissible killings, since permissibility can change when moral status does not.

Those who defend a permission to kill innocent threats will not deny that Falling Person is every bit as innocent as a bystander. What defenders of the permission dispute is that it is their innocence that makes killing bystanders wrong. And, given what we saw in the comparison of *Diversion* and *Barrier*, it seems that we have good grounds for thinking this view can be defended by distinguishing between the ways in which one might kill an innocent person in the course of saving one's own life. If the wrongness of killing bystanders does not generalize to the killing of innocent threats, the Moral Equivalence Thesis is false.[8]

2.3 Ways of Killing

However, Otsuka argues that far from being distinct from a bystander killing, the way in which one kills an innocent threat 'is analogous to the worst type' of bystander killing.[9] This type of killing is depicted in *Human Shield*:

> *Human Shield*: A javelin is heading towards Victim. Victim can save his life only by grabbing nearby Jogger and using her as a human shield, placing her body between himself and the incoming javelin. Jogger will be killed by the javelin.

Otsuka describes such killings as 'paradigm cases of the morally outrageous'—even worse than killing, say, Pedestrian in *Bridge*.[10] In *Bridge*, killing the innocent person is of no use to you, but is merely a side-effect of saving your own life.

> But when you vaporize the body of the falling Threat, your killing of an innocent person is a *means* to save your life rather than merely a *foreseen consequence*. Here your vaporization is analogous to the worst type of killing of a Bystander, in which you initiate a lethal sequence of events that will result in the useful destruction of a Bystander ... The vaporization of the Threat is a means to your end of saving your life, even though the falling Threat is, as I have argued, a bystander, qua agent, to her lethally falling body.[11]

I agree with Otsuka that cases like *Human Shield* are clearly morally wrong. But I do not think that Otsuka has correctly identified the feature that makes this case so abhorrent. It is true in both *Human Shield* and *Ray Gun* that the killing of an innocent person is a means that saves your life. But what is also true of *Human Shield*, and not of *Ray Gun*, is that the innocent person *herself* is treated as a means. When Victim employs Jogger as a human shield, he literally uses her body to save himself, lethally appropriating her as a tool. The same is true in those cases where Victim eats a person to ward off starvation, or takes her organs to save his own life. This explains why *Human Shield* is morally worse than *Bridge*. In killing Pedestrian in *Bridge*, Victim does not exploit her for his own gain. But by killing Jogger, Victim obtains a benefit from her that he could not obtain in her absence.

[8] I adopt this strategy in Frowe, 'Equating Innocent Threats and Bystanders', *Journal of Applied Philosophy*, Vol. 25, No. 4 (2008), 277–90.

[9] Otsuka, 'Killing the Innocent in Self-Defense', 87.

[10] Otsuka, 'Killing the Innocent in Self-Defense', 78.

[11] Otsuka, 'Killing the Innocent in Self-Defense', 87.

In *Ray Gun*, it is, as Otsuka argues, 'your *killing* of an innocent person' (my italics) that is a means to saving your life, not Falling Person herself. Falling Person constitutes the threat to Victim. She thus cannot be something that Victim employs for profit to eliminate that threat. The feature that makes killings like *Human Shield* wrong is that such killings treat the person herself as a mere means. This feature is absent in *Ray Gun*.

Consider the following *Subway* cases from Thomson. In each scenario, a subway train is lethally heading towards Miner and Victim.

(1) There is an alcove in the wall where the train can be avoided, but it's only big enough for one person and Miner is already in it. Victim pulls Miner out of the alcove to where the train will hit him, and gets into the alcove himself.
(2) There is an alcove in the wall where the train can be avoided, but it's only big enough for one person and Miner is already in it. Victim forces his way in, crushing Miner to death.
(3) There is no alcove, but there is Miner. Victim shoves Miner in front of the subway train, causing the train to stop before it reaches Victim. Miner is killed, but Victim escapes unharmed.

Thomson denies that there is, 'any difference in the degree of moral badness' in how Victim behaves in these cases.[12] But Otsuka and I disagree. Whilst Victim acts wrongly in all three cases, both Otsuka and I think that his actions in the third case are worse than those in the first and second cases. Otsuka describes the second case as one in which Victim 'rides roughshod' over Miner. But, '[t]he condemnation of *using* a Bystander gains even greater support than the condemnation of running roughshod over a Bystander ... it would, for example, be particularly outrageous for you to push an innocent person onto the path of a trolley car in order to prevent it from running over five others.'[13]

Why would such a killing be 'particularly outrageous'? Well, I suggest, because this sort of killing manifests the attitude that the innocent person is a tool to be appropriated for gain by others. The above cases are morally distinct because in (1) and (2) the two people effectively compete for a scarce resource, namely the space in the alcove. But whereas in (1) and (2) the alcove is the life-saving resource, (3) treats *Miner* as a resource, with Victim pushing Miner into the subway's path so that Miner's body will stop the train. And this is the source of a more serious moral objection. People are not pieces of apparatus to be appropriated for profit by others. It is, I think, open to argument whether Miner has a greater claim on

[12] Thomson, 'Self-Defense', 291.

[13] Otsuka, 'Killing the Innocent in Self-Defense', 78.

the alcove than Victim.[14] But Miner certainly has a greater claim upon *himself* than Victim has upon him. It is worse to view people as resources to be appropriated for one's gain than it is to kill them in the course of pursuing some other resource. There is something particularly reprehensible about Victim's willingness to lethally employ Miner for his own benefit that is absent in the other cases.

None of the objections to Victim's treatment of Miner in the third case apply to *Ray Gun*. Victim is not seeking to use Falling Person to avoid a harm that he would be forced to bear in her absence. In her absence, there would be no harm to bear. Nor is Victim treating Falling Person as a resource from which he can benefit. He benefits from her destruction, but when this destruction does not also involve exploitation of the sort present in *Human Shield*, this claim amounts to nothing more than the observation that Falling Person is a threat to Victim. This is hardly at issue. The notion of profiting, which is the source of the wrongness of the killings upon which Otsuka builds his case, does not generalize to the killing of innocent threats. It would be very odd to say that Victim makes himself better off by Falling Person's presence, or uses her to save his life, given that it is only because of Falling Person that Victim needs to save his life at all.

Of course, that killing Falling Person is less morally bad than some other impermissible form of killing does not show that killing Falling Person is permissible. But it does show that Otsuka's argument fails to establish that killing an innocent threat is impermissible because it is morally indistinguishable from killing a bystander. This error arises because Otsuka is wrong about why it is impermissible to kill bystanders. As I argued in Chapter 1, the relevant, and essential, feature of bystanders is that they are not lethal. And because bystanders are not lethal—because they do not threaten—any killing aimed at them will necessarily be aimed at exploiting them: at treating the bystander as a tool to be used for profit. *This* is what makes it wrong to kill bystanders: that such killings exhibit a particularly morally abhorrent attitude towards the person one kills.

Any attraction to the idea that it is lethal agency that matters for permissible killing comes in no small part, I suspect, from a concern that not *all* bystander killings will treat people as a means in this exploitative way. For example, if Victim diverts a runaway trolley away from himself and towards Worker, he does not employ Worker as a tool. Nor does Victim exploit Pedestrian when he knocks her off the bridge as he flees Murderer. Jeff McMahan makes precisely this objection in *Killing in War*, arguing that in killing Pedestrian '[o]ne would not be exploiting the innocent bystander's presence in order to save one's life. Yet to kill

[14] I think that whether this is true might depend on the nuances of the case. In *Subway* the two men are engaged in a joint risky enterprise in which it might be rational for them to agree

her is a clear instance of impermissibly killing an innocent bystander as a means of self-preservation.'[15] But given what we have seen in Chapter 1, this objection is misguided. These people are not bystanders. They are innocent threats. And thus we should not be worried that our explanation of the wrongness of killing bystanders does not also explain the wrongness of killing Worker and Pedestrian.

As I will argue, the mere fact that a killing is not exploitative is not sufficient to make it permissible. Rather, to generate a permission to kill, this feature must be combined with some other justification. In section 2.4, I explain why Jon Quong's attempt to provide this justification through agent-relative permissions fails. I argue in section 2.5 that the fact that a direct threat will harmfully interfere with an innocent person's body gives us a better explanation of why killing direct threats is permissible. But, as I've argued, this feature is not true of indirect threats. Thus, even though the killing of an indirect threat is not exploitative—often such killings are side-effects of defensive action—they are not permissible unless some other justification for killing obtains.

2.4 Quong's Account of Permissible Defence

Of course, undermining Otsuka's argument against a permission to kill innocent threats is not enough to show that there is such a permission. Having rejected Thomson's argument in favour of killing innocent threats, I need to offer some alternative explanation of why we are permitted to kill innocent people in self-defence.

Jonathan Quong has independently developed a critique of Otsuka's position along similar lines to those defended here.[16] Quong argues, as I have done, that the correct account of permissible defence must pay attention to the way in which a person is killed—that it matters whether a person is killed using eliminative force, or force that aims at exploiting her.

In this section, I show why we ought not to adopt Quong's alternative account of permissible defence. I argue that his view results in an overly broad permission of defensive killing and commits us to implausibly different results in cases that are morally similar.

2.4.1 Agent-Relative Permissions

Quong's account relies in part on the idea of an agent-relative permission that allows Victim to weight his own life more heavily than that of Falling Person.

beforehand to a coin toss if a train comes along. This seems different to the *Bridge* case, in which the characters are not working together in this way.

[15] Jeff McMahan, *Killing in War* (New York: OUP, 2009).

[16] Jonathan Quong, 'Killing in Self-Defense', *Ethics*, Vol. 119, No. 3 (2009), 507–37.

Consider a case in which Victim can save either a stranger or his wife from drowning. We cannot expect the fact that one of the drowning people is Victim's wife to be of any great significance to the coastguard. This fact does not give *her* any reason to save Victim's wife rather than the other person. But it is certainly an excellent reason for Victim to save his wife rather than the other person. And it probably means that whilst, for example, the coastguard ought to toss a coin to decide who to save (assuming that other things are equal), Victim is under no such obligation. Rather, the fact that one of the people is Victim's wife permits him to go ahead and save her without needing to engage in any sort of randomizing decision process.

The relationship between Victim and his wife is, of course, not the same as the relationship between Victim and himself. And the drowning case is not one in which Victim must kill a person to save his wife. But it is still true that the reason why Victim is permitted to save this person rather than that person is a reason about him (she is *his* wife) that has no moral significance for other people. This reason, despite being no reason at all for others, is an appropriate basis for Victim's choosing between equally innocent lives.

Nancy Ann Davis makes use of this notion of agent-relative permissions to explain the permissibility of killing innocent threats. She argues that even though I realize that my life does not have greater objective value than the life of some other innocent person, it is nonetheless more valuable to me than the life of the other person (just as her life is more valuable to her).

> Because of the greater value that each of us understandably attaches to the continuation of his or her own life, we are (in certain circumstances) permitted to kill another person to preserve our own life, even though we acknowledge that their claim to life is not weaker than our own. Even when I acknowledge that my preference is not one that would be endorsed from a neutral standpoint—it is not better or fairer that *I* should be the one to survive—it is permissible for me to kill another person to preserve my own life.[17]

The central question that agent-relative accounts must address is what falls under the 'certain circumstances' in which one may weight one's own life more heavily than the life of some other innocent person. Most people think that one can weight one's own interests more heavily in cases where one is in a position to prevent harm befalling someone else. I am not required to rescue even an innocent person at significant cost to myself. Davis herself clearly takes the defensive killing

[17] Nancy Ann Davis, 'Abortion and Self-Defense', *Philosophy and Public Affairs*, Vol. 13, No. 3 (1984), 175–207, at 192–3.

of an innocent threat to be justified by reference to the greater value that each of us 'understandably' places on our own life compared to the life of a stranger.

But an agent-relative permission must be in some way constrained if it is to amount to anything more than mere self-preferment. We must avoid the (by now familiar) problem that I ought not to kill a bystander to save my own life. Davis does not explore the constraints that might apply to this permission. But on Quong's account, these constraints arise from a prohibition on treating others as a mere means, which is in turn understood by thinking about the ownership of resources. When certain conditions are met, defensive force against the innocent permissibly infringes, rather than violates, their rights.

Quong proposes the following principle of permissible killing.

> You can permissibly infringe someone else's rights when this is necessary to defend something that belongs to you [including your life] provided: (a) the infringement is proportionate, and (b) you would be able to keep what belongs to you if the other person and all their property were not present.[18]

Quong holds that anyone who has not 'done anything to waive or forfeit their right not to be killed' may use counter-defence against defensive force.[19] So, innocent threats may defend themselves against Victim—provided their defence meets the above conditions—but a culpable threat is not so permitted.

Condition (b) is designed to rule out exploitative killings of the sort involved in *Human Shield*. In *Human Shield*, you can keep what belongs to you (your life) only because of the presence of Jogger. Quong argues that this means that killing Jogger treats her as a mere means—it exploits her in the way that I described above—and is therefore impermissible. Whereas I have argued that exploitative killings are especially bad, Quong argues that only exploitative killings are wrong.

At first glance, it appears that such a position will be far too permissive, since it looks like only killings in which I try to make use of a person's body will fall foul of Quong's principle. But Quong argues that we should not limit our understanding of what it is for a killing to be exploitative to cases in which we exploit the person's body. We should also include killings that exploit those things to which the person has rightful claims. If I can save myself only by lethally making use of something that belongs to another person, this too qualifies as wrongfully exploiting her. Counted amongst the other person's belongings will be the physical space her body occupies, where this qualifies as belonging to her because her occupancy of it gives her a prior claim to it.

[18] Quong, 'Killing in Self-Defense', 530.

[19] Quong, 'Killing in Self-Defense', 520.

Quong suggests that we can identify the killings that will be permitted by his principle by considering the following counterfactual: *If X and all the things currently belonging to X were to suddenly disappear, would your life be saved?* Quong argues that if you can answer yes to this question, your killing of X does not exploit X or take advantage of X. Rather, you simply keep what you would have without them. But if the answer to the question is no, this shows that you *will* be exploiting X to save yourself. Here, you cannot survive *but for* X's presence, or other things over which X has a rightful claim.[20]

The inclusion of X's belongings in the counterfactual is primarily intended to deal with the obstructing cases of the sort that I have discussed at length. For example, take the first of the subway cases that I discussed in section 2.3, in which Victim can avoid the runaway train only by pulling Miner out of the alcove and getting into the alcove himself (call this case *Alcove*). Most people think that it would be impermissible for Victim to remove Miner from the alcove to save himself. But unlike in the case where Victim must use Miner's body to stop the train, it does not seem that the notion of exploiting will explain the wrongness of pulling Miner out of the alcove. After all, Victim would be much better off in Miner's absence. Given this, it seems, prima facie, that he cannot be said to exploit Miner by removing him from the alcove. But if we adopt Quong's wider definition of exploiting, we can account for the wrongness of killing Miner. Quong claims that the importance of having rights over our bodies and the space that they occupy means that we have prime facie claims over the place that we currently occupy.[21] Miner's prior occupation of the alcove means that we should treat the alcove as belonging to him, and thus, by making use of the alcove to save himself, Victim wrongfully exploits Miner. Quong thus claims that killing Miner is analogous to killing Jogger in *Human Shield*. In both cases, Victim cannot save himself *but for* something to which the innocent person has a rightful claim.[22]

For the same reason, Quong thinks it impermissible to kill Pedestrian in *Bridge*. Pedestrian has a rightful claim to the bridge because she was there first. Since Victim needs the bridge to escape, and the bridge is in the relevant sense *Pedestrian's* bridge, he exploits something to which Pedestrian has a rightful claim if he gets on it.

So, the reason why Victim cannot proceed in *Alcove* is not that it is generally wrong to kill innocent obstructors. It is that in *Alcove* he would need to exploit something belonging to Miner in order to save himself. And indeed, Quong's account will

[20] Quong, 'Killing in Self-Defence', 28.
[21] Quong, 'Killing in Self-Defense', 27.
[22] Quong, 'Killing in Self-Defense', 27.

not prohibit killing innocent obstructors across the board. Compare *Alcove* with *Meteor*:

> *Meteor*: A small meteor is heading towards Victim. He can save his life only by pulling an Occupant out of Victim's tiny car, to where Occupant will die, and getting into the car himself.

Quong says that it is clearly permissible to proceed in *Meteor*.[23] So on what does this permissibility turn? Well, Quong claims that since the resource that Victim needs to save his life in *Meteor* is *his* resource, he does not act wrongly if he kills Occupant, who obstructs his access to that resource. It is, after all, *Victim's* car.[24] Victim's keeping what belongs to him depends upon neither Occupant nor anything that belongs to her and thus he does not exploit her if he kills her in the course of saving himself. Similarly, the impermissibility of killing Pedestrian in *Bridge* holds just in case the bridge in question is a public bridge. If Victim owns the bridge, it is permissible for him to get on it, killing Pedestrian.[25] In doing so, he does not exploit something that is rightfully hers, and so he does not treat her as a mere means.

2.4.2 *Quong's Counterfactual*

Quong argues that his counterfactual test shows the impermissibility of killing Miner in *Alcove* because the alcove belongs to Miner in virtue of his prior occupation. Therefore, if he and all that belongs to him were to vanish, there would be no alcove into which Victim could squeeze to avoid being hit by the trolley. Thus Victim cannot save himself *but for* something that belongs to Miner, just as he cannot save himself but for something that belongs to Jogger in *Human Shield*.

Something has gone wrong here. In *Human Shield*, Jogger provides by her presence the only opportunity Victim has to save his life. And so of course, if she and everything belonging to her were to disappear, Victim could not save his life. There is no escape route in her absence because she *is* the escape route. In *Human Shield*, then, the presence of the escape route is contingent on the presence of Jogger, and this is why Victim cannot save his life but for her presence.

But in *Alcove* the reverse is true. Here, Victim could save his life but for Miner's presence. Miner blocks an escape route that Victim would otherwise have. It is incorrect, therefore, to suggest that these are similar cases in which Victim

[23] Quong, 'Killing in Self-Defense', 25.
[24] Quong, 'Killing in Self-Defense', 25.
[25] Quong, 'Killing in Self-Defense', 44 n. 53.

cannot save himself but for something that belongs to someone else. He would die but for Jogger's presence in *Human Shield*, but he would live but for Miner's presence in *Alcove.*

Quong anticipates this objection, and tries to deal with it by specifying that his principle is temporally specific and refers to the other person's presence here and now, rather than their general existence.[26]

> When we evaluate some action and ask whether our action would constitute using someone as a mere means, we are asking, given the facts as they are *now*, does our action have a certain moral feature? To know if a particular course of action requires the use of some particular person or their property we must look to the facts as they are, not as they might have been had the person in question never existed ... The only relevant counterfactual is whether we could save ourselves if the person and their property were suddenly removed from the current situation, but everything else remained as it is.[27]

But this response is unsatisfactory. It makes little sense to insist that you could not save yourself in a person's absence because you cannot save yourself but for their property, when the fact that something *is* a person's property is contingent upon their presence. The rationale behind 'but for' counterfactuals is that they reveal what would have occurred in the absence of certain features of a situation. Quong's principle fails in *Alcove* because Miner's ownership of the alcove is contingent upon the very thing that the counterfactual requires we omit. It will fail in *Bridge* for the same reason. That Pedestrian has a claim to the bridge stems from her presence on it. We cannot, therefore, sensibly suppose that the bridge would be absent in *her* absence, when it belongs to her just in case she is present.

There is, I suggest, a distinction between cases in which something is present because it belongs to a person, and cases in which something 'belongs', in Quong's sense, to a person because (and just in case) she is present. The escape route's belonging to the innocent persons in *Alcove* and *Bridge* is contingent upon their presence. In *Human Shield*, the escape route itself is contingent upon Jogger's presence. The two cases cannot be assimilated as Quong suggests. Thus, Quong's counterfactual does not show that it is impermissible to kill the obstructor in *Alcove*. We cannot plausibly apply his counterfactual to cases in which ownership of a resource depends upon a person's presence.

2.4.3 *Owning*

Quong does note that there are difficulties with applying his counterfactual to *Alcove*. Since a vanished alcove would presumably leave an even larger empty

[26] Quong, 'Killing in Self-Defense', 43 n. 42.

[27] Quong, 'Killing in Self-Defense', 36.

space into which you could move, we cannot understand the counterfactual as requiring us to envisage what would happen if the alcove disappeared. Quong says that we should instead understand it as asking whether Victim could still save his life if the space occupied by the innocent person were suddenly inaccessible: if, for example, it were obstructed by a barrier.

But this way of understanding the counterfactual is rendered rather implausible by what Quong says about the trolley case I discussed in Chapter 1.

Trolley: Victim is stuck on a train track, with a runaway trolley heading towards him. Victim can save his life only by diverting the trolley down an alternative track. However, the trolley will then kill Worker, who is lying unconscious on the other track.

Given what Quong says about killing Pedestrian in *Bridge*—that it would be impermissible for Victim to knock her off to save his own life—it seems likely that he would want to say that killing the person in *Trolley* is similarly impermissible. But this is not what Quong says at all. Rather:

> The proposed [counterfactual] test would permit you to re-direct a runaway trolley which was headed towards you on to a side-track, even if [Worker is] trapped on that side-track. This is true because even if the area where [Worker is] currently trapped was blocked by some barrier, you would still be able to successfully turn the trolley on to the side-track.[28]

Why the radically different permissions between *Trolley* and *Bridge*? Well, because in *Trolley*, assuming that Worker is some way down the track, Victim doesn't need to exploit anything she owns in order to save himself. Quong's account holds that Worker owns only the specific part of the track on which she is actually lying. So, if Worker happens to be quite far down the track, there would be plenty of unowned track before her onto which Victim could divert the trolley. Thus, he can save his life without needing to exploit anything Worker owns. Of course, the trolley will then continue onto her bit of track, but this is not something that Victim *needs* to save himself. The killing therefore passes Quong's counterfactual.

There are two things wrong with this, aside from the intuitive impermissibility of diverting the trolley. The first is that Quong argues against killing Pedestrian on the grounds that since the bridge cannot safely hold two people, it should be treated as an amount of physical space that can hold only one person. If Victim gets onto the bridge, Quong claims, he effectively seizes the *entire* bridge, including the part occupied by Pedestrian. Quong therefore argues that in *Bridge*,

[28] Quong, 'Killing in Self-Defense', 44 n. 48.

Victim needs the physical space that Pedestrian occupies, and to which she thus has a prior claim. Victim cannot save himself without exploiting something that belongs to Pedestrian, and killing her thus impermissibly treats her as a mere means.[29]

These comments seem to apply to *Trolley* just as much as *Bridge*. It can hardly make a difference that in *Bridge*, Victim makes the bridge uninhabitable because he puts himself on it, whilst in *Trolley* he makes the track uninhabitable because he puts a trolley on it. Both things are equally lethal to their respective obstructors. Diverting the trolley is to effectively seize the whole track, since there is no way of halting the trolley's progress once begun. If it is impermissible to seize the bridge when doing so will kill Pedestrian, I do not see how it can be permissible to seize the track when doing so will kill Worker. Quong's account generates inconsistent results in these cases.

The second problem with Quong's position is that if it *is* permissible to turn the trolley, cases like *Bigger Alcove* will also be permissible.

Bigger Alcove: Victim is in a tunnel and sees a runaway trolley headed straight for him that will kill him if he does not escape. There is an alcove in which he can take refuge. However, Miner is already in the alcove, and whilst there is sufficient room for both of them, Miner will suffocate if Victim positions himself in front of Miner.

It is hardly plausible to grant Victim a permission to proceed in *Bigger Alcove* if he may not proceed in *Alcove*. And yet he does not need the actual space that Miner occupies in *Bigger Alcove*. If he and the bit of the alcove that he occupies were to suddenly vanish, or if a barrier were to appear before Miner, Victim could still save his life. But surely if Victim cannot pull Miner out of the alcove when doing so will kill him, he cannot step into the alcove when doing so will kill him. On Quong's account, just this slight revision of the case creates a permission to kill the obstructor. But it's hard to believe that the permissibility of killing an innocent person hangs on this difference.

We can make a similar argument against Quong's analysis of *Trolley*. Quong's account makes the permissibility of diverting the trolley contingent upon exactly where Worker happens to be lying. If she is far down the track, then a barrier before 'her' space would indeed leave room for the diverted trolley, and Quong will think diverting permissible. If, however, she is right at the joint of the track, a barrier here would block the entire track to Victim. By Quong's lights, diverting

[29] Quong, 'Killing in Self-Defense', 30.

the trolley now is impermissible. But surely whether Victim is permitted to kill Worker cannot be contingent upon how far down the track Worker happens to be. Irrespective of whether one thinks diverting permissible or impermissible, we must surely agree that what goes in one case goes in the other. But Quong's account will deem one killing permissible and the other impermissible.

Quong might revise his view to deal with these objections by saying that since Victim inevitably invades the innocent person's space in *Trolley*, albeit in a way that is not itself useful to him, turning the trolley is impermissible. But this doesn't rule out killing Miner in *Bigger Alcove*, since Victim doesn't invade Miner's space at all in this case. More generally, I think that relying upon this idea of prior claims and ownership will leave Quong's account open to all kinds of difficulties. Take a case like *Private Trolley*:

> *Private Trolley*: Victim and Landowner are captured by Villain, who takes them to Landowner's country estate and ties them both to her private train tracks. Villain sets in motion a train that will kill Victim unless he diverts the train down the alternative track to which Landowner is tied.

It looks like it is going to be impermissible for Victim to divert the trolley in this case. Landowner not only occupies the other track: she *owns* all of it. If ownership tips the balance of who gets to live in *Meteor* and *Bridge*, surely Landowner gets to live in *Private Trolley*. It is, after all, *her* track. To save himself, Victim would have to make use of something to which Landowner has a clear prior claim. And yet if Victim is permitted to divert the trolley when tied to public tracks, as Quong argues, it is rather implausible to say that he cannot do so if he is tied to privately owned tracks.

In addition to this implausibility, we should also notice that in this case, if Landowner and everything that belongs to her were suddenly to disappear, Victim's life would be saved, since this would include the train. Perhaps killing Landowner will not exploit her after all, since in the absence of all that belongs to her, Victim's life would be saved. But surely it is not right that since Villain used her property to threaten you, you may kill Landowner. Endorsing this claim would make it hard to resist the idea that just in case a villain has thrown *Jogger's* javelin towards Victim in *Human Shield*, Victim may grab Jogger to use as a human shield after all, even if Jogger is wholly innocent. If this is impermissible, which it surely is, killing Landowner in *Private Trolley* should also be impermissible. And if this is impermissible, it seems plausible that killing Worker in *Trolley* should be impermissible too. But Quong's counterfactual will permit all these killings on the grounds that killing a person does not treat her as a means when one could keep what belongs to one in the absence of her and her property.

A final but, I think, serious difficulty with Quong's account comes from its inability to cope with the *Discovery* case I discussed in Chapter 1.

Discovery: Victim is hiding from Murderer, who wants to kill him. Passer-By is about to stumble upon Victim, whereupon her startled cry will alert Murderer to Victim's hiding place. Only by quietly killing Passer-By before she sees him can Victim save his life from Murderer.

People have disagreed about whether Passer-By is a bystander or an innocent threat. (On my account she is an indirect threat. If he's not permitted or able to kill her, Victim is made very much worse off by her presence, and her causal role is such that she could play that role culpably—deliberately crying out in order to alert Murderer to Victim's whereabouts.) But irrespective of this disagreement, when Passer-By is innocent, it seems clearly impermissible for Victim to kill her to stop her from revealing his hiding place.[30] Can Quong's counterfactual show that this is the case? I do not see how. Victim needs neither Passer-By nor anything that belongs to her in order to save himself. He could keep what belongs to him—his life—if Passer-By were not present. If she were to suddenly vanish, Victim could save himself by continuing to hide. Nothing in Quong's account rules out killing Passer-By. But *Discovery* seems to me, like *Human Shield*, to be one of the central test cases that an account of self-defence ought to deem impermissible. If Quong's account cannot so deem it, I think that's a pretty good reason not to adopt his account of permissible defence. If we want to account for a permission to kill innocent threats, we need to look elsewhere.[31]

2.5 Direct Threats

In Chapter 1, I proposed a distinction between direct and indirect threats. This distinction maps onto an intuitive distinction between people who are going to actually inflict harm upon you, and people who are not going to inflict harm upon you, but who endanger you in some other way. Falling Person is a direct

[30] We should resist any temptation to draw an analogy with the case of the refugees in a boat who are attempting to pass a Nazi ship undetected when a baby on board begins to cry. In this case, the numbers are different, and the baby will (by assumption) also be killed if they are discovered.

[31] Quong's account seems to me a good illustration of why it's probably a mistake to try to identify a single rule or principle that can identify all (but only) cases of permissible defence. I suspect that things are simply more complicated than this.

lethal threat, as is Murderer in *Discovery*. Pedestrian in *Bridge* is an indirect lethal threat, as is Passer-By in *Discovery*. Neither Pedestrian nor Passer-By will kill Victim, but both endanger his life.

I suggest that a person's defensive rights allow her to use necessary and proportionate force against someone who will kill her even when that killing is innocently brought about. The fact that a person is going to kill you is morally significant, and distinguishes that person from an indirect threat. The fact that preventing such interference requires only eliminative force is also part of what makes such killings permissible, since such killings lack the feature of exploitation that make bystander killings so objectionable.

2.5.1 *Flagpoles, Shields, and Wells*

In order to motivate the claim that Victim may kill an innocent person who will otherwise kill him, we will need to look down some more wells. Compare *Spacious Well* with *Stationary Shield*:

Spacious Well: Falling Person is heading towards Victim. If she hits him, the impact will kill Victim, but Falling Person will survive. However, the well is sufficiently large that Victim can move out of Falling Person's path. If he moves, Victim will be unharmed, but Falling Person will be killed when she hits the ground.

Stationary Shield: Falling Person is heading towards Victim. The impact will kill Victim, but Falling Person will survive. However, Victim is lying on top of a shield, under which he can crawl. Hitting the shield, rather than Victim's body, will kill Falling Person, but Victim will survive.

Victim is clearly permitted to move out of Falling Person's way in *Spacious Well*. Even Otsuka agrees that this is permissible.[32] To deny this would be to require Victim to rescue Falling Person from harm at the cost of his own life. Few people think that our obligations to rescue are so stringent.

If Victim may move out of Falling Person's way to prevent Falling Person from killing him, even though his doing so results in Falling Person's death, I think he must also be permitted to move under an object to that same end, as in *Stationary Shield*. This is true even if Victim's moving results in Falling Person's death. But if this is true, it seems that Victim ought to be able to move a shield over himself

[32] Otsuka, 'Killing the Innocent in Self-Defense', 76 n.7.

in order to prevent Falling Person from killing him. And, he must be permitted to continue to hold a shield of which he's already in possession, as in *Existing Shield*:

Existing Shield: Falling Person is heading towards Victim. However, Victim is lying on the ground holding a shield. The impact with the hard shield will kill Falling Person, but Victim will survive. If Victim sets the shield aside, Falling Person will kill Victim, but she will survive when his body cushions her fall.

Again, Victim is surely permitted to continue to hold the shield in order to prevent Falling Person from crushing him to death. He need not cast the shield aside and allow Falling Person to kill him.

We might think that all these cases are examples of letting Falling Person die, and that they therefore cannot establish a permission to kill innocent threats. But I think that this is wrong on two counts. First, I don't think that the *Shield* cases are examples of letting die. Invoking the killing/letting die distinction, therefore, will not distinguish these cases from *Ray Gun*. We can see this by thinking about what Otsuka says about *Flagpole*:

Flagpole: Victim is holding a flag in a display of patriotism. He suddenly realizes that Falling Person is falling towards him. Should Victim continue to hold the flagpole, Falling Person will be impaled upon it. Falling Person will die. If Victim drops the flagpole, Falling Person will crush Victim to death. Falling Person will then survive.[33]

Otsuka insists that Victim must drop the flagpole and allow Falling Person to kill him:

> May you continue to hold the flagpole? Many would insist that you may. But, by so doing, do you not kill the Threat by sustaining a lethal sequence of events? Is it not the case that if you may not shoot and vaporize a falling Threat in order to save your life, then you may not continue to hold the flagpole in order to save your life?[34]

Otsuka says that his use of the term 'killing' 'will refer only to the initiation or sustaining of, or the insertion of somebody into, a sequence of events that results in the death of a person'.[35] So, *Flagpole* is a killing because, in continuing to hold the flagpole, Victim sustains a sequence of events that results in the death of Falling Person. As

[33] This case, cited by Otsuka, 'Killing the Innocent in Self-Defense', 89, was suggested to him by Seana Shiffrin.

[34] Otsuka, 'Killing the Innocent in Self-Defense', 89.

[35] Otsuka, 'Killing the Innocent in Self-Defense', 76 n. 7.

such, continuing to hold the flagpole is impermissible. But of course, *Flagpole* is just *Existing Shield* with a different object. If *Flagpole* is a killing, so too is *Existing Shield.*

If sustaining or initiating a sequence of events of which Falling Person's death is an upshot counts as killing her, then *Spacious Well* and the *Shield* cases are all killings too. In *Spacious Well*, for example, Victim initiates a sequence of events of which Falling Person's death is an upshot, since he initiates moving out of her path when so moving will result in her death. The same is true in *Stationary Shield* and *Existing Shield.*

We might reply that this just shows that Otsuka's account of what it is for something to be a killing needs revising. Perhaps a different account of the killing/letting die distinction will do better. But I don't think it will. This is partly because I think that Otsuka is correct that intentionally sustaining a lethal sequence of events falls on the killing side of the killing/letting die distinction. Even if Victim does not take up the flagpole with lethal intent, his continuing to hold the flagpole renders his action more than a letting die.

But it's also because I think there's a deeper problem with trying to invoke the killing/letting die distinction to deal with these cases. It doesn't matter whether, for example, holding the flagpole is a killing but moving the shield over oneself is a letting die. What matters is whether it is plausible to grant Victim a permission to move the shield over himself, or move himself under the shield, but deny him a permission to continue to hold the flagpole. And I don't see how it can be plausible, because picking up a lethal object—which is what the shield is—looks *more* like a killing than does merely continuing to hold the flagpole.

Just as defenders of a permission to kill innocent threats need to constrain this permission so that it doesn't permit the killing of bystanders, defenders of a prohibition on killing innocent threats need to show that this prohibition doesn't require Victim to rescue innocent threats at the cost of his life. The cases above show that this is pretty difficult: even Otsuka thinks that there's no morally significant difference between *Flagpole* and *Ray Gun* (and it's worth noting that he doesn't seem terribly convinced about the impermissibility of *Flagpole*—'I am prepared to swallow, as a consequence of my argument, the claim that you may not continue to hold the flagpole').[36] It seems to me that the killing/letting die distinction just isn't going to suffice to generate different permissions in these cases. Given that the claim that Victim may move out of the way in *Spacious Well* has overwhelming intuitive force, and given that it's implausible to advocate different permissions between *Spacious Well* and the *Shield* cases, we ought

[36] Otsuka, 'Killing the Innocent in Self-Defense', 89.

to concede the permissibility of Victim's acting to save his life in all these cases, including *Ray Gun*.

2.5.2 *Killing and the Lesser Evil*

What the above cases all have in common is that Victim is acting to prevent Falling Person from killing him, and he seems permitted to so act even though Falling Person will die as a result, irrespective of whether her death counts as an instance of eliminative killing or letting die.[37]

But even if we agree *that* it matters that Falling Person is going to kill Victim, we also want to know *why* it matters. I think that the best explanation of this comes from Victor Tadros. Tadros's view combines a claim about Falling Person's duties with a lesser-evil justification for the inflicting of harm. Tadros argues that Falling Person has a duty to prevent herself from harming (and especially from killing) innocent people. The important connection between our bodies and ourselves means that we have special responsibility for the things that our bodies do. This is partly an instrumental way of realizing certain morally good ends: as Tadros argues, compared with making each of us responsible for threats posed by bodies other than our own, 'distributing responsibility to us for our bodies will typically interfere with our projects and aims to a lesser degree, increasing the control we have over the shape of our lives.'[38] (We might think that a similar concern partly motivates the appeal of holding me more responsible for the things that I do than for the things I allow. Such a distinction allows me to demarcate a field of action over which I have dominion, and thus to more effectively pursue my ends.)

But the connection to our bodies is also of intrinsic significance. As Tadros points out, many of our judgements about impermissible harming make sense only because of the intimate connection between persons and their bodies. For example, I argued in section 2.3 that the particular abhorrence of harming Jogger in *Human Shield* comes from the fact that we employ Jogger's body as a tool. This is thought by most people to be a particularly reprehensible way of treating

[37] The argument does not, then, inadvertently show that whenever one is permitted to let a person die, one is also permitted to kill them. Victim may not, for example, continue to hold a shield when doing so will deflect harm onto an innocent, non-threatening person. The harm that Victim would inflict in that case would not be eliminative harm aimed at someone who is going to harm him. Nor does it show the general irrelevance of the distinction between causing harm and allowing harm. I have argued elsewhere for the moral significance of this distinction (see Helen Frowe, 'Killing John to Save Mary: A Defence of the Moral Significance of the Distinction between Doing and Allowing', in Joseph Keim Campbell, Michael O'Rourke, and Harry S. Silverstein (eds.), *Action, Ethics, and Responsibility* (Cambridge, Mass.: The MIT Press, 2010)). And, in Chapter 3 I argue that when it comes to non-eliminative harm, whether a person has caused herself to threaten or allows herself to threaten matters for what we are allowed to do to her.

[38] Tadros, *The Ends of Harm*, 253.

Jogger—that is, a reprehensible way of treating the *person*, not merely a shoddy way of treating her body. But the sort of reasonable complaint that Jogger could make about such treatment—'but you're just using me'—relies 'on the idea that a person's body is so fundamentally connected with the person that the use of the body amounts to the use of the person for these purposes'.[39]

I have argued that Falling Person's position is not akin to that of a bystander, even if she lacks agency over her movements. Tadros similarly argues that the fact that Falling Person is going to kill Victim makes a difference to her obligations in a case like *Ray Gun*. To see this, consider the following case:

> *Busy Well*: Falling Person is falling down the well towards Victim, and will kill him if she lands on him. She can twist her body to avoid landing on Victim, but doing so will result in the loss of her foot. Tramp, who is in an alcove in the well, could pull Victim out of Falling Person's way, but doing so will result in the loss of Tramp's foot.[40]

Tadros's view holds that Falling Person, but not Tramp, is required to suffer the loss of her foot in this case.[41] This is because Tramp will merely fail to rescue Victim if he does not pull him into the alcove. The loss of a foot exceeds the cost Tramp is required to bear to that end. Falling Person, in contrast, fails to prevent herself from killing Victim. Even though she is not responsible for the fact that she will kill Victim, the threat nonetheless comes from her, and '[i]t is the fact that I am responsible for what my body does, even when that is not a product of my agency, that gives rise to the permission to harm innocent attackers and innocent threats. And I bear that responsibility because my body *is me*.'[42] Frances Kamm similarly argues that Falling Person's position 'is different from that of a natural object—for example, a stone that the wind hurls at a person—because she is not a stone but, rather, a person who should not be in an inappropriate position relative to others'.[43] Because Falling Person would be obliged, if she were able, to avert her body even at the cost of her foot, Tadros plausibly argues that Victim is permitted to inflict some harm on Falling Person if doing so will divert her. If she cannot move herself, she ought to permit Victim to move her. In moving Falling Person, then, Victim simply gets her to comply with her moral duty not to kill him. He does not wrong Falling Person.

Of course, *Busy Well* suggests only that Falling Person must bear *some* cost in averting the threat that she poses to Victim, and that Victim may make her bear

[39] Tadros, *The Ends of Harm*, 254.
[40] Tadros, *The Ends of Harm*, 254.
[41] Tadros, *The Ends of Harm*, 255.
[42] Tadros, *The Ends of Harm*, 255.
[43] Kamm, *Creation and Abortion*, 47.

a cost in getting her to comply with that duty. Tadros must provide an additional argument for why Victim may impose a *lethal* cost on Falling Person: we may think, along with Kamm, that Falling Person is not required to divert herself if doing so involves lethally smashing herself into the wall.[44]

It is here that Tadros invokes a lesser-evil justification. In virtue of her special connection to her body, Falling Person has an obligation to bear serious harm to avoid killing Victim. Say we agree that Falling Person could be required to redirect herself at a cost of paralysis. When we consider the harm that Victim must inflict upon Falling Person as a means of saving his own life—death—Tadros argues that we can discount the harm that Falling Person is obliged to inflict upon herself in virtue of the fact that she poses a threat.[45]

So, what we must consider is whether Victim may inflict the remaining harm—the difference between paralysis and death—upon Falling Person. We can call this remaining harm 'morally weighted' harm to distinguish it from the harm that Falling Person has a duty to bear, the infliction of which is thus already morally accounted for. Victim is himself probably required to bear some harm to avoid defensively killing an innocent person. If he can get out of Falling Person's way at the cost of, say, a broken leg, he should do that rather than kill her. But our duty to avoid defensively killing innocent people is not as stringent as our duty to avoid non-defensively killing innocent people. This means that if Victim is killed, he suffers more morally weighted harm than Falling Person would suffer if she is killed. Ultimately, then, Falling Person's death is the lesser evil, since she bears less harm in excess of what morality requires her to bear.

If this kind of approach is right—and I think it is—it looks like many of our judgements about permissible harming might turn out to based upon this sort of hybrid justification that combines our duties to bear harm for certain good ends (rescuing people, not indirectly endangering them, and so on) with a judgement about the lesser evil. That a harm is the lesser evil entails that it is proportionate to the good achieved in the course of inflicting it, but lesser evil is not the same as proportionality. I may not divert a runaway trolley to where it will break your leg in order to save me from a broken leg and a bruised ankle. Lesser-evil justifications don't permit harming as either a means or a side-effect merely to avert a slightly greater harm to oneself. If Victim is permitted to inflict harm on Falling Person, there must be some fairly significant difference between the morally weighted harm facing him and that which he will inflict upon Falling Person.

[44] Kamm, *Creation and Abortion*, 48.

[45] Tadros, *Ends of Harm*, 251.

It might be tempting to suggest when the harm Victim employs is eliminative—that is, when it is aimed at a person who poses a threat—less disparity between the harms is required. But we've already included the fact that Falling Person is going to kill Victim in our calculation about how much cost she has a duty to bear. We can't invoke this feature of the case again on pain of double-counting. But it nonetheless seems correct that the duty not to non-defensively kill people is much more stringent than the duty not to defensively kill innocent people. As I argue in Chapter 3, we are required to bear very significant harm rather than non-defensively kill other people.

2.5.3 *Innocent Direct Threats and Counter-Defence*

Falling Person has a duty to bear serious harm to prevent herself from killing Victim. This means that she lacks a right not to suffer such harm when it is a means of preventing her from killing Victim. But a portion of the harm that Victim inflicts upon Falling Person goes beyond what Falling Person is obliged to bear. She does have rights against suffering this part of the harm, and this harm is therefore unjust. But it is not always permissible to defend oneself against an unjust harm. Consider, for example, a case in which Attacker tries to kill Victim and Victim can defend himself only by throwing a grenade at Attacker. The grenade will kill not only Attacker, but also five innocent people. In such a case, Victim will lack a right to use the only defensive measures available to him, but it does not follow that he lacks a right not to be killed by Attacker. He simply lacks the right of defence because his defence entails inflicting a more morally weighted harm than it will avert.

Similarly, Falling Person can defend herself against unjust harm only by inflicting more morally weighted harm on Victim than she will suffer herself. Falling Person therefore lacks a right to defend herself. Victim's defence, in contrast, inflicts sufficiently *less* morally weighted harm on Falling Person—that's why it is justified as a lesser evil and permissibly infringes (rather than violates) Falling Person's right.

2.6 Summary

I have argued that my account of what it is to be a bystander undermines Thomson's account of a permission to kill innocent threats. Thomson's position commits her, inadvertently, to the permissibility of killing innocent obstructors like Pedestrian. I have also shown that Otsuka is mistaken in his account of the wrongness of killing bystanders. Since bystanders are not lethal, any killing aimed at a bystander aims at exploiting her presence. It is this that makes killing bystanders wrong, and that this wrongness does not extend to the killing of innocent threats. The killing of an innocent threat involves only eliminative agency. Otsuka's argument for the impermissibility of killing innocent threats therefore fails. I rejected Quong's alternative account of permissible defence, which also draws on the notion of exploitation defended here, as overly permissive. Quong's view permits the killing of characters that I have identified as innocent indirect threats. As I have argued, since these characters are not going to kill Victim, he may not kill them to save his own life. I also argued that Quong's reliance on property rights commits us to implausibly different results in morally similar cases.

I have defended the claim, outlined in Chapter 1, that there is a morally significant distinction between threats who will kill Victim, and threats who will not. I suggested that those who oppose a permission to kill innocent threats must resist a requirement for Victim to rescue innocent threats at the cost of his own life. By comparing variations on the original *Ray Gun* case, I suggested that it is implausible to grant Victim a permission to move himself out of Falling Person's way in *Spacious Well*, but not to move himself under a shield knowing that Falling Person will be killed when she hits the shield. And, once we grant a permission for Victim to move under the shield, it's hard to see why he may not continue to hold a shield—or a flagpole—knowing that Falling Person will be killed when she hits it. But this seems to me to count as a killing. What these cases suggest is that, when he acts to stop himself being killed by someone who will otherwise kill him, it is not important whether Victim's actions constitute a killing or a letting die.

Drawing on recent work by Victor Tadros, I suggested that the best explanation of why it matters that Falling Person will kill Victim is that Falling Person has a duty to avoid killing Victim, and that Victim may force Falling Person to bear costs to this end. Combined with a lesser-evil justification, this generates a permission to kill innocent threats. But, as I will explore in Chapter 3, the duty to prevent oneself from non-defensively killing an innocent person is much more stringent than the duty not to indirectly endanger an innocent person.

3

Moral Responsibility and Liability to Defensive Harm

I have suggested that there is a morally significant distinction between a person who poses a direct threat and a person who poses an indirect threat. I have argued that an innocent person, Victim, may kill an innocent direct threat in self-defence. But, Victim is not permitted to kill an innocent indirect threat in self-defence. It is permissible to kill indirect threats—such as Pedestrian in *Bridge* or Passer-By in *Discovery*—only if they are morally responsible for the fact that they pose a threat.

I will argue that morally responsible threats can be *morally liable to defensive harm*. The notion of liability has played an increasingly important role in the literature on defensive killing, thanks in no small part to the work of Jeff McMahan. Some people find the concept 'liability' rather opaque, but, at least as I understand it, it's not an especially mysterious term. If I say that Attacker is liable to a defensive harm, this is just a concise way of expressing the following claim: 'Attacker lacks a right against having the defensive harm inflicted upon him, because he has forfeited his usual rights against such harm as a result of behaving in a particular way.' A person who is liable to a harm is not wronged by its infliction—she has no justified complaint against being harmed—and she may not, ordinarily, harmfully defend herself against its infliction. On most accounts of liability to defensive harm, 'behaving in a particular way' is going to be cashed out in terms of being morally responsible or culpable for a threat of unjust harm (usually abbreviated to 'an unjust threat'). A threat of harm is unjust if it is aimed at someone who possesses a right not to suffer the harm.

Some theorists add what they take to be an essential caveat to this account of liability, namely that Attacker has forfeited his right not to be harmed in *the pursuit of a particular goal*. As I argue in Chapter 4, this caveat can be interpreted in two ways. The first, McMahanian, interpretation holds that Attacker is liable only to harm that is necessary for achieving that goal—that is, harm that is the *least harmful means* of achieving that goal.[1] The second interpretation, which is the novel view that I will defend, holds that Attacker is liable only to harm that is a *proportionate means* of achieving the goal.

Other theorists deny that this kind of goal-orientated caveat attaches to liability at all. On purely 'backwards-looking' accounts of liability, Attacker's behaviour renders his rights forfeit irrespective of whether harming him is necessary for, or instrumental in, averting a threat. I argue in Chapter 4 that this kind of view cannot succeed as an account of liability to defensive harm.

I think that a person can be liable to defensive harm only if she is morally responsible for posing an unjust threat.[2] In this chapter, I investigate the circumstances in which a person can be described as morally responsible for posing an unjust threat. The account developed here is not intended as an account of moral responsibility in general, but specifically of what makes a person morally responsible for posing an unjust threat, such that this responsibility can ground liability to defensive harm. I argue that a person is morally responsible for posing an unjust threat if she had a reasonable opportunity to avoid posing the unjust threat and she intentionally failed to avail herself of that opportunity. These formal conditions for moral responsibility are the same irrespective of the sort of threat one poses. But, as I will argue, they have different implications in different cases, because whether an opportunity to avoid posing a threat counts as reasonable is sensitive to a variety of factors, including the sort of threat that one poses.

I suggest that an agent counts as *intentionally failing* to take a reasonable opportunity to avoid posing a threat of unjust harm to Victim if (i) Victim has a right not to suffer the harm, (ii) the agent believes that a given course of action will endanger Victim, (iii) the agent believes that she has alternative courses of action available to her that are not unreasonably costly to her or other innocent people and that will not endanger Victim (or will not endanger him to the same degree), and (iv) she chooses not to take any of those alternative courses of action. Endangering Victim includes helping to bring about a harm to Victim or obstructing a valuable escape route of which Victim could avail himself.

Whether or not an opportunity to avoid posing a threat is *unreasonably costly* to an agent is sensitive to a range of considerations: (i) the cost to the agent (and to other innocent people) of taking the opportunity; (ii) the prospective harm to Victim (and to other innocent people) if she fails to take the opportunity; (iii) whether the

[1] McMahan, *Killing in War*, 10.

[2] Of course, there can be other grounds of liability to *other kinds of harm*. As I argue in Chapter 4, this includes liability to harms that one's victim inflicts in the course of trying to defend herself (even when, as I shall explore, these are not defensive harms because either (a) there is no genuine threat, or (b) the harms fail to avert a threat).

agent will threaten directly, indirectly, or as an indirect cause; (iv) whether the agent will be causing herself to threaten, or allowing herself to threaten.

I suggest that the threshold at which an opportunity to avoid posing a threat becomes unreasonable is set lowest in the case of indirect threats who will be allowing themselves to threaten. People posing these types of threats must bear some non-trivial cost to avoid endangering Victim, but they need not bear high costs to do so. The threshold at which an opportunity becomes unreasonable is set highest with respect to direct threats who will be causing themselves to threaten. People who will pose this type of threat ought to bear even lethal harm rather than kill Victim. The threshold is also high with respect to those whose actions will be an indirect cause of what kills Victim. A person who fails to take a reasonable opportunity to avoid posing an unjust threat is morally responsible for posing a threat, and is liable to defensive harm.

3.1 Agential Responsibility and Moral Responsibility

We should begin by distinguishing between *agential responsibility* and *moral responsibility*. Agential responsibility is about whether we can sensibly describe an action as belonging to an agent. Moral responsibility, my primary interest here, concerns intention and belief. Agential responsibility is a prerequisite of moral responsibility. One cannot be morally responsible for an action unless it can be traced back to one's agency. When, for example, a defendant enters a plea of insanity, she is claiming that she was not agentially responsible for her actions—that they are not attributable to her in the sense required for punishment or blame.

Falling Person is an agentially innocent threat.[3] Her falling towards Victim is not an action, and thus she can be neither agentially responsible nor morally responsible for it. This is one way in which a person can be an innocent threat: if the threat that she poses does not proceed from any action of hers.

Light Switch depicts a morally innocent, but agentially responsible threat:

Light Switch: Unbeknown to Neighbour, Villain has wired up her electricity so that when she turns on her light switch, she will detonate a bomb in Victim's house, killing Victim. Neighbour turns on her light switch.[4]

[3] McMahan calls agentially innocent threats like Falling Person *non-responsible projectiles* to distinguish them from threats who are e.g. acting but ignorant.

[4] I've adapted this from Jeff McMahan's example in 'The Basis of Moral Liability to Defensive Killing', *Philosophical Issues*, Vol. 15 (2005), 397.

Neighbour is certainly acting when she turns on the light switch. Her movements stem from her agency, and can be properly described as hers. We can also describe Neighbour as having had a reasonable opportunity to avoid threatening Victim—she could have not turned on the light without incurring any cost to herself. But she isn't morally responsible for threatening Victim because she did not intentionally fail to take this opportunity, where an intentional failure requires that the agent believe that this is an opportunity to avoid posing an unjust threat. Because of her ignorance of the trap set by Villain, I do not think that Neighbour is morally responsible for the threat that she poses to Victim's life.[5]

We can easily think of cases in which a person is agentially *and* morally responsible for posing a threat, such as *Attack*:

Attack: Murderer is shooting at Victim, trying to kill him, because he hates Victim and wants him to die.

Murderer is the paradigm culpable threat. He not only endangers Victim, but is also morally responsible for doing so.

3.2 Moral Responsibility

3.2.1 Prospective Costs

Here's another variation of the *Bridge* case from Chapter 1:

Snappy Bridge: Frightened Pedestrian sees Victim fleeing Murderer. She could get off the bridge and swim to shore, allowing Victim to escape (Victim cannot swim to safety, since Murderer will shoot him as he swims). However, there is an enormous crocodile in the river that will eat Frightened Pedestrian if she gets in the water. She decides to stay on the bridge, knowing that this will impede Victim's escape.

[5] On my account, Neighbour is an innocent direct threat, and thus Victim may kill her in self-defence. She is going to kill Victim by way of a tool (in this case, by turning on the lights and detonating the bomb). This case is thus analogous to a case in which, say, Neighbour and Victim are playing Cowboys and Indians with what Neighbour believes is a toy gun, but what is in fact a real, loaded gun. Neighbour's innocent mistake—she has no reason at all to think it a real gun—means that she is not morally responsible for threatening Victim. But she is nonetheless agentially responsible for threatening him. Her pointing of the gun and pulling the trigger are actions that are hers. I think that Victim is permitted to kill Neighbour to stop her from killing him in this case too. (What makes this permissible, though, is not that Neighbour is agentially responsible for posing a threat to Victim, but that, as in *Light Switch* and *Ray Gun*, she will non-defensively kill Victim unless Victim kills her.)

Frightened Pedestrian believes that staying on the bridge will endanger Victim, that she has an alternative available course of action that will not endanger Victim, and she chooses not to take that alternative course of action. But she is not morally responsible for the threat that she poses, because her only alternative course of action will expose her to a lethal cost. Even though she endangers Victim's life, the cost to her of taking the opportunity not to do so is too high for us to deem the opportunity reasonable. Thus, she is not liable to be killed by Victim, and Victim may not knock her off the bridge even if that is the only way in which Victim can save his own life.

But things are different in *Selfish Bridge*:

Selfish Bridge: Victim is fleeing Murderer, who wants to kill him. Victim's only escape route is across a narrow bridge that can hold only one person. Selfish Pedestrian is out for a walk on the bridge. Selfish Pedestrian could easily get off the bridge, but doing so will involve getting her feet wet and she has on her lovely new shoes. She decides, with a certain amount of regret, to stay on the bridge, realizing that her doing so impedes Victim's escape.

In this case, the cost to Selfish Pedestrian of getting out of Victim's way is very low. She not only intentionally fails to take an opportunity to avoid threatening Victim—she intentionally fails to take a *reasonable* opportunity to avoid threatening him. I think Selfish Pedestrian is therefore morally responsible for threatening Victim's life and liable to be killed by him.

This is true even though Selfish Pedestrian is not initially required to bear a lethal cost to avoid posing a threat to Victim. As we saw in *Snappy Bridge*, there is no requirement to cease posing an indirect lethal threat at lethal cost to oneself, and thus Victim may not knock Frightened Pedestrian off the bridge if she refuses to bear a lethal cost to get out of his way. It's Selfish Pedestrian's initial refusal to bear a *reasonable* cost that makes her liable to bear a much higher cost as part of Victim's defence of his life. By getting off the bridge at the cost of wet shoes, Selfish Pedestrian could have ensured that neither she nor Victim needed to bear a serious harm. In refusing to bear this reasonable cost, she becomes morally responsible for endangering Victim's life. What it is proportionate to do to her at that point is judged not by how much cost she was initially required to bear to cease posing a threat to Victim, but by the magnitude of the harm to which she wrongly exposes Victim. Since her presence endangers Victim's life, it is proportionate for Victim to use lethal defensive force against her.

Cases like *Selfish Bridge* show that one needn't have harmful intent towards Victim in order to be morally responsible for endangering him. Selfish Pedestrian does not intend to endanger Victim (she even feels rather bad about it). Her intention is only to keep her shoes dry. But she nonetheless foresees that by staying on the bridge she will indirectly threaten Victim. Even absent lethal intent, this foresight is sufficient to make her liable to defensive harm.

So what counts as a reasonable opportunity to avoid posing a threat? It's unlikely that we will be able to establish a clear threshold at which the cost to an agent becomes unreasonable. It seems plausible that Pedestrian needn't jump into the river with a crocodile, but that she ought to get off the bridge even if doing so will ruin her shoes, break her ankle, or perhaps even break her leg. But comparing harms is always difficult, and once we move beyond certain paradigm cases in which there is a clear disparity (Pedestrian's wet shoes versus Victim's death), it becomes harder to distinguish the cases of permissible threatening from the cases of impermissible threatening.

Still, it's worth emphasizing two things. The first is that a 'reasonable opportunity' does not mean 'an opportunity that isn't too bad'. An opportunity can be reasonable and yet be very costly and extremely unattractive, requiring considerable sacrifice on the part of the agent. This is partly because what is reasonable is sensitive to both the cost to the agent of taking the opportunity *and* the prospective harm to Victim that taking the opportunity avoids. When the prospective harm to Victim is very serious—as when, for example, the agent's actions or presence endangers Victim's life—it can be reasonable for the threatening agent to bear a very serious cost to cease or avoid posing that threat. Second, as I'll explore below, the reasonableness of a cost is also sensitive to other considerations, and identifying these considerations can help guide our judgements about whether a person threatens permissibly or impermissibly. In section 3.2.2, I consider the relevance of the distinction between direct and indirect threats. In section 3.2.3, I consider the relevance of the distinction between causing oneself to threaten and allowing oneself to threaten. In section 3.2.4, I consider the implications of being an indirect cause of a direct threat.

3.2.2 *Direct Threats and Indirect Threats*

Consider *Duress.*

> *Duress:* Villain holds a gun to Hostage's head, and threatens to shoot Hostage unless Hostage kills Victim.

Most people think that it is impermissible for Hostage to kill Victim even if doing so is the only way in which Hostage can avoid being killed by Villain. This is reflected in many legal systems, which do not permit duress as a defence of homicide. Of course, we might say that Hostage is excused if she caves in to Villain's threats and tries to kill Victim. But we would not, I think, say that she acted permissibly.

This suggests that although the cost to Hostage of not killing Victim is very high, it is nonetheless a reasonable cost, since it is a cost that we expect her to bear rather than kill Victim. The cost facing Hostage is not so much greater than the harm she must inflict on Victim that inflicting it could be justified as the lesser evil. Things would be different if, for example, Villain wanted Hostage to shoot Victim in the foot. Here, Hostage could invoke the disparity between the lethal cost facing her and the lesser cost facing Victim as a justification for inflicting harm on Victim. But when the cost to Hostage is equal to the harm she will inflict on Victim, she has no such justification.

If this is correct, there must be some difference between *Snappy Bridge*—in which Frightened Pedestrian is not required to bear a lethal cost to avoid endangering Victim's life—and *Duress*—in which Hostage *is* required to bear a lethal cost to avoid endangering Victim's life. I think that the different requirements in each case are partly explained by the fact that Frightened Pedestrian indirectly threatens Victim, whereas Hostage directly threatens him. But remember that the importance of this difference can't be one of straightforward proportionality—it's not that killing indirect threats like Pedestrian is simply disproportionate to the contribution they make to the threat to Victim's life. It *is* proportionate to kill a person who plays Pedestrian's causal role in the threat to Victim's life—otherwise it would not be proportionate to kill even Malicious Pedestrian, who deliberately blocks the bridge because she wants Victim to die. As I argued in Chapter 1, Pedestrian's causal role is the same irrespective of whether she is innocent, selfish, frightened, or malicious. If Victim may kill Malicious Pedestrian, this entails that the role Malicious Pedestrian plays is sufficient to make killing her proportionate, and this must be true in all the *Bridge* cases since her causal role does not change. Lethal force is proportionate because proportionality is judged not by the extent of one's contribution to a threat, but, as I suggested above, the magnitude of the threat to which one contributes. If a group of ten people set about kicking Victim to death, they are not each liable to one-tenth of lethal defensive force. Rather, each is liable to lethal defensive force—which entails that lethal defence against each is proportionate—because what each contributes *to* is a lethal threat. Victim may therefore kill any and all of them in order to save his own life. (I return to this idea in my discussion of non-combatant liability in Chapter 6.)

The reason why it matters that Hostage is a direct threat is not, then, that it's proportionate to kill only direct lethal threats. Rather, being a direct threat influences whether her opportunity to avoid posing a threat counts as reasonable. We must bear greater costs to avoid killing (or directly harming) people than to avoid endangering them in other ways. Thus, whilst a lethal cost exceeds what Pedestrian is required to bear to avoid indirectly threatening Victim's life, it does not exceed what Hostage is required to bear. It is reasonable to expect people to bear very great costs if the alternative is that they will non-defensively kill an innocent person who is not going to kill them.

3.2.3 *Doing and Allowing*

The attentive reader will now want to know why, if this is true, we need any sort of lesser-evil justification to permit Victim to kill Falling Person in *Ray Gun*. Why isn't Falling Person also required to bear very great, even lethal, costs, to avoid killing innocent Victim?

I think the answer lies in the difference between allowing oneself to threaten and causing oneself to threaten, which has its roots in the moral significance of the broader distinction between doing and allowing. If this distinction is sound, it is morally worse for a person to intentionally turn herself into a threat than it is to intentionally allow herself to threaten. Notice that what all the *Bridge* cases have in common is that Pedestrian must act if she is to *cease* posing a threat. If she does nothing, she allows herself to continue to non-defensively endanger Victim. The same is true in *Ray Gun*. Falling Person has not intentionally caused herself to non-defensively threaten Victim. Even if she were able to divert herself but intentionally failed to do so, she would still be allowing herself to kill him, not causing herself to kill him. Whereas one ought to bear lethal costs rather than cause oneself to non-defensively kill an innocent person, one need not bear lethal costs rather than allow oneself to non-defensively kill an innocent person.

However, that Falling Person would be allowing herself to *kill* Victim, rather than indirectly endanger him, is still morally significant. She must, as I suggested in Chapter 2, bear significant costs to avoid allowing herself do this. If she fails to take a reasonable opportunity to avoid killing Victim—say she can divert herself at the cost of paralysis but decides not to do so—I think that Falling Person then becomes a morally responsible threat. That she is responsible for the unjust threat she poses will render her liable to defensive killing. In *this* case, there is indeed no work for a lesser-evil justification to do, since Falling Person has forfeited her right not to be killed. But when she is an innocent threat, she need not bear such high costs to cease posing a non-defensive threat as a person is required to bear rather than intentionally turn herself into a non-defensive threat.

In *Duress*, Hostage not only directly threatens, but also *causes* herself to threaten. She intentionally turns herself into a non-defensive threat to Victim in order to avoid costs to herself. If causing oneself to threaten is morally worse than allowing oneself to threaten, as correlates with the moral worseness of causing harm rather than allowing harm, this explains why Hostage is required to bear greater costs than Falling Person. A failure to bear these costs renders Hostage morally responsible for the threat that she poses to Victim.

3.2.4 *Causes*

Turning oneself into an indirect *cause*—into part of the causal chain that kills Victim—also seems to be morally significant. Consider *Drive By*:

> *Drive-By*: Terrorist holds a gun to Driver's head, and orders him to drive the car for a drive-by shooting, in which Terrorist will kill Victim.

I do not think that Driver is permitted to drive the car. He ought to let himself be shot rather than help bring about the shooting of an innocent person.[6] Even though this is a very high cost to bear, it is a reasonable cost because the alternative is, again, to help inflict an equally costly, non-defensive harm on an innocent person. If he drives the car, he might be excused for doing so, but he cannot invoke the cost of the alternative as a justification for doing so. Driver must bear greater cost to avoid causing harm to Victim compared to the cost that other indirect threats, such as Pedestrian, must bear rather than allow themselves to threaten in ways that are not instrumental in bringing about the direct threat to Victim.

If Driver has a reasonable opportunity to avoid endangering Victim's life, his intentional failure to take it renders him liable to be killed by Victim. If Victim can save his life only by killing Driver, sending the car off the road, he is permitted to do this. This is true even if Victim knows that Driver is acting under duress—he still need not let Terrorist shoot him rather than defend himself by killing Driver.

3.3 Mistakes and Reasonable Opportunities

So far, I've looked at cases in which the threatening agent is fully informed about the relevant facts. For example, in *Selfish Bridge*, Selfish Pedestrian knows that

[6] British law has been inconsistent on the availability of duress as a defence for murder in cases in which the defendant was not the principal killer. See e.g. *DPP for Northern Ireland v. Lynch*, 1975 AC 653, in which members of the IRA forced Lynch to drive the car for the shooting of a policeman. Lynch was originally convicted of murder, but his conviction was eventually overturned by the House of Lords who ruled that Lynch could use a defence of duress because he was only an accomplice (but there is, I think, a difference between a legal defence that functions as an excuse, and a moral justification). In *Howe v. R* (1984, AC 417), the House of Lords ruled that the defendant could not invoke duress as a defence even though he had not killed the victim. In *Abbot v. R* (1977, AC 775), the defendant was the principal killer, and received a life sentence for murder despite acting under serious duress.

Victim will be killed unless she gets off the bridge, and that if she gets off the bridge, her shoes will be ruined. She is not mistaken about her situation, then. Rather, her mistake is that she judges Victim's life to be less important than her shoes. This kind of moral mistake is what makes her not just morally responsible for staying on the bridge, but morally culpable.

But what about someone who makes an epistemic mistake? Consider *Mistaken Bridge*:

> *Mistaken Bridge*: Pedestrian knows that if she doesn't get off the bridge, her presence will obstruct Victim's escape. But Pedestrian mistakenly believes that there is a huge crocodile in the river. She stays on the bridge because she believes that the only alternative will involve her incurring a very serious cost.

Compare *Mistaken Bridge* with Michael Otsuka's *Hologram*:

> *Hologram*: Villain projects a holographic gun onto Victim's hand as he extends his hand to greet Dignitary. Dignitary, taking the gun to be real, pulls her own gun on Victim, planning to kill him in what she takes to be a justified instance of self-defence.

In both these cases, the agent has a reasonable opportunity to avoid posing a threat. Pedestrian can get off the bridge at no cost to herself, since there are no crocodiles, and Dignitary will suffer no harm at Victim's hands if she doesn't shoot him.

Otsuka argues that Victim may kill Dignitary in self-defence because, in choosing to threaten Victim, Dignitary 'takes a gamble', engaging as she does in 'such avoidable risky behaviour'.[7] The gamble is that if it turns out that she has made a mistake, she forfeits her right not to be killed. Of course, the difficulty is that Dignitary believes that if she doesn't kill Victim, Victim will kill her. Whilst she has a reasonable opportunity to avoid posing a threat, she doesn't *know* that it's a reasonable opportunity because she thinks that it involves letting Victim unjustly and non-defensively kill her.

Notice that Dignitary is not like Neighbour in *Light Switch*. Dignitary knows that she threatens Victim, but does not know that the threat she poses is unjust, or that she has a costless opportunity to avoid posing it. Neighbour, in contrast, is an innocent threat because she has no reason to think that her actions constitute a threat at all. I suggest that when one is not knowingly harming, or knowingly

[7] Michael Otsuka, 'Killing the Innocent in Self-Defense', *Philosophy and Public Affairs*, Vol. 23, No. 1 (1994), 74–94, at 91.

contributing to an endeavour that aims at harming, one's moral responsibility depends on the reasonableness of one's belief that one is not posing or contributing to a threat. Neighbour in *Light Switch* is reasonably ignorant about the fact that her light switch is wired to a bomb in Victim's house. She is thus not morally responsible for posing a threat when she turns on the light because she reasonably believes that, in doing so, she poses no threat at all.

I think the same is true of Bob in *Baseball* in Chapter 2. Bob is somewhat like McMahan's Careful Motorist:

> *Careful Motorist*: Careful Motorist keeps her car well maintained and always drives carefully. One day, she faultlessly loses control of the car and hurtles towards Victim. Victim can stop himself from being killed only by blowing up both Careful Motorist and her car with a grenade.

McMahan thinks that Careful Motorist is liable to be killed because she knows that there's a risk that in driving she will endanger someone's life. I think that this is a mistake. When the risk of endangering someone is sufficiently small, one can reasonably believe that one is not going to endanger anyone. I don't think Careful Motorist is morally responsible for posing a threat to Victim (although, as she is a direct innocent threat, I think that Victim may kill her to save his own life). Bob is not a direct threat, and since he does not intentionally threaten, I don't think that he fails in a sufficiently stringent duty to make it permissible for Victim to kill him on lesser-evil grounds.

But when one *knows* that one is harming (like Dignitary in *Hologram*) or contributing to a project that aims at harming (like Driver in *Drive-By*), the relevant reasonable belief is that one lacks a reasonable opportunity to avoid posing this threat. This demands a much higher standard of evidence if one is to evade moral responsibility for posing the threat. And, as I have argued, good evidence one will otherwise bear a lethal cost oneself is not enough—one must have good evidence, as Dignitary does, that one will otherwise be non-defensively and unjustly endangered by the person whom one intends to threaten. If a person reasonably believes that the opportunity is too costly because it involves letting Victim non-defensively and unjustly kill her, she does not count as *intentionally failing* to take a reasonable opportunity to avoid posing a threat.[8] The standard of reasonableness that applied to the agent's belief is sensitive to the factors I have described above. If one will be causing oneself to intentionally kill a person, one's belief that

[8] This means that she also believes that if she kills Victim, the harm she inflicts is not unjust. I don't think this belief matters for determining Dignitary's own responsibility (and liability). What matters for her responsibility is the standard of evidence for her belief that the opportunity

doing otherwise is too costly must be based upon very good evidence. If one has such a reasonable belief, one is not morally responsible for posing a threat in a way that can ground liability to defensive killing even if it turns out that one is mistaken.[9]

This doesn't entail that if one decides to pose a threat on the basis of insufficient evidence, one is liable to be killed even if it turns out that one's unreasonable belief is correct. Say that Dignitary decides to try to kill Victim because a member of the audience looks at Victim suspiciously as he extends his hand. Her belief in this case is not based on sufficient evidence to make it reasonable. But if it so happens that Victim really *is* going to try to kill her, Dignitary does in fact lack a reasonable opportunity not to shoot Victim and is therefore not liable to defensive harm. This is because one becomes liable to defensive harm only if one is morally responsible for an *unjust* threat. If it turns out that, however improbably, Victim actually poses a threat, then Dignitary gets lucky. The threat for which she's morally responsible isn't unjust, and thus in posing it she hasn't forfeited any of her rights.

Of course, Victim may still make a non-liable person bear some costs to avoid exposing him to unjust harm, since this is to make her comply with her duty not to threaten him (which obtains independently of Dignitary's beliefs). This can be true of cases in which the threatening person cannot prevent herself from posing a threat (like Falling Person in *Ray Gun*) and of the sort of case we are discussing here, in which the agent refuses to take an opportunity to avoid posing a threat because she reasonably believes that it is too costly. Such a person is not morally responsible for threatening Victim's life, and so isn't liable to be killed. But she still has a duty to bear costs to avoid threatening Victim. Indeed, when she has intentionally caused herself to threaten, I think her duty to prevent herself from killing Victim requires her to bear lethal costs. She is not *liable* to defensive

to avoid posing a threat is too costly to be reasonable. We can see this by thinking about a case in which Dignitary believes that she can save her own life simply by ducking Victim's bullets, but she instead chooses to try to kill Victim because she mistakenly believes that he's liable to be killed and that killing him is therefore not unjust (assuming that one can be liable to unnecessary harms). I don't think Dignitary evades liability in this case, even if her belief in Victim's liability is a reasonable belief, precisely because she also believes that she has a reasonable opportunity to avoid posing a threat and she intentionally fails to take it. Choosing to try to *unnecessarily* kill someone is an especially serious gamble, therefore, since it renders one liable to lethal defence if one is mistaken about the justness of one's killing, no matter how reasonable a mistake it is.

[9] The idea that standards for reasonable belief can be context-sensitive is fairly uncontroversial. As McMahan argues, the fact that your car is not in your drive can suffice for my having a reasonable belief that you are not at home when all that is at stake is whether or not I play my music loudly. But if your house is on fire, I should not assure the firefighters that the house is empty on that same basis.

harm—she hasn't *forfeited* her rights. But she nonetheless lacks a right not to be harmed because in harming her—even lethally—Victim imposes only costs that she has a duty to bear. Unlike in the case of an innocent threat who merely allows herself to threaten (like Falling Person), there is no work for a lesser-evil justification to do when a person intentionally turns herself into a lethal threat, and that threat turns out to be unjust.

This has implications not only for the permissibility of harming direct threats, but also for the permissibility of harming those who indirectly cause a direct threat to Victim.

Mistaken Drive-By: Friend convinces Driver that Victim is going to kill Driver, and that the only way to avoid this is to kill Victim first. Driver drives the car for the drive-by shooting because he believes that doing so is necessary for saving his life.

I think the standard of evidence required in *Mistaken Drive-By* is on a par with that required in *Hologram*. In cases where the agent is either an indirect cause or the direct threat to Victim, she contributes to an endeavour that aims at harming Victim. In *Mistaken Drive-By* and *Hologram*, the threatening agents knowingly contribute to such endeavours. This means that if he is to escape liability to defensive harm, Driver, like Dignitary, must believe on the basis of very good evidence that he lacks a reasonable opportunity to avoid threatening Victim. And, I think that the duty to avoid contributing to an endeavour that aims at unjust killing (even if one thinks that it is just killing) is sufficiently stringent that here too Victim can make Driver bear lethal costs to conform with that duty.

But I think that a much lower standard of evidence is required in order for Pedestrian's mistaken belief in *Mistaken Bridge* to count as reasonable. Some of the considerations to which I drew attention above can help explain why these cases are different. Whilst both Dignitary and Pedestrian take a risk, they do not take the same risk. This is partly because Pedestrian has not chosen to engage in threatening behaviour. Rather, she finds herself in the position of inadvertently threatening Victim, and must now decide whether to cease posing that threat. If she stays on the bridge, she allows herself to continue to threaten Victim as a foreseen side-effect of refusing to expose herself to harm, but she has not intentionally turned herself into a threat in a bid to avoid costs to herself. And, it is partly because Pedestrian is not going to kill Victim, and she is not a cause of the direct threat to his life.

In cases like this, the agent's belief need not be based on such strong evidence as required in cases of direct threats or indirect causes in order for her to permissibly treat the opportunity to avoid posing a threat as unreasonable. If Pedestrian has some reason to believe that there are crocodiles in the river—if there are official-looking signs up, for example—her belief can count as reasonable. Since this means that she is not intentionally failing to take a reasonable opportunity to avoid posing a threat, she is not liable to defensive killing. This means that whilst Victim might inflict some harm on Pedestrian to get her off the bridge, he cannot inflict serious harm upon her. It would therefore be impermissible for Victim to use lethal force to get Pedestrian off the bridge even if there are no crocodiles. The obligation not to allow oneself to indirectly threaten is not so weighty as the obligation to refrain from turning oneself into a (direct) threat. And the discrepancy between the amount of harm that she has a duty to bear and the lethal force Victim needs to inflict to move her is too great for inflicting that amount of additional harm to be justified on lesser-evil grounds.

3.3.1 More Mistakes

What about a different sort of mistake, as depicted by *Apparent Murderer*?

> *Apparent Murderer*: Enemy hates Victim and therefore wants to kill him. He points what he mistakenly believes to be a loaded gun at Victim. Victim, thinking that the gun is loaded, believes that only by killing Enemy can he save his life.

I have suggested that two things are entailed by liability to a defensive harm—that the harm does not wrong you, and that you may not harmfully defend yourself against its infliction. It seems to me that both of these things would be true of any harm that Victim inflicts upon Enemy. I do not think that Victim wrongs Enemy if he kills him. Nor do I think that if Enemy suddenly realizes that his gun is not loaded, and that therefore he never actually posed a threat to Victim, he is permitted to kill Victim and claim to be acting in legitimate self-defence. So, it looks as if Enemy is liable to be killed. But how can this be? He hasn't intentionally failed to avail himself of a reasonable opportunity to avoid posing an unjust threat, because he doesn't pose a threat at all.

I think that to explain this sort of case, we must look outside liability to defensive harm to liability to other kinds of harm. As I shall argue in Chapter 4, any harm that Victim inflicts upon Enemy cannot be defensive harm, because there is no threat against which Victim needs to defend himself. Thus, an account of liability to defensive harm will not explain why Victim may harm Enemy. But Enemy can be liable to other sorts of harm, such as harms that Victim inflicts in the course of trying to defend himself. The relevant moral responsibility for forfeiting rights against this sort of harm is responsibility for the fact that

Victim believes that if he does not kill Enemy, Enemy will kill him. The criteria for judging moral responsibility for this fact are the same as those by which we judge responsibility for posing a threat. We ask whether Enemy had a reasonable opportunity to avoid making Victim form this belief and whether he intentionally failed to avail himself of it. Since Enemy is morally responsible for bringing it about that Victim believes that either he or Victim must bear a lethal cost, Enemy lacks a right that Victim not kill him and may not defend himself against Victim. This helps explain why Enemy's position vis-à-vis Victim is not akin to Victim's position vis-à-vis Dignitary in *Hologram*. Victim is not morally responsible for making Dignitary believe that she must kill him to avoid a threat to herself.

3.4 Summary

The account of self-defence that I have developed draws a distinction between direct threats and indirect threats. It permits Victim to kill even an innocent person who will otherwise kill him. However, Victim may kill an indirectly threatening person only if she is morally responsible for posing an unjust threat.

In this chapter, I have argued that a person is morally responsible for posing an unjust threat if she intentionally fails to avail herself of a reasonable opportunity to avoid posing the threat. A person *intentionally fails* to avail herself of a reasonable opportunity to avoid posing an unjust threat if she believes that (a) a given course of action will endanger Victim (who has a right not to be harmed), (b) that she has at least one alternative course of action that would not so endanger him and that action is not unreasonably costly for her, and (c) she chooses not to take that alternative course of action. An alternative course of action is not *unreasonably costly* for an agent if it does not impose upon her more cost than she is required to bear for Victim's sake. What counts as 'too costly' varies depending on the severity of the harm that will befall Victim if the agent does not take the opportunity to avoid posing a threat, whether she threatens Victim directly, indirectly, or as an indirect cause, and whether, in failing to take the course of action that does not endanger Victim, she will be allowing herself to threaten him or causing herself to threaten him.

I suggest that the point at which a course of action becomes too costly is set lowest in cases where a person would be allowing herself to indirectly threaten Victim. Pedestrian is an example of this sort of threat. The point at which a course of action becomes too costly is set highest in cases where a person would be causing herself to directly threaten Victim. Hostage in *Duress* is an example of this sort of threat. Hostage ought to bear a lethal cost rather than non-defensively kill Victim. When a person intentionally fails to bear a reasonable cost in order to avoid threatening Victim, she is morally responsible for the threat she poses to him. Such a person renders herself liable to defensive harm—that is, she forfeits her rights against defensive harm and harming her does not wrong her.

The final part of the chapter considered cases in which an agent endangers Victim because she has made a mistaken about the reasonableness of an opportunity to do otherwise. I argued that an agent does not count as intentionally failing to take a reasonable opportunity to avoid posing a threat if she has sufficient evidence that the opportunity is in fact unreasonable. However, again, the standard of sufficient evidence varies depending on the sort of threat that one will be posing. A person who will be intentionally turning herself into a direct threat to Victim—such as Dignitary—must be responding to very good evidence that she lacks a reasonable opportunity to do otherwise (which, in *Hologram*, means that Dignitary must have very good evidence that Victim is going to unjustly and non-defensively kill her). But the reasonable belief standard is set lower when a person is neither a direct threat nor a cause, but threatens only indirectly. It is lower still when that person will be allowing herself to threaten rather than causing herself to threaten, as Pedestrian does in *Bridge*.

4

Liability and Necessity

4.1 Accounts of Liability

A division has emerged in the recent self-defence literature between those who hold what I will call *internalist* accounts of liability to defensive harm, and those who hold what I will call *externalist* accounts of liability to defensive harm.[1] For the purposes of this chapter, I'll assume that both accounts treat moral responsibility for an unjust threat as a condition of liability to defensive harm. What's of interest here is whether the *necessity* of harming a threatening person is also a condition of that person's being liable to defensive harm.

Consider *Lucky Escape*:

Lucky Escape: Murderer is shooting at Victim to try to kill him because he dislikes Victim. He chases Victim to the edge of a cliff. Unbeknown to Murderer, Victim has both a gun and a parachute. He can thus save his own life by either (a) jumping to safety, using no force against Murderer, or (b) shooting and killing Murderer.

Internalism holds that one can be liable to a harm on grounds of defence only if the infliction of that harm is necessary for averting a threat—that is, only if it is the *least harmful means* of averting the threat.[2] On this sort of account, then,

[1] Quong and Firth use the labels 'instrumentalism' and 'non-instrumentalism' to refer to internalism and externalism respectively (Jonathan Quong and Joanna Firth, 'Necessity, Moral Liability and Defensive Harm', *Law and Philosophy*, Vol. 31 (2012), 673–701). But, as will become apparent, this is a mistake because there's a difference between a harm's being *instrumental* in averting a threat and a harm's being *necessary* for averting a threat. In a case in which Victim can escape Murderer by either killing Murderer or running away, killing Murderer is still instrumental in averting the threat that Murderer poses. But internalists will not think that Murderer is liable to be killed in such a case, even though killing him is instrumental in averting the threat he poses, because killing him violates the necessity condition—it's not the *least harmful means* of averting the threat Murderer poses. As will become apparent, I think that instrumentality is key in this debate.

[2] I'm going to understand necessary force as the 'least harmful means' even though, of course, there could be cases in which Victim has various means of averting a threat, all of which are equally

liability has an internal necessity condition (hence the name). Absent any other justification for harming, a person who is unnecessarily harmed in self-defence suffers a harm to which she is not liable, and is therefore wronged by the infliction of this harm. This is true even if the person meets other conditions for liability, such as being morally responsible for an unjust threat. The internalist will therefore argue that Murderer is not liable to defensive harm in *Lucky Escape*, even though he is morally responsible for an unjust threat. Harming him is not necessary for avoiding the threat that he poses, and harming him will wrong him.

But the proponent of a standard externalist account will disagree. According to this sort of account, liability is fixed solely by facts about the person's moral responsibility for posing or contributing to an unjust threat. It is thus immune to thoughts about the necessity of harming a person, since this does not influence whether the person is morally responsible for an unjust threat. Murderer is morally responsible for an unjust threat to Victim, and it's this that makes him liable to defensive harm. An externalist can still hold that unnecessarily harming a person is wrong. But necessity is viewed as an external constraint on the *overall permissibility* of inflicting harm, not constitutive of liability itself. Harming Murderer may be impermissible, but it is not impermissible because it wrongs him.

In section 4.2 of this chapter, I briefly elaborate on both internalist and externalist accounts of liability and outline the implications of holding either an internalist or externalist view. In section 4.3, I argue that moral luck-based objections to internalism fail. In section 4.4, I consider cases of ineffective defence, in which there is nothing that can be done to avert a threat. Jonathan Quong and Joanna Firth have argued that such cases undermine internalism. I argue that their claims about these cases show that Quong and Firth have misunderstood what internalism entails. Properly understood, these cases do not undermine internalism.

Section 4.5 explores cases of 'insufficient defence'—that is, cases in which a victim can only inflict a certain amount of harm, *h*, upon her attacker, but *h* is insufficient to avert the threat her attacker poses. Again, Quong and Firth argue that these cases undermine internalism. I argue that a harm can count as defensive

harmful. As Åsa Wickforss pointed out to me, what we really mean by necessary force is that 'there are no less harmful means available'. I intend my use of 'least harmful means' as a less cumbersome way of saying this. 'Harmful means' includes both eliminative force (e.g. shooting a person who is going to kill Victim) and uses of force that harm an attacker as a side-effect (e.g. throwing a grenade that destroys a projectile that an attacker has hurled at Victim and that also kills the attacker as a side-effect). In what follows, 'averts a threat' should be understood as including 'sufficiently mitigates a threat'.

only if it is a means of averting a threat. Given this, an account of liability to defensive harm can and should justify the infliction only of harms that are means of averting threats. If *h* is not a means of averting a threat, *h* should not be justified by an account of liability to defensive harm. Contra Quong and Firth, then, cases of 'insufficient defence' do not undermine internalism. On the contrary—they undermine purely backwards-looking externalist accounts, since these accounts do justify inflicting *h*, whether or not *h* is a defensive harm.

Section 4.6 argues that Quong and Firth's own pluralist view, which combines backwards externalism with a humanitarian duty not to harm, produces largely unconvincing results. We should reject this account in favour of a new account of liability to defensive harm that I call *proportionate means externalism*. This account is externalist because it does not treat necessity as a condition of liability. However, this account takes seriously the insight that liability to defensive harm must mean liability only to harm that is capable of defending a person against a threat.[3] Instrumentality is a condition of liability, because only instrumental harms are defensive.

Section 4.7 argues that, contrary to what we might expect, it is not liability to punitive harm that best explains why an attacker is liable to harms that are insufficient to avert the threat he poses. Rather, as I argue in section 4.8, a culpable attacker poses two threats to her victim: the physical threat and a supervening threat to the victim's honour. Drawing on Daniel Statman's work, I argue that an attacker is thus liable to harm that defends her victim's honour even if there is no harm the victim can inflict that will avert the physical threat.[4]

In sections 4.9 and 4.10, I consider what both the proportionate means account and internalism should say about attackers' rights of counter-defence. I conclude that, in terms of explaining the cases under discussion here, it's not obvious that we have much reason to prefer either internalism or proportionate means externalism: combined with an honour-based justification for harming, I think that both can capture our intuitions about these cases fairly well. However, I do think that proportionate means externalism can help us explain the difficult case of using one person to avert a threat posed by someone else. I explore these cases in Chapter 6. In section 4.11, I briefly say something about the relationship between liability and proportionality. I explore the proportionality requirement in more detail in Chapter 5.

[3] Or, of course, defending some other good (such as property) against a threat. For simplicity's sake, I'll focus on defence of persons.

[4] Daniel Statman, 'On the Success Condition for Legitimate Self-Defence', *Ethics*, Vol. 118 (July 2008), 659–86.

4.2 Internalism and Externalism, and the Importance of Liability

Internalism holds that one can be liable to a harm on grounds of defence only if the infliction of that harm is the least harmful means of averting a threat. Jeff McMahan is an internalist, holding that 'the assignment of liability is governed by a requirement of necessity. If harming a person is unnecessary for the achievement of a relevant type of goal, that person cannot be liable to be harmed.'[5] According to McMahan, one reason why non-combatants in war are generally not liable to attack even if they are morally responsible for unjust threats is that attacking them is generally unlikely to be an effective means of averting those threats.[6]

Internalists distinguish liability from desert by noting that a hallmark of desert is that when a person deserves a harm, that is itself a reason to give it to her. As McMahan puts it, it's impartially good that people get what they deserve. If a person deserves a harm, inflicting that harm 'is an end in itself'.[7] Desert entails liability: you are liable to actions that are a means of giving you the harms you deserve.

But for an internalist, liability is about harms that are a means, not ends in themselves. Such harms are bad 'not only for those who suffer them but also from an impersonal point of view'.[8] Liability does not entail desert.

On an externalist view, the distinction between liability and desert looks something like this: to say that a person deserves a harm implies a positive reason to inflict it upon her. But to say that a person is liable to a harm means only that a usual reason not to harm her—that she has a right not to be harmed—is absent. It entails no claim that it is desirable to inflict harm on her. It is not a claim that it is impartially good that she be harmed, in the way that it is generally impartially good that people get what they deserve.

In many cases of self-defence, the internalist and externalist will give the same headline judgement concerning whether Victim is permitted to use force to defend himself. In the *Lucky Escape* case considered above, force is unnecessary for averting a threat because it is not the *least harmful means* that the victim has for averting the threat. Therefore, internalists and externalists will both say that it is impermissible for Victim to kill Murderer. But, as we saw, they will differ on whether Murderer is liable to be killed. The internalist thinks that Murderer is not so liable, since killing him is not the least harmful means of averting the threat.

5 McMahan, *Killing in War*, 9.

6 He also suggests that force will usually be disproportionate compared to the non-combatant's contributions, but we can set that aside here. We'll come back to it in Chapter 6.

7 McMahan, *Killing in War*, 8.

8 McMahan, *Killing in War*, 8.

The externalist thinks that he is so liable, since he's morally responsible for an unjust lethal threat.

Why does this difference in liability matter, if not for the purposes of determining what Victim may do in self-defence? Well, liability has implications for at least three important issues. The first concerns Murderer's right to compensation. Typically, if one inflicts a harm upon a non-liable person, that person is entitled to compensation for the harm she suffers. So, if Murderer is not liable to defensive harm, but Victim nonetheless inflicts harm upon him, Murderer seems to have a claim that Victim compensates him.

More importantly, one is typically permitted to defend oneself against the infliction of a harm to which one is not liable. So, Murderer's liability may be crucial to the question of what he may do to Victim should Victim use defensive force against him. If he is not liable to harm, he may acquire a permission to harm Victim in counter-defence. So, it's possible, on the internalist view, that by wrongly trying to kill Victim in circumstances where Victim is able to escape, Murderer acquires a moral permission to kill Victim if Victim uses even proportionate force against him. This, in turn, could ground a permission or even an obligation for third parties to assist Murderer. This is pretty counter-intuitive.

The third implication of the internalism/externalism debate concerns the purposes for which a person who poses a threat may be harmed. The role we grant to necessity can determine whether we adopt either a narrow or a broad view of liability. A person is *narrowly* liable to be harmed if she is liable to be harmed only to avert the particular unjust threat for which she is responsible. A person is *broadly* liable to be harmed if, once she is morally responsible for posing an unjust threat, she is liable to harm to avert any unjust threat, provided the harm we inflict upon her is proportionate to the threat for which she is responsible.

We can illustrate this distinction using the following case:

Alley: Roof Shooter is shooting at Victim from the roof, maliciously trying to kill him. In an independent (but simultaneous) attack, Better Shooter is shooting through a basement window at innocent Victim. Victim can hide from Roof Shooter's bullets, but not from Better Shooter's bullets. However, he can shoot Roof Shooter, whose body will then fall from the roof and block Better Shooter's line of fire, saving Victim's life.[9]

The narrow view of liability holds that Roof Shooter is liable only to harm that averts the particular threat for which he is responsible. Since he's not responsible

[9] I've adapted this from a set of cases in Jeff McMahan, 'Self-Defense and Culpability', *Law and Philosophy*, Vol. 24 (2005), 751–74, at 757.

for Better Shooter's attack, he is not liable to be killed to avert it (even if killing him is necessary to avert it). But the broad view of liability holds that Roof Shooter can be liable to be killed so that he blocks Better Shooter's line of fire. Once he is liable to be defensively killed by Victim, Victim can kill him in defence against another threat to his life.[10]

Internalism is neutral between narrow and broad liability. Internalists need only require that a harm be instrumental in averting *a* threat—they needn't say that it must avert the very same threat for which the target is responsible.[11]

The sort of externalist account I've described above—which determines liability exclusively on the basis of backwards-looking features—is compatible only with broad liability. Since Roof Shooter can, on this account, be liable to be killed even if killing her serves *no* purpose, she can surely be liable to be killed for *any* purpose—as on the broad view. But this kind of 'backwards' externalism is not compatible with narrow liability. If one doesn't tie liability to averting a threat at all—as on the backwards externalist account—then one cannot tie it to averting a particular threat, which is what the narrow view of liability requires. If, in order to be liable to be killed, the target of force must be morally responsible for the particular threat one is trying to avert, this will entail that she can be liable to be killed only if killing her aims at trying to avert a threat. The narrow view of liability doesn't require *necessity*—that force aims at averting a threat doesn't mean that it's the least harmful means of averting it. But it does require *instrumentality*—that the force be *a* means of averting a threat. This makes it incompatible with backwards externalism.

Prima facie, this distinction has significant implications for the ethics of war, if (as I will argue) the moral rules that govern harming in war are reducible to the moral rules that govern harming in ordinary life. If the narrow view of liability is correct, a person on the unjust side of a war will be liable to harm only to avert the particular unjust threats to which she responsibly contributes or that she responsibly poses. Whereas conventional accounts of killing in war hold that enemy

[10] These two kinds of liability correspond to views expressed by McMahan and Hurka in their debate about proportionality in war. Hurka defends the broad view, arguing that once a country makes itself liable to attack, it also makes itself liable to force aimed at achieving additional goods, such as disarmament, even if it would otherwise be disproportionate to pursue disarmament by means of war. McMahan, in line with the narrow view, argues that only those ends that do themselves warrant pursuit by military force (i.e. serious rights violations) can be factored into the proportionality calculation. The country is liable only to force necessary for the correction of those particular wrongs that made war permissible. See Jeff McMahan, 'Just Cause for War', *Ethics and International Affairs*, Vol. 19, No. 3 (2005), 1–21, and Thomas Hurka, 'Proportionality and the Morality of War', *Philosophy and Public Affairs*, Vol. 33, No. 1 (2005), 34–66.

[11] Some internalists do say this—McMahan ties liability to averting the threat for which the attacker is responsible. But they don't *have* to say this.

combatants may be targeted at any time for any military purpose, the narrow view of liability potentially restricts the range of justifications for killing enemy combatants to the aversion of the particular threats that they pose or for which they are responsible. I will not defend either the narrow or broad account here, but merely note the potential importance of this debate, and that adopting a backwards externalist view seems to rule out adopting the narrow account of liability. I'll return to this issue in my discussion of non-combatant liability in Chapter 6.

4.3 Moral Luck

I used to think that an important strike against internalism is the way in which it makes Murderer's liability dependent on a range of variables.[12] For example, in the event that it would be risky for Victim to use his parachute (perhaps the parachute is old and unreliable, or the cliff very high), it seems permissible for Victim to kill Murderer rather than risk his own life by jumping. And I don't think the risk to Victim would have to be very high to make this permissible: I think that if Victim is just not sure whether he will be able to jump to safety because the wind is quite strong, then he is not required to jump. He may instead shoot Murderer to save his own life.

But we might think that there is something troubling with imagining Murderer's liability to defensive harm to pop in and out of existence on the basis of Victim's confidence in his parachuting skills, or the condition of his parachute. The internalist view generates the peculiar result that if he inadvertently attacks a world-class parachutist, who is utterly confident in his ability to jump to safety, Murderer is not liable to be killed. But, if he attacks a novice parachutist, or one who hasn't looked after his equipment—well, then he might be so liable. And yet in both cases Murderer is responsibly trying to inflict lethal harm upon an innocent person. It seems more plausible to think that Murderer's liability remains constant across these variations, whilst the overall permissibility of harming him changes. This captures the intuition that Murderer ought to have control over his liability to being harmed, but that there's less reason to think he ought to have control over whether harming him is all-things-considered permissible.

Quong and Firth argue that the role internalism allows for moral luck is indeed a central reason to reject the internalist view, for precisely the kind of reason I have given—that the right not to be non-consensually killed is an important agency right, and its forfeiture 'should not be influenced by the sort of luck to which the

[12] See Helen Frowe, 'Non-Combatant Liability in War', in Helen Frowe and Gerald Lang (eds.), *How We Fight: Ethics in War* (Oxford: OUP, 2014).

[internalist] account is sensitive'.[13] But I'm no longer sure that this kind of moral luck-based objection is very successful against the internalist view. There are two reasons for this. The first is that even on an externalist account, liability is already sensitive to luck. The second is that on closer inspection, the moral luck objection seems ill-founded.

4.3.1 *Externalism and Luck*

I've been assuming here that on both the internalist and externalist accounts, moral responsibility for an unjust threat is a condition of liability to defensive harm. But whether or not one poses a threat can be a matter of luck. If, unbeknown to you, I've emptied the chamber of your gun, then it will turn out that you don't pose a threat to me when you later point the gun at me and pull the trigger. And, if there's no threat, then you can't be morally responsible for an unjust threat, and so you can't be liable to defensive harm on either the internalist or externalist account.

Quong and Firth argue that this feature of a case—whether one poses a threat—is sufficiently central to determining liability that we must deem it relevant even if it is based on luck. But this doesn't mean that we should allow other sources of luck, such as necessity, into our determinations. They argue that it's a mistake to think that 'if moral luck is unproblematic with regard to the issue of whether one threatens unjust harm, moral luck must be similarly unproblematic when we consider any other condition that is alleged to be relevant to liability to defensive harm'.[14]

But this reply doesn't quite capture the point of the objection to excluding necessity on the grounds that it makes liability sensitive to luck. The objection doesn't claim that if some forms of moral luck are relevant to liability, any form of moral luck can or must be relevant. Rather, it claims that if one allows that some forms of moral luck can be relevant to determinations about liability, the mere fact that necessity is a luck-based element cannot be a reason to exclude it from those determinations. To exclude it on these grounds alone is arbitrary. If we are to rule out necessity because of its dependence on luck, we need a good argument for why allowing luck to play this particular role is unacceptable. The claim about some forms of luck being too central to liability to do without doesn't strike me as such an argument. Indeed, it threatens to beg the question against the internalist, since the debate between internalism and externalism is a debate about precisely whether or not necessity *is* central to liability.

[13] Quong and Firth, 'Necessity, Moral Liability and Defensive Harm', 680.
[14] Quong and Firth, 'Necessity, Moral Liability and Defensive Harm', 684.

One can, of course, come to lack rights through events beyond one's control—for example, one might lose one's liberty rights because of insanity. But as I have been using the term forfeiture, it refers to losing one's rights by *acting* in a particular way. One cannot forfeit rights through wholly involuntary behaviour. Whilst forfeiting one's right not to be killed must therefore be to some extent under one's control, it seems to me that this element of control is adequately captured by accounts that make moral responsibility a prerequisite of liability to defensive harm.

Furthermore, the objection to allowing moral luck to play this greater role in determining liability might disappear if we think more carefully about the baseline against which this moral luck can operate. Murderer is culpably and unjustly threatening Victim's life. The normative baseline here is that Victim may kill Murderer without wronging him if he needs to do so to save his own life: this permission obtains on either an internalist or externalist view. The sensitivity to moral luck, then, can serve only to *improve* things for Murderer: he gets *good* moral luck if it turns out that Victim doesn't need to kill him, because he then retains his immunity to being harmed. The luck-free alternative suggested by Quong and Firth—according to which Victim can kill Murderer without wronging him whether or not he needs to—is surely much less appealing to *Murderer*. Given this, Murderer is very unlikely to make the kind of complaint that Quong and Firth make on his behalf—that his rights shouldn't depend on this kind of variable. If these agency rights protect our normative control over our lives, as Quong and Firth claim, Murderer is surely going to prefer a situation in which he retains his right against being non-consensually killed to one in which this right is forfeit. And there doesn't seem to be any other moral objection to allowing luck to be relevant to a person's liability when we do so only when it makes the agent whose rights are in jeopardy better off, and makes nobody else worse off. Doing so is certainly not objectionable from Murderer's perspective, which is the perspective from which Quong and Firth ground their objection.

Quong and Firth might reply that allowing luck to play this role does make someone else worse. It makes Victim worse off. He is not worse off because he must now suffer some harm—he can still avoid that by using the parachute. But he's *morally* worse off because if he uses force against Murderer, Murderer is permitted to fight back or to claim compensation. But again, I think this reply threatens to beg the question against the internalist. Whether or not this forms the basis of a legitimate complaint from Victim is precisely what is at issue between the internalist and the externalist. The internalist thinks Victim *should* be morally worse off if he uses unnecessary force against Murderer, because he wrongs Murderer in doing so.

4.4 Ineffective Force

Lucky Escape illustrates one type of necessity problem that we can call the *least harmful means* problem: it is a case in which force against the attacker is not the least harmful means of avoiding or averting a threat. *Unjust Aggression* illustrates a different type of necessity problem:

> *Unjust Aggression*: Carla is preparing to unjustly attack Dan in order to steal some of his property. She draws up two possible plans of attack. Under the first plan, she will wait until the next time he invites her over, slip a sedative in his coffee, and steal the goods. Under this plan, Dan will be left relatively unharmed (except for the stolen property). But there is a reasonable chance that he will be able to successfully thwart her since she can't get hold of a very strong sedative, and he might notice her slipping the sedative into the coffee. Under the second plan, Carla will break into Dan's house while he is watching TV, kill him using a gun, and steal the goods. Under this second plan, Carla is certain to succeed and kill Dan.[15]

Quong and Firth claim that because in the second scenario 'any attempts at self-defence by Dan are certain to be instrumentally ineffective', the internalist account must pronounce that Carla is not liable to defensive harm. Internalism thus 'yields the very odd result that Carla can ensure moral immunity from defensive harm by choosing to act in a far more harmful and unjust manner'.[16]

What Quong and Firth say about this case (and some of the other cases they discuss) suggests to me that they just haven't understood internalism, or at least that they're not addressing the most plausible version of it. The internalist view will not hold that Carla is immune to defensive harm because she attacks Dan with overwhelming force that he cannot defeat. Rather, it will hold that Carla is liable to be killed by Dan because (let's assume) killing her would avert the threat, and nothing less than killing her will avert the threat. If Dan could kill her, then, this would be the least harmful means of averting the threat to his life. The fact that he can't kill her doesn't show that killing Carla isn't necessary, and doesn't show that she isn't liable to be killed on the internalist view. Whether or not a given amount of force will stop Carla from killing Dan is not determined by Dan's capabilities.

[15] Quong and Firth, 'Necessity, Moral Liability and Defensive Harm', 688.
[16] Quong and Firth, 'Necessity, Moral Liability and Defensive Harm', 688.

There's a difference between whether proportionate defence is *possible*, and whether proportionate defence would *work*, where to work would be to avert the threat. Internalists reject liability to defensive harm in cases where (a) one can escape the threat using less harmful means, as in *Lucky Escape*, or (b) even if one used proportionate defensive force, that force would not avert the threat. This is why McMahan says that non-combatants are generally not liable to be killed. The reason is not that killing non-combatants is impossible—it clearly isn't—but because *even if one killed them*, this would not avert the threats for which they are responsible. As he puts it, 'a person is liable to be harmed only if harming him will serve some further purpose—for example, if it will prevent him from unjustly harming someone else'.[17] Killing Carla *would* serve the purpose of saving Dan, and so she's liable to be killed on the internalist view.[18]

To see this difference, contrast *Unjust Aggression* with *Unjust Poisoning*:

Unjust Poisoning: Carla has been slowly poisoning Dan over several weeks. Dan has already consumed a lethal dose of the poison (for which there is no antidote) and will certainly die no matter what.

In this case, killing Carla will serve no purpose and in *this* case the internalist will say that Carla is not liable to defensive killing. But this is because killing Carla would not *work*, irrespective of whether killing her is possible. In these cases of ineffective force, in which there is no amount of force that could avert the threat for which she is responsible, no harm inflicted on Carla can be instrumental. Thus, as I shall argue below, no harm inflicted upon Carla can be defensive—irrespective of the kind of account of liability one holds. But internalists needn't reject liability to defensive harm in cases where killing the aggressor would be proportionate and would avert the threat, but defence is not possible because the victim lacks the strength or means to inflict the necessary harm.[19]

[17] McMahan, *Killing in War*, 8.

[18] Another way in which we can see that Carla is liable to be killed is by thinking about what a third party could do. It's obvious that a third party could shoot Carla to save Dan, and most people think that a third party's right of other-defence to kill Carla must derive from Dan's right of self-defence against Carla. If Carla really did have moral immunity against being harmed, it's hard to see why a third party would be permitted to kill her.

[19] Of course, there's a different sense in which the necessity condition *is* tied to the defender's capabilities. If Attacker would be stopped by a pinch on the nose, but Victim is too short to reach his nose, kicking Attacker in the shin could count as necessary force. We should not understand the necessity condition as requiring that one use the least amount of force that would in fact avert the threat. Rather, it requires that individuals use the least harmful means available to them.

4.5 Insufficient Force

Another sort of necessity problem that's been discussed in the literature involves the use of force that is unnecessary because it is *insufficient* to avert the threat the victim faces, and yet it is the maximum amount of force the victim has at her disposal. Quong and Firth explore the problem of insufficient force with the following case, *Rape*:

> *Rape*: Eric is in the midst of culpably raping Fran. Eric is much bigger and stronger than Fran, and consequently there is nothing she can do to stop him from continuing to rape her. While being raped, Fran threatens to break Eric's wrist, though this will do nothing to stop the rape from occurring. The only way Eric can stop Fran breaking his wrist is to quickly break her wrist first.[20]

Suzanne Uniacke has pointed out that a harm must have some chance of averting a threat to count as necessary defence.[21] If so, it looks like the moderate harm Fran can inflict fails the necessity condition and is impermissible. She'd be permitted to kill Eric to stop the rape, but she may not inflict lesser harms that won't even mitigate the rape.

Rape raises two questions: whether Fran may break Eric's wrist when doing so won't curtail the rape, and whether Eric may do anything to stop her. Quong and Firth argue that the internalist account will tell us that because breaking Eric's wrist 'stands no chance' of averting the rape, and is thus not necessary for averting it, Eric cannot be liable to it. Internalism must therefore deny Fran a permission to break Eric's wrist, and permit Eric to defend himself against the infliction of the broken wrist by breaking Fran's wrist first.

As Quong and Firth say, that seems a pretty dreadful result. But contrary to what Quong and Firth suppose, I think that rather than undermining internalism, *Rape* shows why purely backwards-looking externalist views are false.

4.5.1 Defensive Action and Defensive Harm

To see why this is, we need to recognize a distinction between defensive action and defensive harm. I mentioned above Uniacke's claim that a harm must have

[20] Quong and Firth, 'Necessity, Moral Liability and Defensive Harm', 689. I've slightly altered their description of the case, because they describe Fran as 'trying to resist', which makes it sound like Fran doesn't know that her attempt will be futile. For the sake of clarity, I will treat Fran as knowing that she can't stop the rape.

[21] Suzanne Uniacke, 'Self-Defence, Just War and a Reasonable Prospect of Success', in Frowe and Lang (eds.), *How We Fight*, 66.

some chance of averting a threat if it is to count as *necessary* defence. But we can make a stronger claim: a harm must have some chance of averting a threat if it is to count as *defensive*. It might be helpful to think about a roulette case to see how defensive action and defensive harm can come apart. If all the chambers of your gun are empty when you point it at my head, killing you cannot avert a threat to me (because there is no threat) and thus to kill you is not to inflict a defensive harm. But I can still sensibly be said to be *acting* in self-defence when I kill you because I believe that killing you will avert a threat to my life. And I think that you are liable to harms that I inflict in the course of trying to defend myself—they're just not defensive harms.

Whether an action is defensive, then, is determined by the agent's beliefs and intentions. But one can inflict a defensive harm even if one is not acting defensively. Consider *Sprinkler*:

> *Sprinkler*: Gunman is just about to shoot Victim through Victim's kitchen window. Victim has no idea that Gunman is there, but since he's off to bed, he turns on his powerful garden sprinkler. A jet of water hits Gunman in the eye as he pulls the trigger, causing his bullet to miss Victim.

I don't think we should say that in turning on his sprinkler, Victim acted defensively, because he lacks the requisite beliefs about there being a threat and lacks any defensive intent. But I do think the harm he inflicts on Gunman is a defensive harm, because it is in fact a harm that defends his life.

Now imagine that Victim knows that Gunman is about to shoot him, but he has no sprinkler and there's no time to do anything else to stop Gunman from killing him. Victim spits at Gunman. He does not believe that this can avert the threat—he correctly believes it will do nothing at all to deter Gunman or deflect the bullet. Is Victim acting in self-defence when he spits at Gunman? Again, I don't think he is, because not just anything that one does whilst knowing that one's life is in danger can count as acting in self-defence. The category of defensive actions must be demarcated in some way, and the most plausible way to do this is to look at the agent's beliefs and intentions: at what they think their actions can achieve. If Victim does not believe that there is a threat, or does not believe that his actions can avert a threat, he doesn't count as acting in self-defence. And, like in the roulette case, spitting at Gunman when this will not avert a threat is not an unnecessary defensive harm—rather, it is not a defensive harm at all.

We can now see why cases like *Rape* undermine purely backwards-looking accounts of liability to defensive harm. The problem is that such accounts will deem attackers liable to harm irrespective of whether or not such harms will avert a threat—that is, irrespective of whether or not such harms are even defensive. But an account of liability to defensive harm should not justify the infliction of harms that are not defensive. Backwards externalism proves too much.

How does internalism fare in *Rape*? Well, Quong and Firth are correct that if harming Eric cannot avert a threat, internalism will not pronounce Eric liable to harm. But, as I've suggested, that's the correct result. If harming Eric cannot avert a threat, an account of liability to defensive harm should not declare him liable to harm.

However, as I will argue in section 4.8, harming Eric in *Rape* does, in fact, avert a threat. It averts a threat to Fran's honour, even though it does not avert the rape. Thus, internalism can pronounce Eric liable to harm after all. But unlike backwards externalism, it does so only when harming Eric can avert a threat—that is, only when harming him can be defensive. It does not pronounce him liable irrespective of whether harming him can be defensive.

If purely backwards-looking externalism fails, are there any other alternatives to internalism? Quong and Firth propose a pluralist account of liability to defensive harm. In section 4.6, I argue that we should reject their pluralist account in favour of what I call proportionate means externalism.

4.5.2 *Averting a Threat*

First, though, we should notice that there's some equivocation in what I say above between a harm's being unable to avert a threat and a harm's failing to avert a threat. A harm might, prior to infliction, seem to have some prospect of averting a threat, and then fail to do so. On what we might call more 'objectivist' accounts, we might say that such a harm was never able to avert the threat. Combined with my account of defensive harm, this entails that such harms do not count as defensive (although, as outlined above, this is compatible with the claim that inflicting the harm is a defensive *action*, and that the attacker is liable to the harms even if they are not defensive).[22] But we might also take a more probabilistic view of defensive harm, according to which a harm counts as defensive as long as it has or had some prospect of averting a threat—judged perhaps by inference from previous instances of self-defence—even if it fails to avert it. Combining this claim with my account of defensive harm will result in a wider range of harms counting as defensive harms. The debate here is over whether having some chance of success is both necessary and sufficient for a harm's counting as defensive, or

[22] In Chapter 5, I suggest that a harm that seems to have some prospect of averting a threat is best described as a *potentially* defensive harm. If the harm fails to avert a threat, we can say *ex post* that it was *merely potentially* defensive, and not in fact defensive. But we can set that aside for now.

whether this is a necessary, but not sufficient, condition, since the harm must also actually avert the threat in order to count as defensive.

Since I'll be treating *Rape* as a case in which Fran knows that the harm has no prospect of averting the threat, it shouldn't matter for the discussion here whether one prefers the objectivist view or the probability-based view. All that's needed for my purposes is that we grant that there can be cases in which a person faces a threat and inflicts a harm on her attacker knowing that it will not avert that threat.

4.6 The Pluralist Account

Quong and Firth argue that we should reject internalism in favour of their pluralist account of liability, which combines backwards externalism with a humanitarian duty to aid when one can do so at a low cost to oneself. According to this view, even when a person forfeits her right not to be killed by being morally responsible for an unjust threat, she retains a general humanitarian right to be aided when aiding her will impose only a low cost on others. From this right to be aided when the cost of aiding is low, we can derive a right not to be harmed when the cost of not harming is low, since our obligations not to harm are weightier than our obligations to aid. If there's a duty to aid, there is certainly a duty not to harm.

So, a person who lacks a right not to be killed is only partly liable to be killed, since she retains her general humanitarian right to be aided. To be fully liable, such that killing her in no way wrongs her, she must also lack a right to this kind of basic humanitarian consideration. In cases where Victim can refrain from killing Murderer at only a low cost to himself, he violates Murderer's humanitarian rights if he nonetheless kills him. This captures Quong and Firth's view that Victim wrongs Murderer by killing him unnecessarily. But they argue that it also limits what Murderer can do to Victim if Victim uses force against him: 'by breaching a low-cost duty such as the humanitarian duty, one becomes liable to only a low degree of force because this duty is only a duty to bear a low degree of cost'.[23] So, if Victim tries to kill Murderer, Murderer can use *some* force to try to stop him, but only a pretty moderate amount, because any more would exceed Victim's liability. (Presumably any claim to compensation would be similarly limited.)

This is Quong and Firth's attempt to deal with the problem I mentioned at the outset: reconciling the impermissibility of killing Murderer with denying Murderer a right to counter-defence. Externalism is, to a large extent, motivated

[23] Quong and Firth, 'Necessity, Moral Liability and Defensive Harm', 699.

by the intuition that Murderer shouldn't have a right of counter-defence. And yet, if also we want to say that Victim acts impermissibly in needlessly killing Murderer, we seem committed to the view that Victim fails in some sort of duty if he harms Murderer. If that's right, Victim must render himself liable to *something*, it seems, in light of this failure. Quong and Firth's compromise is to permit Murderer to use some force, but to ground this permission in a right to make Victim comply with his humanitarian duty rather than Murderer's right not to be killed (which is of course forfeit). They then limit the force Murderer may use to the low cost that it would be proportionate to make Victim bear to comply with this humanitarian duty.

Quong and Firth argue that although the pluralist account does not produce perfectly intuitive results in the cases they discuss, it does a significantly better job than the internalist account. But, as I have argued above, they've largely misunderstood what internalists would say about the cases they discuss. Properly understood, internalism fares just as well or better than the pluralist view in many of Quong and Firth's own cases. For example, of *Unjust Aggression*, Quong and Firth say that '[o]n our account [Carla] cannot make herself immune to defensive harm by choosing to unjustly attack others in a manner that is certain to succeed. On the pluralist account, whether an attacker is fully liable to defensive harm in cases like *Unjust Aggression* depends on whether the attacker retains her humanitarian right, and this is determined by the cost to the defensive agent of refraining from harm, and not by the probability of the defensive harm being successful.'[24] They claim a difference of 'real moral significance' compared to the internalist, because even though Dan is effectively defenceless, 'it remains true that Carla is, as a matter of morality, liable to his defensive actions'.[25]

But as I have argued, whether the internalist pronounces Carla liable to be killed does not depend on whether Dan can kill her. It depends on whether killing her would stop her from killing Dan. Assuming it would, internalism pronounces Carla straightforwardly liable to be killed. There's no victory for the pluralist account here.

This is especially so given that it looks like the pluralist account will accord Carla a humanitarian right against Dan. Since Dan is certain to die, the cost to him of refraining from non-lethally harming Carla—of fulfilling his humanitarian duty—is nothing. And so Carla does not look to be 'fully liable' to defensive harm on the pluralist account after all. By Quong and Firth's own lights, this seems to be a worse result than the result we get on the internalist account.

[24] Quong and Firth, 'Necessity, Moral Liability and Defensive Harm', 699.

[25] Quong and Firth, 'Necessity, Moral Liability and Defensive Harm', 700.

In a case like *Unjust Poisoning*, however, the internalist will not pronounce Carla liable to be killed. But, as I've argued, this is the correct result. If harming Carla cannot avert a threat to Dan, harming her is not defensive and should not be justified by an account of liability to defensive harm. The pluralist view, in contrast, will prohibit harming Carla only because of her humanitarian rights, just like in *Unjust Aggression*. Dan can refrain from harming her at no cost to himself. The pluralist view fails to recognize that this case is different to *Unjust Aggression*, because this is a case in which there is no defensive harm to which Carla can be liable.

4.6.1 Less-Than-Culpable Aggressors

It seems to me that unnecessarily killing a person gets worse the less morally responsible she is for posing a threat.[26] Consider *Breakdown*:

> *Breakdown*: Victim's car breaks down in a remote area. He knocks on the door of an isolated farm to ask to use the phone. Unbeknown to him, there's been a series of gruesome murders in the local area. Warnings have been issued to local residents to be wary of strangers. When Resident opens the door, she thinks Victim is the violent murderer come to kill her and tries to shoot him. Victim can either shoot Resident before she shoots him, or he can jump off her porch, getting out of her line of fire.[27]

Let's assume that Resident is morally responsible for the unjust threat she poses to Victim.[28] Neither the internalist account nor the pluralist account distinguishes between unnecessarily killing culpable and less-than-culpable aggressors. This isn't such a pressing problem for internalism, since it prohibits unnecessarily killing either sort of aggressor. But it is a problem for Quong and Firth's pluralist account. Their humanitarian duty—the source of the prohibition on using unnecessary force on the pluralist account—is sensitive to the cost to Victim of refraining from killing a person. But it isn't sensitive to the worseness of killing Resident compared to killing Murderer, as long as the cost to Victim of refraining from killing either is the same. The cost one has to bear to fulfil one's humanitarian duty

[26] Thanks to Jonathan Parry for first drawing my attention to this problem.

[27] Based on a case in Jeff McMahan, 'The Basis of Moral Liability to Defensive Killing', *Philosophical Issues: Normativity*, Vol. 15 (2005), 387–405, at 387.

[28] There's probably some disagreement about this. I'm assuming that Resident's belief isn't based on sufficiently good evidence to meet the reasonable belief standard that I explored in Chapter 3. Those who reject responsibility in this case can substitute some other case in which there seems to be only minimal moral responsibility for the unjust threat.

is a fixed cost, being grounded in 'urgent need and not by appeal . . . to responsible choices'.[29] It is thus explicitly insensitive to a person's culpability or lack thereof. And this isn't something Quong and Firth can easily change, since making the duty sensitive to an attacker's responsibility will of course undermine the idea that there is a duty to refrain from harming a culpable attacker such as Murderer, which is the reason for including this humanitarian duty in the pluralist account in the first place. There is, therefore, no requirement on the pluralist account that Victim bear more of a cost to avoid killing a person who is only minimally morally responsible for posing a threat compared to the cost he must bear to avoid killing a fully culpable attacker.

This means that, as well as being unable to capture the moral worseness of certain killings, there will be cases in which the pluralist account holds that killing Resident is permissible when (it seems to me) killing her is impermissible. I think that if Victim can jump off the porch at the cost of breaking his arm, he ought to do that rather than kill Resident. Assuming that a broken arm counts as a serious cost, Quong and Firth's humanitarian duty has no purchase in these cases since that duty requires that Victim bear only a low cost to fulfil it.[30] This means that, counter-intuitively, they cannot deem it impermissible to kill Resident to avoid a broken arm.

Given what I have argued so far, I suggest that we reject both backwards externalism and Quong and Firth's pluralism. The only genuine rival to the internalist account is something that I will call proportionate means externalism. Proportionate means externalism denies that aggressors can be liable only to necessary harms—that is, only to the least harmful means of averting a threat. But it recognizes that liability to defensive harm means liability to harm that can avert a threat. So, to be liable to harm on this account, an attacker must be morally responsible for an unjust threat and the harm inflicted upon her must be a proportionate means of averting a threat.[31] In *Lucky Escape*, the proportionate means account will hold that since killing Murderer is a proportionate means of averting the lethal threat he poses to Victim, Murderer is liable to be killed. But, as I'll outline below, properly understood, the necessity condition that is standardly included in accounts of permissible defence can do the work that Quong and Firth want their humanitarian duty to do: it explains why Victim ought not to kill Murderer even if Murderer is liable to be killed, but combined with Murderer's liability to honour-defending harms, it explains why Murderer may not lethally defend himself.

[29] Quong and Firth, 'Necessity, Moral Liability and Defensive Harm', 693.

[30] Quong and Firth, 'Necessity, Moral Liability and Defensive Harm', 699.

[31] Again, 'proportionate means' includes not only eliminative harms, but harms that are a side-effect of force that Victim uses to avert a threat.

Proportionate means externalism can also preserve the distinction between liability and desert. As I outlined in section 4.2, backwards externalists distinguish liability from desert by saying that liability does not give us a positive reason to harm someone. It merely denotes the absence of a usual reason against harming them. But the natural way to capture this idea is to invoke the means/ends distinction. Harms to which we are merely liable are instrumental harms: the reason why there's no positive reason to inflict them is that they are not ends in themselves. But by divorcing liability to defensive harm from averting a threat, backwards externalists struggle to gain purchase on the distinction between liability and desert, because they cannot distinguish between harming for a further purpose and harming as an end in itself. On a purely backwards externalist account, one can be liable to 'defensive' harms that serve no purpose at all. Proportionate means externalists, in contrast, can agree with the internalist that deserved harms are ends in themselves, whereas harms to which we are merely liable are valuable only as a means of achieving a goal.

This is why a person who is liable to defensive harm may use non-harmful means to prevent herself from suffering that harm, even though she may not harmfully defend herself. The same would not be true if I were inflicting a harm that you deserved to suffer. If you are liable to be defensively killed by me, you may not deflect my defensive bullet back to where it will kill me in order to save your life. But if you can non-harmfully deflect the bullet into empty space, you may do this. This is because, unlike with desert, harms to which we are merely liable aren't ends in themselves. Of course, 'non-harmfully' is to be broadly interpreted here: if you deflect the bullet in order to continue your unjust attack on me, then this is not an instance of non-harmful defence and is impermissible. But this is just another way of saying that you're not allowed to defend yourself in a way that undermines the goals of the harm—and that's something that we can make sense of only when the harm *has* a goal.

4.7 Against Punitive Justifications for Harming

Many people's intuitive reaction to cases such as *Rape* is probably to think that the reason Fran may break Eric's wrist is that Eric is liable to punitive harm. There is, we might think, a clear sense in which Eric deserves to suffer that makes it very hard for us to condemn Fran for breaking his wrist, or permit Eric to try to harmfully defend himself.

Assuming that all culpable aggressors deserve to be punished, identifying punishment as the justification of defensively unnecessary harms will explain why one may use unnecessary force against all but only culpable aggressors.

This has the advantage of retaining a prohibition on unnecessarily killing minimally morally responsible attackers such as Resident, and explains why a culpable attacker such as Eric or Murderer is not permitted to engage in counter-defence. If they are liable to punitive harms, they may not defend themselves against being harmed.

Relatedly, we might think that part of what justifies harming Eric is the deterrent value of doing so. Even if harming Eric can't fend off his attack, it may be that other potential rapists are discouraged from carrying out attacks if they know that rape victims tend to inflict harms on their attackers. If we grant that culpable attackers can be liable to be harmed as a means in this way, we might think that this helps to explain why Eric is liable to non-defensive harms.

But although punishment is the most obvious candidate for justification for harming Eric, it fails to provide a satisfactory justification for inflicting harm in the cases under discussion.

There are two objections to a punishment-based justification for harming that I think we can overcome. One is that we don't typically allow private individuals to dish out punishment – especially not corporal punishment. There are thus reasons that apply to Fran (for example, of institutional stability or preserving the rule of law) that could mean that she should refrain from punishing Eric herself.

But this objection isn't persuasive because even though a victim ought not to inflict punishment herself, a culpable aggressor is nonetheless liable to punitive harm, and thus may not try to avert it. Given this, Eric may not defend himself against Fran unless she is inflicting harm greater than that to which he would be liable as punishment. In some cases, the punitive harm inflicted by the victim could be deducted from any later punishment by the state.

The second surmountable objection to punishment-based justifications concerns our epistemic fallibility. One reason we don't want individuals to carry out punishments is that they might make mistakes. But this objection seems to have only limited force in Fran's case—probably because our primary concern when it comes to punishment is making sure that we have the real culprit. Under the circumstances, Fran is unlikely to make any kind of mistake about that. The kinds of mistake she might make concern Eric's moral responsibility for what he is doing, and how much punishment he deserves for what he is doing. But again, the first of these concerns has a fairly limited application in this sort of case. It's much easier to imagine a person's having an excuse for posing a lethal threat (like Resident), or some other sort of physical threat, than it is to imagine why Eric would non-culpably believe that he and Fran are engaged in consensual sex.[32] As for how much harm Eric is liable to—Fran might make a mistake about this, but a broken wrist doesn't seem like an excessive punishment for rape. Most people would probably opt for a broken wrist over, say, several years in prison.

More problematic is that a punishment-based justification will permit what I will call deferred harming—that is, harming that takes place once the attacker no longer poses a threat. For example, consider *Late Rape*:

> *Late Rape*: On Monday, Eric rapes Fran. Fran inflicts no harms upon Eric during the rape. On Tuesday, Fran sees Eric in a bar, having a drink. Fran breaks Eric's wrist.

Whether Fran is permitted to break Eric's wrist, and whether Eric can fight back, will depend on whether the justification for harming Eric that seems to obtain in *Rape* still obtains the next day when (let's assume) Eric no longer poses a threat to Fran or anyone else. If it is his liability to punishment that permits harming Eric in *Rape*, then it certainly looks like the deferred harming described in *Late Rape* is also permissible. Liability to punishment is triggered by engaging in wrongdoing, but persists once the wrongdoing has ceased.

Whilst I think most people's intuitions will support the permissibility of Fran's harming Eric during the rape, there is likely to be much less consensus about whether Eric then becomes liable to be harmed by Fran at any time after the rape, or at least until Eric is punished by the state. The permissibility of deferred harming is even less plausible, I think, in *Lucky Escape*: even if we think Victim is permitted to kill Murderer rather than use his parachute whilst Murderer is trying to kill him, it seems unlikely that Victim may use his parachute and then kill Murderer a week later on punitive grounds. Of course, this is probably in part because Murderer hasn't killed Victim: he's guilty only of attempted murder. Perhaps at this point, what it's proportionate to do to Murderer decreases. But attempted murder is still a very serious wrong, and so Murderer should still be liable to some significant harm at Victim's hands if it's punishment that's doing the justificatory work here. And this kind of justification also implies that if Murderer had succeeded in his attack and killed Victim, he would be liable to very significant punitive harm at the hands of third parties. But it doesn't seem

[32] Note the 'non-culpably': doubtless there are many examples of people believing that e.g. having sex with an unconscious person is not rape as long as you had consensual sex with them before they passed out, but this kind of ignorance isn't sufficient to make the rapist's mistaken belief non-culpable.

permissible for Victim's brother to hunt Murderer down and kill him or seriously harm him once Murderer has killed Victim. We might partially excuse such behaviour, but we would not think it a permissible killing.

To permit victims to use force against their attackers on punitive grounds whilst a threat is ongoing, but then prohibit their doing so once the threat has ceased, we would have to hold that the reasons that apply to victims to let the state punish attackers somehow get stronger once the threat has ended. But it's hard to see why this would be the case—unlike defensive action, there's typically no urgency about punitive measures. If we do not think that Murderer and Eric are liable to suffer deferred harm at the hands of their victims, we will need to reject punishment as the source of a liability to non-defensive harm.

4.8 Honour-Based Justifications for Harming

4.8.1 *Statman's Account*

I think that thus far, Daniel Statman has come closest to explaining why Fran is permitted to harm Eric. Statman argues that defending honour can ground a person's right to inflict harm on an aggressor even if this will not avert the rape:

> We realize that, in the eyes of the aggressor, we are just items to be used, mere objects. Given the power of the aggressor and his ability to force his will upon us, we fear that by doing so he will quite literally degrade us. We feel that we must protect not only our body or our property but our *selves* ... To reaffirm our honor in the face of such threats, we need more than abstract thoughts such as 'I'm proud to be who I am, and nobody can diminish my inner sense of worth.' Concrete acts of resistance are needed in order to communicate to the aggressor, to ourselves, and to an actual or potential audience that we are not just passive objects to be trodden upon. By carrying out such acts, we reaffirm or protect our honor.[33]

To be clear: the claim is not that victims lack honour in the sense of being shamed by the attack. Rather, Statman's claim is that victims of aggression are subject to two threats: the primary threat (for example, a threatened rape or killing), and a parasitical threat to their honour. Victims are treated in a way that involves the attacker's refusing to recognize their moral status—a harm that is related to, but distinct from, any physical harm being visited upon them. Barbara Herman, in her exploration of possible Kantian justifications of self-defence, similarly suggests that what makes it permissible to resist an attack is that an attacker's maxim (in the Kantian sense) 'involves ... the discounting of my agency. The aggressor

[33] Statman, 'On the Success Condition for Legitimate Self-Defence', 669.

would use me (take my life) for his purposes. This is what I resist and claim moral title to refuse ... it is not the fact of death but the death as a means to the aggressor's purposes that gives moral title to resistance and self-defense.'[34]

The honour-based justification for harming is appealing because it captures our sense that victims need not be passive in the face of attacks that they cannot avert. The scope of the justification is also likely to be restricted to culpable aggressors. Those who pose unjust threats because, for example, they mistakenly believe that Victim is trying to kill them do not threaten Victim's honour in the way that a culpable attacker such as Murderer does.[35] Resident in *Breakdown* is correct about the sorts of reason that justify trying to harm someone. If Victim really were trying to kill her, she'd be permitted to kill him. Thus, her threatening of Victim doesn't demonstrate some inappropriate lack of regard for him, and therefore the threat that Resident poses to Victim's life doesn't simultaneously threaten his honour.

I think that both internalists and proportionate means externalists can employ this kind of explanation of why Fran may break Eric's wrist in *Rape*. But I think Statman's account of this justification for harming needs some improvement. In what follows, I defend a revised version of Statman's account and explain its implications for internalist and proportionate means accounts.

4.8.2 Honour and Proportionality

Statman argues that the proportionality of the force that honour-assertion justifies in cases like *Rape* is determined by the seriousness of the primary threat posed by the attacker.[36] This solves the problem that an honour-based account might justify, for example, a person's very harmfully defending her honour against some mild unwanted touching. What is proportionate for defending her honour in this case is limited by what is proportionate to avert the touching. But it will allow Fran to use very harmful means to assert her honour in *Rape*. Assuming that lethal force is a proportionate response to rape, harms up to lethal force—for example, permanent paralysis or blindness—will be proportionate for defending the parasitic threat to her honour.

Statman doesn't seem to regard this as an objection to his view: on the contrary, he thinks that what we are seeking to explain is the *permissibility* of, for example, a rape victim's killing two of five attackers even though she knows that this will

[34] Barbara Herman, *The Practice of Moral Judgement* (Cambridge, Mass.: Harvard University Press, 1993), 129.

[35] Thanks to Krister Bykvist for interesting discussion of this point.

[36] Statman, 'On the Success Condition for Legitimate Self-Defence', 681.

not prevent her being raped by the others. A moral theory that prohibited such killings would, he says, demand 'submission to evil and passivity in the face of wickedness'.[37] But I suspect that many people who think that Fran is permitted to break Eric's wrist in *Rape* might nonetheless be reluctant to permit Fran to very seriously harm Eric—perhaps to blind or paralyse him—when she knows that doing so will do nothing to mitigate the rape.

Why is Statman not troubled by this implication of his view? I think the answer lies in the fact that Statman develops his account in the context of defence against multiple attackers, where killing some of the attackers does not ultimately save the victim from harm. His central cases are that of a rape victim who can kill only two of five attackers, John Wayne's killing two of five people who are trying to kill him, and the Warsaw ghetto uprising. Requiring capitulation in these cases does indeed seem to be, as Statman claims, a *reductio* of a moral theory of self-defence.[38] But I don't think any plausible account of self-defence—including those based upon the accounts of liability to defensive harm that are under discussion here—would prohibit these killings.

What theories of permissible defence are looking to explain is what we may do to individuals who endanger us. A rape victim who kills two of her five attackers might not thereby prevent the others from wronging her, but she does prevent *those two men* from wronging her. She averts any threat that they pose, even if other threats persist. It seems to me that such killings are permissible even if, for example, the two people whom she kills were never planning to rape her themselves but only to keep watch or hold her down whilst she is raped by another member of the group (perhaps these are the only two of the five at whom she has a clear shot). Lethal force is a proportionate response to these contributions to a serious wrong such as rape, and thus killing the two men is a proportionate and (let's assume) necessary way of preventing them from performing these wrongs. The same goes for the John Wayne case: Wayne might not prevent other people from killing him by killing two of his attackers, but he prevents *those men* from killing him. There's no reason to think that the targets are not liable to be killed and that such killings could not be all-things-considered permissible on most accounts of self-defence. Such accounts don't typically demand that one's defence be necessary for making oneself better off overall, but only necessary for averting a threat. I may, for example, kill a (culpable) person who will otherwise kill me even if I'm certain to die of an illness the next day.

[37] Statman, 'On the Success Condition for Legitimate Self-Defence', 664.
[38] Statman, 'On the Success Condition for Legitimate Self-Defence', 664.

Statman's mischaracterization of the problem is important not only because it both fails to illustrate the puzzle of unnecessary (or in his terms, unsuccessful) defence with which he's supposed to be dealing and misrepresents what theories of self-defence say about such cases. His use of these cases also lends credence to his claim that killing can be a proportionate defence of honour. If we present these as cases of unnecessary defence against physical threats, and combine that with our intuition that the killings are nonetheless permissible, this supports Statman's conclusion that killing is a proportionate response to threats to honour. But, as I've argued, these are not really cases of unsuccessful or unnecessary defence at all. That killing is proportionate in these cases cannot, therefore, show that it's proportionate to kill to defend honour.

Once we suppose that harming the attacker does not avert or mitigate the primary threat that he poses, as we do in the Eric and Fran *Rape* case that I have been discussing, we get a genuine case of unnecessary (or unsuccessful) defence. But now it's much less clear that very harmful measures are justified for the defence of honour alone. May Fran really permanently paralyse or blind Eric when this will not even mitigate the rape? I do not think that she may.

I agree with Statman that the proportionality of defence of honour is indeed sensitive to the seriousness of the primary threat. The gravity of the threat to honour is likely to increase as the seriousness of the primary threat increases because a threat to honour is about the wrongness of thinking that one may do this sort of thing to one's victim.[39] The worse that one is treating one's victim in terms of the primary threat, the more one denies her status as a person deserving of a certain sort of consideration. Thinking that you are the sort of thing that I can slap because I feel like slapping you is not as significant a threat to your honour as thinking that you are the sort of thing I can rape or kill or seriously assault because I feel like raping, killing, or seriously assaulting you.

But even though the threat to honour increases the more serious the primary threat becomes, this does not entail that the threat to honour is *as bad as* the primary threat, and that therefore whatever is proportionate in warding off the primary threat must also be proportionate in averting the threat to honour. The wrongness of being treated as the sort of thing that may be subjected to a harm is not the same (and is not as bad) as being subjected to that harm. This partly explains the difference in punishment between inchoate and choate crimes: it's

[39] As I suggested above, this is why this sort of justification doesn't hold against someone like Resident—because she is not wrongly attributing to Victim some kind of inappropriate status ('I can kill you because I don't like you'). On the contrary, she is correct about the sort of circumstances under which she may kill Victim—namely, when he will otherwise unjustly kill her.

very bad when I treat you as someone whom I'm permitted to kill because I don't like you, but it's not as bad as actually killing you because I don't like you. There is, therefore, a limit to what defence of honour alone can justify, even where the threat to honour is at the most serious end of the scale. As always when judging proportionate harms, it's hard to say exactly what the defence of a particular good warrants—especially when it's an intangible good such as honour. But it seems to me that a moderate harm like a broken wrist or arm falls below the threshold, and that serious harms such as blindness, death, or paralysis fall above it. Whilst honour in the sense under discussion here is important, it is not as important as not being raped or killed, and its defence does not justify the infliction of very serious harms. (It's also likely that anything beyond such moderate harms would not be necessary for defending one's honour. When we think about what it is that such harms try to convey—a refusal to be passive, a refusal to be complicit, a means of asserting oneself as a person worthy of better treatment—it seems that even in the face of a serious threat to one's honour such as that present during rape, inflicting a moderate harm upon one's attacker (a broken limb, for example) would suffice to manifest such an attitude, which is what constitutes the defence of one's honour.)

4.8.3 Deferred Harming

Can the honour-based justification avoid sanctioning deferred harming? Statman seems to think that it cannot: 'Unlike the defense of life, in which Victim must act before the threat materializes, acts to restore Victim's honor can take place afterward ... it might never be too late to get even.'[40] Absent the kind of institution-preserving reasons that I mentioned in relation to punishment, Statman suggests that there might be no way to limit the time frame in which victims can harm their attackers.[41]

But I think this is too quick. Statman is somewhat ambiguous about whether the harms that he is trying to justify defend or 're-assert' honour (see, for example, the material quoted in section 4.8.1). But the view is most plausible when it is conceived of as defence against a threat to honour rather than an attempt to restore honour *ex post*. Statman says that the threat to honour is parasitical on the primary threat. If we take this to mean that the honour-based justification for harming supervenes upon the existence of the primary threat, this entails that once the primary, physical threat is over, the threat to honour (notice: not the harm to honour)

[40] Statman, 'On the Success Condition for Legitimate Self-Defence', 673.

[41] And as I suggested above, these institution-preserving reasons wouldn't show a lack of liability on the part of the attacker, but only give the victim reasons to refrain from inflicting harm.

is also over. Once the threat to honour has ceased to exist, nothing that the victim can do can avert that threat to her honour. Thus, neither the proportionate means account nor the internalist account will deem an attacker liable to physical harming of the attacker *ex post*.

The attacker can, of course, still be liable to other, non-physical methods of *ex post* restoration. Why only non-physical methods? Well, it is generally preferable that people avoid unjust harms rather than suffer such harms and be compensated later. Even if giving me a certain amount of money fully compensates me for a broken leg, there's nothing odd or irrational about my preferring that you not break my leg in the first place. And since we might think that there are some harms that cannot be fully compensated, there will be many cases in which it's morally better that harm be avoided rather than suffered and partially compensated later on. Thus, if a victim can defend herself against a threat to her honour—that is, if she can prevent her honour's being compromised in the first place—this is better than giving her access to restorative measures later on.

This gives us a reason to allow a victim to physically defend her honour whilst denying her a permission to physically harm her attacker later on, because such harming is justified only when it achieves the good of averting or mitigating the threat, not the lesser good of restoration *ex post*. Contra Statman, then, we need not sanction deferred physical harming if we take defence (and not restoration) of honour to justify harms that cannot avert the primary threat. Moreover, as Statman argues, such harms don't seem to raise the kind of success concerns that we encounter when thinking about defence against physical threats. We don't have the problem that, for example, Fran might inflict harm on Eric and somehow this would fail to avert the threat to her honour, as it might fail to avert the rape. This is because it is in part the *trying* that defends honour, and thus 'such actions necessarily succeed ... in achieving their goal'.[42] And, successfully averting the primary threat is also a way of averting a parasitic threat to one's honour. Thus, if Fran were able to fend off the rape, she would thereby fend off the threat to her honour. The account does not, therefore, justify the inflicting of additional harms when there has been successful defence against the primary threat.

So, both internalism and proportionate means externalism can account for the permissibility of Fran's breaking Eric's wrist. What should they say about least harmful means cases such as *Lucky Escape*?

[42] Statman, 'On the Success Condition for Legitimate Self-Defence', 679.

Internalism and the proportionate means account face asymmetrical challenges in such cases. The proportionate means account holds that an aggressor is liable even to unnecessary harms, as long as they will avert a proportionate threat. This explains why an aggressor may not fight back against unnecessary harms—the harms do not wrong him. But the account then needs to explain the intuition that a victim ought not to inflict such harms, even though the aggressor is liable to them. Of course some proponents of this view might simply deny that a victim does anything wrong if she harms an aggressor unnecessarily. But, as I have argued, thinking about less-than-culpable aggressors shows us that this response is implausible. It seems clearly impermissible to kill Resident rather than jump off the porch. And, I think it's also impermissible to kill Murderer in *Lucky Escape*.

Internalism, in contrast, holds that an aggressor is not liable to unnecessary harms. This explains why a victim ought not to inflict such harms—the harms will wrong the aggressor. But internalism then needs to explain the intuition that aggressors may not fight back should their victim choose to inflict unnecessary harm. Again, some internalists may simply reject the claim that an aggressor may not fight back. Perhaps Murderer does acquire a permission to kill Victim if Victim tries to defend himself rather than use the parachute. But in conversation at least, several internalists agree that there are restrictions on what an aggressor may do to a victim who uses unnecessary defensive force. The aggressor is not in the same position as a wholly innocent person who finds himself suffering an unjust attack. The internalist thus needs to explain what grounds these restrictions.

4.9 Prohibitions on Counter-Defence

4.9.1 Moral Responsibility

Some internalists have suggested that if Victim chooses to try to harm Murderer, we can deny Murderer a right of defence, even though he's not liable to the harms that Victim will inflict. Kai Draper and Jeff McMahan have both suggested that this is because Murderer bears greater responsibility than Victim for the situation in which Murderer is harmed.[43]

This seems plausible when it's applied to rights to compensation rather than rights of defence. The connection between liability and compensation is more tenuous: whilst there is perhaps a presumption in favour of compensation when a person suffers a harm to which they are not liable, this presumption can be

[43] McMahan put forward this argument in 'The Limits of Self-Defence: Retreat, Submission and Conditional Threats', at a workshop on self-defence at Bowling Green State University, April 2013. Draper suggested it in discussion at the same event.

defeated.[44] But I'm not sure that it shows that Murderer lacks of a right of defence. For a start, it's not obviously true that Murderer is more responsible than Victim for the current situation. Murderer did have an opportunity to ensure than neither he nor Victim need bear a cost, since he could have refrained from attacking Victim. But Victim also has such an opportunity, since he could have jumped to safety without harming Murderer. If he chooses not to, it *is* his choice. This is not a case in which someone other than Victim is solely—and therefore more—responsible for bringing it about that someone must suffer a harm. Murderer may be partly responsible—presumably Victim wouldn't have tried to harm Murderer at all if Murderer hadn't try to kill him. But this doesn't show that Murderer is *more* responsible than Victim for the fact that, now, one of them must bear a cost.

Even if we grant that Murderer is more responsible than Victim for the unjust threat that Victim poses, I'm not sure that this is helpful to the internalist. Being morally responsible for an unjust threat usually rules out one's having defensive rights because it is a ground of liability to harm. But taking this line here is effectively a denial of the internalist view, because it means that Murderer is liable to unnecessary force. Moreover, it looks incoherent. What would make Murderer liable to harm is his moral responsibility for an unjust threat. In this case, what grounds Murderer's liability is his responsibility for the very unjust threat that internalists are saying he may not fend off—the threat posed by Victim. But if he's liable to suffer the harm that Victim will inflict, in virtue of his moral responsibility for it, Victim's responding threat is no longer an *unjust* threat. And if it's not an unjust threat, how can Murderer's moral responsibility for it be a ground of liability? Something has gone wrong here. I don't see how invoking Murderer's greater moral responsibility will help bring internalism in line with our intuition that Murderer may not fight back. The internalist will need to come up with some other explanation of why Murderer may not kill Victim in counter-defence.

4.10 Honour and Necessity

The most plausible way for a proponent of the proportionate means account to explain why Victim ought not to unnecessarily harm even a liable attacker is to invoke the necessity condition that is standardly attached to accounts of

[44] See e.g. Victor Tadros, 'Orwell's Battle with Brittan: Vicarious Liability for Unjust Aggression', *Philosophy and Public Affairs*, Vol. 42, No. 1 (2014), 42–77, at 48. Tadros suggests that it can be wrong to make a person who owes compensation pay up under certain circumstances (if, for example, my doing so would leave me unable to provide for my children). We might think that it can be wrong to make a victim of aggression pay compensation when the beneficiary triggered the harm by subjecting her to an unjust attack.

permissible defence. The existence of this condition must be grounded in a more general moral requirement not to cause unnecessary harm to people and other sentient beings—I take the existence of such a requirement to be relatively uncontroversial.[45] Even if killing an attacker does not wrong her and she has no special complaint against being unnecessarily harmed, it can still be all-things-considered impermissible to harm her.

Victim's unnecessarily killing Resident strikes me as much worse than his unnecessarily killing Murderer (assuming that Victim realizes that Resident threatens him only because she has made a pretty reasonable mistake). Given that Victim will fail in his duty not to cause unnecessary harm if he kills Resident, third parties (and Resident) may use force to prevent his killing her. The proportionality of the force they may use is established by the extent of the breach of his duty—that is, the seriousness of the harm he will unnecessarily inflict on Resident. If Victim tries to kill Resident, they may kill him in defence of her life.

But although the necessity condition also applies to the all-things-considered permissibility of killing culpable aggressors, it will not permit lethal defence by (or on behalf of) culpable aggressors, even if Victim is trying to unnecessarily kill the aggressor.

Since culpable attackers threaten Victim's honour, some harm inflicted upon Murderer can be necessary as a means of Victim's defending his honour, even if it is not necessary for averting the threat to Victim's life. So, even if Victim is going to kill Murderer rather than use his parachute, not all of the harm that Victim inflicts in killing Murderer breaches his duty not to inflict unnecessary harm. Since Murderer poses a lethal threat, it will be proportionate for Victim to inflict quite significant harm to defend his honour, and thus a substantial component of the lethal harm Victim inflicts will satisfy the necessity constraint. Whilst Murderer may inflict some defensive harm on Victim to prevent the remaining, unnecessary harm, he may not use lethal force against him. The amount of force that it's proportionate for Murderer to use is determined by reference to the amount of *unnecessary*, morally weighted harm that Victim will inflict, not the total harm that Victim inflicts. Once we subtract the harm that it is necessary for Victim to inflict in defence of his honour, the remaining unnecessary harm will not permit a lethal response from Murderer. Only less than lethal harm will be a proportionate response.

If the internalists adopt something like the honour-based justification for harming that I have defended, they too can get this kind of result in *Lucky Escape*.

[45] Of course, different moral theories will explain the requirement's existence in different ways.

Murderer will be liable to the harm that's necessary to avert the threat to Victim's honour. He may therefore use force to defend himself only against the excess harm that exceeds what Victim may inflict in defending his honour. This will afford Murderer some limited right of counter-defence to avert the remaining harm to which he is not liable, just as the proportionate means account allows Murderer to use some force to make Victim comply with his duty not to cause unnecessary harm.

Overall, then, it seems to me that combined with an honour-based justification for harming, both accounts of liability can explain why Victim ought not to harm an attacker unnecessarily, and also why culpable attackers like Murderer may not employ lethal counter-defence against unnecessary lethal defence. So do we have any reason to prefer one account over the other? I think we might, since I think the proportionate means account is better at dealing with cases like *Alley*, in which Victim can harm one aggressor in order to avert a threat posed by someone else. I return to these cases in Chapter 6.

4.11 Liability and Proportionality

The relationship between proportionality and liability is less controversial than the relationship between necessity and liability. This is because it seems that proportionality must be internal to liability, because one cannot simply 'be liable', but must rather be liable *to something*—namely, to suffer a certain amount of harm. Stipulating the amount of harm one is liable to seems to be the work of the proportionality requirement. We might disagree about how one ought to judge proportionality, but it does nonetheless seem that this will be a disagreement about how much harm a threatening person is liable to.

The only alternative to this picture seems to be a kind of 'all or nothing' approach to liability. On this picture, once one is liable to any defensive harm, one is liable to maximum force.[46] This could mean the maximum force necessary for averting a threat, if one thinks necessity internal to liability. Or, if one does not think necessity internal to liability, it could mean simply unlimited force: that once one is liable to defensive harm, one lacks rights against having any amount of force inflicted upon one. Of course, as with necessity, those who

[46] As far as I know, the only person who defends this sort of view is Peter Vallentyne. See e.g. 'Defense of Self and Others against Culpable Rights Violators' (unpublished manuscript, 2013, available at time of going to press at <http://www.bgsu.edu/content/dam/BGSU/college-of-arts-and-sciences/philosophy/documents/conferences/2013/defense.pdf>).

hold this view could still grant that proportionality is required for defence to be all-things-considered permissible. But whereas an external necessity constraint can be explained by reference to a more general moral requirement not to cause unnecessary harm, it's not clear what would explain the existence of an external proportionality constraint. That a harm is proportionate doesn't mean it's necessary. Unlike with necessity, it seems that the only thing that can explain a proportionality requirement is a connection between the wrong that one performs and the rights that one forfeits as a result. But this makes the requirement internal to liability. If we reject this, we effectively deny that permissible defence is governed by a proportionality condition at all. This seems to me an unappealing and implausible view. Thus, while I say more about judging proportionality in Chapter 5, I won't further defend here the view that proportionality is internal to liability.

4.12 Summary

Internalist accounts of liability to defensive harm hold that one can be liable only to the least harmful, proportionate means of averting a threat. Externalist accounts hold that one can be liable to proportionate harm that is not the least harmful means of averting a threat. Until now, externalists have taken this to mean that one can be liable to harm that is not a means of averting a threat at all. The purely backwards-looking externalism that I have described here holds that liability to defensive harm requires only that an attacker be morally responsible for an unjust threat. But, as I have argued, this does not give us an account of liability to defensive harm, since it justifies the infliction of harms that are not instrumental in averting a threat, and only instrumental harms count as defensive harms.

I have thus proposed a new externalist account. Proportionate means externalism holds that a person can be liable only to harms that are instrumental in averting a threat, and that are proportionate to the threat that the person poses. I have argued that what explains the permissibility of inflicting harm in insufficiency cases such as *Rape* is that the victim is defending her honour, even if she cannot avert or mitigate the physical threat. Both internalists and proportionate means externalists can avail themselves of this explanation. But proponents of either account must recognize that since this justification for harming rests upon an attacker's culpability, it will likely have force in other cases involving culpable attackers in which Victim can defend himself by harming the attacker.

The real difference between the internalist and proportionate means accounts emerges in cases like *Lucky Escape* and *Breakdown*, where we want to know whether (and why) an attacker has a right of counter-defence against Victim. I argued that the proportionate means account can explain these cases by thinking about the necessity condition and the weighting of harm. The internalist, in contrast, will have to insist that culpable attackers such as Murderer are not liable to any unnecessary harm that Victim inflicts, but that Murderer nonetheless lacks a right to defend himself against such harm. I suggest that such arguments are not yet convincing, and that the proportionate means account thus offers the best account of liability to defensive harm.

PART II

War

5

War and Self-Defence

A prominent theme in recent just war theory is the debate between those who hold that war is *sui generis*, subject to its own special morality, and those who hold the reductivist view that war is part of ordinary life, to be judged by ordinary moral rules. Generally, those who hold that war is *sui generis* combine this with a collectivist view of moral responsibility, according to which there is a distinctive way in which moral responsibility can be ascribed to groups, such as corporations or states. On this view, war is an essentially collective, political enterprise, irreducible to the relations between individuals.[1]

Those who hold the reductivist view typically reject this collectivist approach to morality in favour of an individualist view, according to which individuals are the proper focus of moral guidance and evaluation. This view holds that we can judge the morality of war by thinking about what individuals are permitted to do to each other. The rules governing killing in war are simply the rules governing killing between individuals, most obviously (but not exclusively) the rules of self-defence and other-defence. Jeff McMahan is the most influential defender of this view.[2]

I am a reductivist individualist about war. Like McMahan, I think that there is one morality, and that everything falls under its remit. War is not a special moral sphere with special moral rules. Rather, it is a particular aspect of ordinary life to which we apply our ordinary moral rules. I thus endorse McMahan's claim that when it comes to what we ought to do, the conditions of war 'change nothing at all; they simply make it more difficult to ascertain relevant facts.'[3]

I also agree with McMahan that moral responsibility in war attaches to individuals, not collectives. We cannot, in my view, hold that Germany acted wrongly

[1] Michael Walzer's *Just and Unjust Wars* is the classic defence of this position. See also Christopher Kutz, 'The Difference Uniforms Make: Collective Violence in Criminal Law and War', *Philosophy and Public Affairs*, Vol. 33, No. 2 (2005), 148–80 and Noam Zohar, 'Collective War and Individualistic Ethics: Against the Conscription of "Self-Defense"', *Political Theory*, Vol. 21, No. 4 (Nov. 1993), 606–22.

[2] See e.g. McMahan, *Killing in War*.

[3] Jeff McMahan, 'Killing in War: Reply to Walzer', *Philosophia*, Vol. 34 (2006), 47–51, at 47.

in fighting the Second World War, but that no German soldier acted wrongly in fighting it. To be clear: reductive individualism does not deny that there are such things as collectives. Rather, it denies that collectives enjoy a privileged moral status when it comes to inflicting harm. I do not believe that the collective nature of war, or the fact that war is political violence, generates special permissions that allow soldiers to inflict harms in war that they would not be permitted to inflict in a relevantly similar domestic context.

There are various challenges for those who defend a reductive individualist view of war, and I will be able to address only some of these here. Some writers challenge the assumption just made—that there are domestic situations that are relevantly similar to war. Others deny that the scope of interpersonal morality can adequately explain important aspects of the just war tradition. My aim here is not to offer a full reductivist account of just war theory—another book in itself—but rather defend reductivist individualism against some recent objections and indicate how we might develop a plausible, comprehensive individualist account of the ethics of war.

To this end, in this chapter I consider whether a reductive individualist can properly account for certain aspects of *jus ad bellum*—the rules that govern the resort to war. I consider specific challenges based on the requirements of just cause, proportionality, and a reasonable prospect of success. I argue that a reductive individualist view can indeed capture these requirements.

McMahan has primarily focused on the implications of reductive individualism for the *in bello* moral status of combatants, famously arguing that 'as a matter of basic morality', combatants who fight for an unjust cause cannot be the moral equals of those combatants who fight for a just cause.[4] Since so much of the debate has already focused on combatants, in Chapters 6 and 7 I consider what an individualist account of *jus in bello* tells us about the moral status of non-combatants—more specifically, non-combatants on the unjust side of a war.

5.1 Just Cause and *ad bellum* Proportionality

5.1.1 *The Conditional Force Argument*

Conditional force is military aggression by one state towards another that will become violent only if it is resisted. So, imagine that France decides that it would like to have political and territorial control of the Basque region in Spain. It sends

[4] Jeff McMahan, 'The Moral Equality of Combatants', *Journal of Political Philosophy*, Vol. 14, No. 4 (2006), 377–93, at 379.

its soldiers to occupy the Basque Country and to make the region sufficiently secure that the happy transition to becoming part of France can begin. The French have no particular desire to harm any of the Basque population, and will not use any sort of force against them, unless, of course, Spain resists the invasion.

It is widely accepted that, in the circumstances described, Spain would have a just cause for a defensive war against France. The annexing of populated land is generally thought to be the appropriate sort of wrong to warrant a military response. And, most people would think that, given the scale of the annexing, war would be a proportionate response. One plausible explanation of why war would be a proportionate response to this sort of aggression is that the goods directly threatened by the invasion—those of political and territorial control—warrant protection by lethal force. It is not only life and limb that can be protected by military means: other important goods, such as sovereignty, can warrant this sort of defence.

The Conditional Force Argument holds that this widely accepted claim about what counts as a just cause for war poses a problem for reductive individualists. David Rodin, for example, argues that when it comes to individual self-defence, lethal force is a proportionate response only to threats to what Rodin calls *vital interests*.[5] An individual may kill to defend herself against very serious harms such as death, torture, slavery, and rape, but she may not kill to defend her *lesser interests*, which for Rodin includes property and other resources, and political rights like the right to vote. She may not, for example, kill a person who deliberately tries to prevent her from voting, perhaps by damaging her only means of transport to the polling station. Even though this person violates her right to vote and to political representation, these rights are lesser interests, insufficiently important to warrant lethal defence. Just as importantly, she may not endanger bystanders' lives in order to defend her political rights.

If this is true for individuals, reductivists must grant that it applies at the national level. If no single member of the polity may kill or endanger lives to defend her democratic rights, then the polity as a whole cannot kill or endanger lives to defend those rights. Seth Lazar has echoed this thought, arguing that '[s]oldiers defending their country against territorial incursions positively seek out a fight, to protect something other than human life, which could often be conceded without any blood being spilt. This is a really important point, which casts doubt on the whole project of justifying killing in war by appeal to principles of individual self-defence.'[6] According to Rodin, the only way to explain why

[5] David Rodin, 'The Myth of National Self-Defence', in Cécile Fabre and Seth Lazar (eds.), *The Morality of Defensive War* (Oxford: OUP, 2014), 81.

[6] Seth Lazar, 'The Moral Importance of Winning', unpublished manuscript.

something like sovereignty warrants lethal protection is to attribute some kind of inherent value to the state or political community. But such an attribution seems inimical to the reductivist view, given its rejection of the idea that states enjoy special moral permissions when it comes to the use of force.

Thus, it looks like the reductivist is committed to saying that sovereignty may not be defended by means of war, since war nearly always involves inflicting lethal harms and will therefore be disproportionate. The same will go for the defence of ownership of territory or resources—unless one thinks that an individual may kill to defend her property, one cannot grant individual members of states the right to lethally defend land or resources. If an aggressor threatens only these goods, and has no plans to kill, enslave, or otherwise seriously harm the citizens unless they resist, reductivism must require capitulation. Military force would be a disproportionate response to this purely political aggression.

5.1.2 Lesser Interests and Vital Interests

Central to Rodin's version of the Conditional Force Argument are the categories of lesser interests and vital interests, corresponding to which are two types of aggression. Aggression that directly threatens only lesser interests counts as political aggression. Aggression that directly threatens vital interests counts as genocidal aggression. (By calling it 'genocidal', Rodin is stretching our ordinary usage of that term to include, for example, widespread raping or maiming, but that needn't trouble us here.)

According to Rodin, it is only genocidal aggression that may be resisted. Rodin argues that political aggression and genocidal aggression 'have a fundamentally different moral structure. Resistance to political aggression will typically produce greater loss to vital interests among individuals within the defended group, compared with engaging in no defence at all.'[7] Given this, it is usually 'straightforwardly self-defeating and hence morally irrational' to resist such aggression, as well as being disproportionate and thus impermissible.[8]

A natural response to the proportionality argument is to point out those members of a state faced with merely political aggression need not make immediate recourse to all-out war. Rather, they could engage in more limited acts of resistance, such as reinforcing their borders, refusing to cooperate, and so on. Surely, we might say, only full-scale military resistance is disproportionate—non-violent resistance is not disproportionate. And should the aggressor state respond violently to such non-violent resistance—well, then the vital interests of the citizens

[7] Rodin, 'The Myth of National Self-Defence', 82

[8] Rodin, 'The Myth of National Self-Defence', 82.

are directly threatened, and forceful resistance will be a proportionate defence of those vital interests. By working in stages, using only proportionate force at each stage, it seems that the victim state can permissibly defend itself until the situation escalates to the point at which lethal force is a proportionate response.

But Rodin argues that this reply fails because any calculation about the proportionality of this non-violent resistance must take into account the harms that the victim state foresees will be inflicted by the aggressor in response.[9] If the victim state predicts that initial defence will cause the aggressor to escalate the situation, that initial defence can be disproportionate. We can see this with cases like *Pinch*:

> *Pinch*: Bully wants to pinch Victim's arm, which will hurt. Victim knows that if (and only if) he tries to prevent this, Bully will become so enraged that he will kill five people.

It seems plain (to both me and Rodin, at least) that Victim may not try to prevent Bully's pinching his arm.[10] Rodin grants that since these 'mediated' harms will be inflicted by Bully, they don't weigh as heavily in the proportionality calculation as harms that Victim will inflict himself. But the fact that the harms will arise through someone else's intervening agency doesn't make them irrelevant to what one ought to do. On the contrary, they make defending himself against Bully a very bad thing for Victim to do. So, Rodin argues that whilst mediated harms are 'discounted'—they don't count as much as harm that one directly inflicts

[9] Rodin, 'The Myth of National Self-Defence', 77.

[10] We might object that to prohibit Victim's defending himself is to incentivize wrongdoing. If people know that they can render your defence disproportionate and impermissible by credibly threatening to do dreadful things if you prevent them from harming you, this gives them a reason to threaten to do such things. There are two reasons why I don't think this shows us that Victim may defend himself in *Pinch*. The first is simply that having any kind of proportionality condition makes it possible for a person to threaten you under circumstances in which it is impermissible for you to respond. Imagine that I desperately want to flick your ear, but you hate having your ear flicked and so refuse to let me. If I carefully arrange my ear-flicking for a time when the only way you can stop me is by shooting me with your hunting rifle, then I've managed to make it impermissible for you to prevent my flicking your ear. It's just a feature of having constraints on permissible defence that sometimes it will be impermissible for you to defend yourself against wrongdoing. Second, there's no reason why Victim can't factor predicted long-term mediated harms into his proportionality calculation, along with the harms that an aggressor is immediately threatening to inflict. If, in the long run, it seems likely that acquiescing to a particular threat will incentivize wrongdoing that causes more mediated harm overall than resisting the threat, it could be proportionate for Victim to resist. See, for example, Noam Zohar's argument for the permissibility of attacking combatants who employ non-combatants as human shields in 'Risking and Protecting Lives: Soldiers and Opposing Civilians', in Helen Frowe and Gerald Lang (eds.), *How We Fight: Ethics in War* (Oxford: OUP, 2014). Zohar argues that to refrain from attacking combatants in such cases only incentivizes the using of non-combatants as human shields, endangering more lives overall than attacking the combatants.

oneself—they are not discounted to zero. They still matter for determining what one is permitted to do.[11]

On a reductivist view, the same reasoning must apply at the level of war. When the members of a state face a threat, they cannot judge whether war or even non-violent resistance would be a proportionate response unless they factor in what the aggressor will do in reply. If they predict that the aggressor state will respond by waging a war that endangers the lives of many people, they must take those harms into account.

Of course, the harms that the aggressor state will inflict are discounted in the victim state's proportionality calculation. But, Rodin argues, this discount is effectively cancelled out because of the duty of care that the members of the victim state owe their fellow citizens, which he illustrates with the following case:

House: A villain invades and occupies your home without justification. He lives in your house and eats your food, forcing you and your family to do all the work. He makes it clear that he will not use force unless you resist. There is no end in sight. You could tackle the invader, but if you do so, it is likely that one of your children would be killed, either as a side-effect of the struggle, or as a punishment for your resistance.[12]

Rodin argues that most people would think it impermissible to tackle the villain, because 'the value of a child's life—especially since this is your child and you owe a profound duty of care to him' outweighs the good of evicting the occupier.[13] He thinks that a similar duty obtains when members of a state are considering going to war. The people whom they will be endangering through their resistance are 'people who are bound to [them] by relationships of loyalty, community and kinship'. They are '[their] comrades in arms, [their]family members, [their] neighbours'.[14] So, any discount that arises from the fact that it is the aggressor state that will be endangering these people is undone by the fact that the members of the victim state owe a duty of care to the people who are endangered.

The members of the victim state must therefore proceed as if they themselves are harming their co-citizens as a side-effect of their self-defence. Most people think that one may not, for example, kill a bystander as a side-effect of defending oneself against a broken leg. Similarly, Rodin argues that one may not endanger

[11] Notice that this way of 'causing' harms is very different from the facilitating of harms that we have considered in earlier chapters. Victim doesn't help Bully to kill people if he resists, as Driver helps Terrorist kill Victim in *Drive-By*.

[12] Rodin, 'The Myth of National Self-Defence', 79.

[13] Rodin, 'The Myth of National Self-Defence', 80.

[14] Rodin, 'The Myth of National Self-Defence', 78.

one's fellow citizens' vital interests for the sake of defending something of lesser interest, which for Rodin includes land, resources, and political independence. Exposing people to such harms is disproportionate compared to the goods threatened by purely political aggression. Reductivism is therefore unable to allow that resistance against political aggression can be just.

In what follows, I offer an account of how it can be proportionate to kill unjust combatants in defence of political interests and to foreseeably endanger the lives of innocent non-combatants in defence of political interests. I undermine the Conditional Force Argument in two ways. First, I argue that merely foreseen mediated harms are heavily discounted in an agent's proportionality calculation. Second, I argue that the Conditional Force Argument both underestimates the wrongs involved in lesser aggression, and mistakenly overlooks the role of aggregation in making defence against lesser aggression proportionate.

5.2 Responsibility for Mediated Harms

A central issue raised by Rodin's argument concerns our responsibility for mediated harms. Given that Victim in *Pinch* foresees that significant harm will result if he defends himself, he may not defend himself, even though someone else will inflict that foreseen harm.

5.2.1 *The Defence Account*

One way in which we might explain this impermissibility is to say, as Rodin does, that the mediated harms render Victim's defence disproportionate. Call this the Defence Account of mediated harms. On this account, when Victim is calculating the proportionality of defending himself, he must factor in any unjust harms that he foresees other people will inflict as a result of his defence. Even when the lethal harms that Bully will inflict are heavily discounted in virtue of the fact that Victim will not inflict them himself, they still greatly outweigh the harm of being pinched. Thus, even if Victim's defence against Bully consists in merely pushing Bully away, it is nonetheless disproportionate defence given the resulting harms.

Part of the difficulty with Rodin's version of the Defence Account is that whilst his claim about the importance of meditated harms seems correct in *Pinch*, it's less plausible in others. Take *Angry Rape*:

Angry Rape: Angry Rapist tries to rape Alice. If (and only if) Alice fends him off, he will be so angry that he will go and rape two other women. If (and only if) Alice kills Angry Rapist, Angry Rapist's friend will go and rape two other women.

It seems to me very implausible to think that Alice may not defend herself against Angry Rapist even if she foresees that her defence will trigger the rape of two other people. And yet, the harm she predicts will arise from her defence is twice that which will befall Alice herself. Even if we discount the harm by 50 per cent, Alice would still be triggering the equivalent of one rape as a side-effect of defending herself against rape.

On the Defence Account, Alice must proceed as if she would be inflicting the discounted harm herself—as if she would be inflicting the rape upon the other woman. Most accounts of permissible defence do not allow someone to inflict as a side-effect a harm that is equal to the harm she is seeking to avoid. For example, I may not divert a runaway trolley from where it will kill me down a sidetrack to where it will kill some other innocent person. Rather, I would be permitted to divert the trolley only if the person on the sidetrack would suffer a significantly lesser harm than the harm facing me. So, it looks like Alice may not defend herself if we treat her as inflicting one rape on another woman.

Things get only more implausible once we factor in a duty of care. Rodin claims that in war, any discount arising from the fact that the harms of war will be inflicted on members of the victim state by the aggressor state is cancelled out by the duty of care that members of the victim state owe to their co-citizens. The result is that the members of the victim state must treat any harms that they predict the aggressor will inflict on their co-citizens as if they will directly inflict those harms themselves. It's this that gets Rodin his conclusion that defensive war against political aggression is disproportionate. The members of the defending state must proceed as if they are directly killing and maiming to protect their lesser, political interests, and Rodin thinks that it's always disproportionate to kill and maim to protect lesser interests.

But if the duty of care is a duty owed to co-citizens, why does Alice not owe it to the other potential rape victims (assuming they are co-citizens)? If duties to co-citizens matter for making war disproportionate, they will matter for making individual defence disproportionate as well, not least on a reductivist view. But this entails that Alice may not defend herself unless the harm she faces significantly outweighs the harm Angry Rapist will inflict on others. Defence will thus be prohibited in cases where Angry Rapist will go on to rape or even seriously assault just one other person. By forcing her to treat Angry Rapist's actions as if they are her own, the Defence Account places implausible limits on Alice's right of self-defence.

Of course, *Angry Rape* illustrates the defence of a vital interest—the right not to be raped—and so we might think that we should treat it differently to *Pinch*, which involves the defence of a lesser interest. We might say that whilst mediated harms can make defence of lesser interests disproportionate, they can't make the defence of vital interests disproportionate.

But this response is pretty ad hoc: it's not clear why our account of responsibility for mediated harms should be sensitive to this distinction between lesser and vital interests. Our accounts of foreseen but unintended harms do not generally permit us to ignore foreseen harms when we are defending our vital interests (as if I may always divert the runaway trolley to save my life, no matter what the foreseen harm). Moreover, it's not clear that this response is even open to a proponent of the Defence Account. Given, for example, Rodin's claim that '[t]he morality of resisting the direct threat component of a conditional attack cannot be determined independently of the conditional threat', we cannot simply stipulate in advance that vital interests always or even usually warrant defence by lethal force, irrespective of the consequences.[15] Whether or not they do so will depend on what the aggressor has threatened to do if the vital interest is defended. That's the central tenet of the Defence Account: the proportionality of defence is partially dependent upon the predicted mediated harms. But once we apply Rodin's version of the Defence Account to defending vital interests—as in *Angry Rape*—it just doesn't look very plausible.

5.2.2 The Preventing Harm Account

So, we can either try to improve the Defence Account, or jettison it in favour of something else. Frances Kamm opts for jettisoning the account. Kamm imagines the following pair of cases, *Defence* and *Deflection*:

Defence: Suppose that Attacker attacks Victim, and Victim wishes to defend himself. If his act of self-defence will, without any other agents' wilful intervention, cause harm not only to Attacker but also to innocent bystanders, then Victim would be morally responsible for the harms and it may be impermissible for him to act.

Deflection: By contrast, suppose the harm to bystanders comes about because Attacker responds to Victim's act of self-defence by deflecting toward bystanders the object Victim hurled at him.

Kamm argues that in *Deflection*, '[t]hough [Victim] can predict that [Attacker] will do this, the fact that it is [Attacker's] act that will cause the harm to bystanders, not [Victim's], makes it permissible (I think) for [Victim] to defend himself.

[15] Rodin, 'The Myth of National Self-Defence', 77.

One could say of this case that because [Attacker], not [Victim], will be morally responsible for the harm to bystanders, it is permissible for [Victim] to act. When [Victim] determines that he will not be responsible, this gives him a reason to act, by defeating the harm-to-bystanders objection to his act, even though his act, its aim, and its ultimate effects remain the same.'[16]

For Kamm, the fact that the harm to third parties arises from Attacker's intervening agency means that Victim is not morally responsible for the harm, and therefore may act (or at least, a reason for his not acting is defeated). This is not compatible with the Defence Account, according to which Victim still bears responsibility for the foreseen harms, but the discounting could make the harms proportionate (depending on their severity). On Kamm's view, Attacker's intervening agency seems to preclude Victim's being responsible for the harms, even if Victim foresees that Attacker will bring them about.

If Kamm is correct that Attacker's intervention precludes Victim's being responsible for the harms in this sort of case, this suggests that foreseen mediated harms can never render Victim's action impermissible on the grounds that it would be disproportionate defence. This is because the predicted harms are not to be understood as part of Victim's defensive action at all.

But this does not mean that the foreseen harms could never render Victim's action impermissible. There could be other reasons why Victim is not permitted to defend himself, even if his action would not be disproportionate defence. An alternative to the Defence Account is what we can call the Preventing Harm Account. The Preventing Harm Account assumes that we can be obliged to bear some cost to prevent harm from befalling others, and holds that mediated harm cases are best understood as cases in which Victim has an opportunity to prevent harm befalling other people—that by refraining from defending himself, Victim *saves* the five people whom, for example, Bully will otherwise kill. We should then treat these cases as we treat other cases in which one has the opportunity to save others from harm.

Given the comparatively small harm he must suffer to rescue the five in *Pinch*, Victim is required to rescue them. Defending himself would be wrong—not because it is disproportionate defence, but because it amounts to an impermissible

[16] Frances Kamm, 'Substitution, Subordination and Responsibility: A Reply to Scanlon, McMahan and Rosen', *Philosophy and Phenomenological Research*, Vol. 80, No. 3 (2010), 702–22, at 715. Kamm uses 'A' and 'B' where I have used 'Attacker' and 'Victim'. It seems that Kamm thinks it permissible for Victim to act even if he predicts that his defence will be unsuccessful—because Attacker will simply deflect the missile—but let's set that aside for now. We can easily imagine a case in which Victim's defence succeeds but nonetheless results in Attacker's causing harm to bystanders.

failure to rescue. But if Victim were to be threatened with a serious harm, such as paralysis, rape, or death, a rescue-based account would not require him to suffer this harm rather than defend himself, assuming that we need not bear such serious harms even to save other people's lives. If I needn't wade out into a dangerous river to try to pull a life raft carrying five people into shore if doing so endangers my own life, then I needn't refrain from defending my life even if doing so causes my attacker to kill five other people.

The Preventing Harm Account will appeal to those who think that, ordinarily, when Victim is deciding whether to defend himself against a serious harm, he need not take into account the fact that his attacker will go on to harm other people if he defends himself, even if by failing to defend himself Victim could have prevented this. Most people probably have this intuition. And, the account explains that intuition whilst preserving the further intuition that it would nonetheless be wrong for Victim to ignore mediated harms entirely. If very grave consequences will arise from his defence, much graver than the harm he himself faces, then he ought not to defend himself. In other words, it permits Alice to defend herself in *Angry Rape*, but prohibits Victim's defending himself in *Pinch*, which seems like the right result.

Whilst this view is attractive in its implications about what Victim is permitted or required to do, I don't think that it is sound. To say that one is preventing a harm implies that one acts to rescue someone from a harm that is already set to befall them, as in *River*:

River: Five people are drowning on a life raft in dangerous waters. Jogger can pull the life raft to shore, but will suffer the loss of his hand in doing so.

The causal chain that endangers the five people on the life raft has occurred independently of Jogger's actions or presence, and five would be harmed in his absence (assuming that nobody else rescues them). But in *Pinch* and *Rape*, any harm that befalls the relevant people is causally downstream of Victim's actions. This seems like endangering people—Victim certainly makes the five worse off by his actions—and I don't think that if you fail to endanger someone, you count as rescuing them. Not all instances of bearing costs for the sake of others count as rescuing people, even if we might, for example, heap similar praise upon both rescuers and those who bear costs to avoid endangering others. Given that we are typically more responsible for the harms that we are instrumental in bringing about—for harm that is causally downstream of our actions—it seems a mistake to treat our responsibility for mediated harms as equal to our responsibility for failing to prevent harm.

A proponent of the Preventing Harm Account might argue that in a mediated harm case like *Pinch,* we lack the right kind of causal connection between Victim's actions and the harms that befall others for attributing responsibility for those harms to Victim. But this seems like a mistake, because it's not the causal connections that make these harms an inappropriate basis for attributing responsibility. We can see this by thinking about a provocation or incitement case, where the agent intends that others cause harm as a result of his or her actions. Take a case from Robert Fullinwider:

Mad Wife: Wife attempts to seduce Gardener. Gardener rejects Wife's advances. Wife tells Husband that Gardener has raped her, hoping that Husband will try to kill Gardener. Her plan succeeds, and Husband attacks Gardener.[17]

The causal connections between the agent and the harm are the same in this case and *Pinch*. Wife knows that if she performs a certain action (lying to her husband), it will cause Husband to try to harm Gardener, just as Victim knows that if he performs a certain action (pushing Bully away), it will cause Bully to try to harm other people. But it certainly seems like Wife is partly morally responsible for Husband's attack on Gardener. The difference between the cases is not one of causal connections, but of intention. What we intend will result from our actions can affect our moral responsibility for an outcome, but a lack of intention does not make our actions any less a part of the causal chain.

The waters are, however, somewhat muddied by cases like *Surgery*:

Surgery: Surgeon is trying to chop off Victim's hand as part of an unjust attack on Victim. Victim knows that Surgeon has five life-saving operations scheduled for the next day, and that if he kills Surgeon in defence of his hand, nobody else will be available to operate on those people, so they will die.

At first glance, *Surgery* looks like a mediated harm case because the suffering of harm by the five is a foreseen consequence of Victim's defence. But the five people who need operations are already endangered by an independent causal chain (whatever has caused their illnesses). Surgeon can save them, but if he fails to save them, their deaths are not something he causes but something he allows. Thus, if Victim prevents Surgeon from saving them, their deaths cannot be something that Victim causes. So, we should not treat cases like *Surgery* as mediated harm cases akin to *Pinch* or *Angry Rape*.

[17] Robert K. Fullinwider, 'War and Innocence', *Philosophy and Public Affairs*, Vol. 5, No. 1 (1975), 90–97, at 92

Given that mediated harm cases are not cases in which Victim prevents harm if he refrains from defence, I think that we must reject the Preventing Harm Account. It's just not plausible as an account of the causal structure of mediated harms. But it does much better than the Defence Account when it comes to matching our intuitions about what an agent is permitted or required to do. If the Defence Account is to do as well at capturing our intuitions about cases like *Angry Rape*, mediated harms must be heavily discounted, and this discount cannot be cancelled out by duties to co-citizens.

5.3 The Revised Defence Account

I think the plausibility of the Preventing Harm Account primarily derives from setting the limit to the costs that Victim must bear in a mediated harm case to that which obtains in rescue cases. This seems roughly right to me. The connection between the two sorts of case might be explained by something along the lines of Victor Tadros's suggestion that both the restrictions on harming people as a means for the greater good and the restrictions on requiring people to bear costs to rescue other people 'have as their source our status as ends. Because we are not available as tools for the sake of each other, we cannot be harmed as a means to a greater good and duty does not require us to act for the greater good.'[18] If Alice were not permitted to defend herself against Angry Rapist, we would effectively be requiring Alice to treat herself as a means, permitting Angry Rapist to harm her for the sake of others. We can sometimes be so required, but there are limits to how much cost we can be required to bear to such ends, just as (and for the same reason as) there are limits on the costs we must bear to rescue others.

Compare *River* with *Bomb*:

River: Five people are drowning on a life raft in dangerous waters. Runner can pull the life raft to shore, but will suffer the loss of his leg in doing so.

Bomb: Attacker attacks Victim. If (and only if) Victim fends Attacker off, Attacker will detonate a bomb that will kill five people. If Victim doesn't fend Attacker off, Attacker will cut off his leg.

Let's stipulate that for any cost lower than the loss of his leg, Runner would be required to rescue the five on the life raft. Since, in *River*, he can rescue them only at the cost of his leg, he isn't required to rescue them. I also think that Victim is not required to

[18] Tadros, *The Ends of Harm*, 250.

suffer the loss of his leg in *Bomb*, even though I have suggested above that we are typically more responsible for mediated harms than for harms we fail to prevent.

This is because the kinds of mediated harm case we're discussing—defence cases—involve a further cost to Victim that isn't usually present in a rescue case. In *River*, even if Runner bears the cost of the loss of his leg, it doesn't look as if his rights have been violated. Either saving the five is supererogatory, in which case Runner has chosen to sacrifice his leg, or it's obligatory. It's hard to see how in this case doing what's obligatory could also constitute a rights violation. In *Bomb*, in contrast, Victim must suffer not only the loss of his leg if he refrains from defence, but also a serious rights violation at the hands of Attacker. This additional cost—the fact that losing his leg will violate his rights—could counteract his greater responsibility for the harms in *Bomb* compared to Runner's responsibility for the harms in *River*. The upshot would be that, in defence cases, Victim is required to bear roughly the same amount of cost to prevent mediated harms to others as he would be to rescue others from harm, but our explanation of this is quite different from that of the Prevented Harm Account.

Of course, we can imagine rescue cases in which rights violations are in play—say the five have been sent down the river by a villain, and that morality requires Runner to suffer a broken wrist to save them. Runner would then have a legitimate complaint against the villain for imposing this duty (and corresponding cost) upon him. But then, this seems to increase the cost on the five's side too, if we think it's worse that the five be murdered by a villain than be killed in an accident.[19] If this means that the five are threatened by a worse harm, since they will not only die but have their right not to be killed violated, this could require Jogger to bear a greater cost—a broken wrist *and* a rights violation—to save them.

Jonathan Parry has pointed out that by discounting mediated harms in the way I suggest, we might encounter difficulties in cases like *Factory*:[20]

> *Factory*: Bomber, who is on the just side of a war, can achieve a proportionate good if he bombs either Factory A or Factory B. If he bombs Factory A, his bomb will kill 50 innocent people as a side-effect. If he bombs Factory B, his bomb will not kill anyone. However, Bomber predicts that the enemy will then kill 100 innocent people in retaliation for the bombing.

[19] See e.g. Frances Kamm, 'Self-Defence, Resistance and Suicide: The Taliban Women', in Frowe and Lang (eds.), *How We Fight*. Kamm suggests (at 76) that 'it could be reasonable to prevent indignity or unjust acts to one set of people rather than prevent even greater material harm, but due to natural causes, to another set of people. (We do this on a mass scale, e.g., if we invest more money in a police force rather than in heath care.)'

[20] At a workshop on this manuscript at the Centre for Ethics, Law and Public Affairs, University of Warwick, November 2013.

It seems that Bomber ought to bomb Factory A, even though the harms that will arise if he bombs Factory B are mediated and thus (according to me) heavily discounted. If we discount the harms by, say, 50 per cent, it looks like there's no morally relevant difference between bombing A or B, which can't be right if bombing B involves 50 extra innocent deaths. It would, we think, be impermissible for Bomber to bring about an objectively more harmful state of affairs—50 extra deaths—even if bombing Factory B is objectively more harmful only because of mediated harms.

But *Factory* is different to *Angry Rape*, because in *Angry Rape* bringing about the objectively less harmful state of affairs—where only Alice is raped—imposes a serious cost on Alice. As I have argued, it is more cost than Alice can be required to bear to bring that state of affairs about. In *Factory*, in contrast, it doesn't cost Bomber any more to bring about the objectively less harmful state of affairs compared to bringing about the objectively more harmful state of affairs. Bombing either factory achieves Bomber's goal equally well. So, to know how an agent is permitted to act in these sorts of cases, we need to think about the comparative costs to the just side of each course of action, and whether the difference in those costs would warrant bringing about the additional harms, or whether those on the just side could be required to bear that difference in cost to save innocent people from those additional harms. Since, in *Factory*, there's no difference in cost to the just side, my view supports the intuition that it's impermissible for Bomber to bomb Factory B.

If foreseen, but mediated, harms are heavily discounted in a defender's proportionality calculation, we are a good way to explaining why it can be permissible for a victim state to defend itself against political aggression that is only conditionally violent. Even if members of the victim state foresee that their resistance will cause the aggressor state to wage a war that endangers the lives of their co-citizens and of innocent non-combatants in the aggressor state, the members of the victim state need not proceed as if they are themselves inflicting these harms. Moreover, since those co-citizens' political interests are also endangered by the aggression, the members of the victim state are acting not only in self-defence, but in other-defence, which has a bearing on the amount of foreseen harm it would be proportionate to bring about.

On this version of the Defence Account, it would be permissible for the members of the victim state to defend themselves against invasion unless they predicted that doing so would result in sufficiently graver harm to a sufficient number of innocent people. The harms are sufficiently graver if the people in the victim state would be required to save the sufferers from those harms even at the cost of harms to themselves equal to an invasion. As I shall argue in section 5.4, the disparity between the cost to the victim state and the cost to innocent people if they resist is not generally so great that the victim state is required not to defend itself.

5.3.1 *Duty of Care*

This result is more permissive than Rodin's view. Rodin denies that there might be this sort of ratio between foreseen mediated harms and the defended good, holding simply that whenever resistance will harm a greater number of vital interests, the aggression is political and the state must capitulate. This is, in part, because of Rodin's view that the discounting of harms caused by an aggressor state in war is neutralized by the duties of care that one owes to one's co-citizens. One must proceed as if one were directly inflicting the harms upon those co-citizens. But, as I argued in section 5.2.1, if the duty of care extends so widely as to cover co-citizens generally, it really doesn't seem that Rodin can resist the conclusion that Alice may not fend off Angry Rapist when doing so will cause him to rape or seriously assault just one other woman, assuming that the other woman is a co-citizen.

We should also be more generally sceptical of the role that Rodin attributes to a duty of care. I think it possible that familial ties and ties of friendship can sometimes make a difference to what we are allowed to do, although it's not clear to me that this is best explained as owing a duty of care to these people. But if I do owe a duty of care as generally as Rodin supposes—essentially, to all those people who participate in my state—it seems to me unlikely that I owe it to them in virtue of the fact that they participate in my state. Such a duty must rather be grounded in more general properties shared by all persons. That this is simply a general duty owed to all persons explains why, for example, I may not drive more recklessly in a popular tourist area, or in a foreign country, than I drive at home.[21] Such reckless endangerment could not be justified by appeal to the absence of a duty of care, or the claim that any such duty is less stringent when it comes to foreign people. Nor would my duties to rescue be less stringent when I'm abroad, where all the imperilled people are foreign. Nor would the fact that only one of two drowning people happens to be British give me a reason to save her rather than the other person. If there is a duty of care that explains why I must care about all these harms, I should think that it applies equally to foreigners and co-citizens. If I can divert a runaway trolley away from where it will harm five to where I foresee that it will harm either

[21] Rodin does say that the duty of care is less important when it comes to intentionally harming. But reckless endangerment is not intentionally harming, and the tort law duty of care is generally thought to cover just such endangerment.

Local or Foreigner, I don't think a duty of care requires me to harm Foreigner rather than Local.

But once this alleged duty is so widespread, it doesn't make much sense to describe it as an extra aspect of morality that must be factored in to what we may ordinarily do. Invoking such a general requirement to treat all people in a certain way is simply to recognize the requirements of morality, not to discover an additional constraint on top of what morality usually requires. If the demands that such a duty makes generalize across all people, there is nothing in particular that the duty picks out: it does not single out some people for special treatment. The best that Rodin can do is simply stipulate that morality doesn't allow us to expose anyone to such foreseen harms, but that is not much of an argument, and is anyway in direct tension with his own arguments about discounting—if it is never permissible to foreseeably bring about such harms, what would be the point of saying that such harms are discounted? We may have some duties towards our co-citizens that we do not have to other people, but I don't think that these duties are relevant when it comes to determining whom we may harm or place at risk of harm.

5.4 Political Interests and Reductivism

5.4.1 Aggregating Lesser Interests

In a vein similar to Rodin's argument, Jeff McMahan suggests that lesser interests just are those interests that don't warrant protection by lethal force.[22] Certainly, it seems correct that an individual cannot kill a person who damages her car and thereby prevents her from voting. And the putative worry for reductivist individualists is that it looks like they can't invoke the natural response that the numbers matter—an aggressive occupation impedes *lots* of people's right to vote—because this looks prima facie incompatible with their focus on individuals.

But I think this concern *is* only prima facie. It doesn't follow from the fact that it would be disproportionate to lethally defend one person's lesser interest that it must be disproportionate to lethally defend many people's lesser interests. There's nothing in reductivism that prohibits caring about numbers. The central claim of reductivism is that the moral rules of war are the moral rules of ordinary life, and aggregation is certainly a feature of morality in ordinary life. Most people accept this when it comes to protecting vital interests. Part of the explanation of

[22] Jeff McMahan, 'What Rights May be Defended By Means of War?', in Fabre and Lazar (eds.), *The Morality of Defensive War* (Oxford: OUP, 2014), 115–56.

why most people think it permissible to kill the one to save the five in the trolley problem is surely that one is saving five lives at the cost of one. There's nothing collectivist about this: it's the *number* of individuals' lives at stake that matters, not the relationship between those individuals. And this also seems to be true with respect to the defence of lesser interests, provided that a sufficient number of lesser interests are at stake. If you are going to culpably break my arm, it will be disproportionate to kill you to prevent this. But there surely comes a point at which if killing you is the only way to stop you going around breaking *lots* of people's arms, I may kill you. I don't think there's anything in this claim that's unfriendly to a reductivist, because aggregation and other-defence are familiar parts of ordinary, interpersonal morality.

If the category of lesser interests does indeed correspond to interests that don't warrant lethal defence, as Rodin and McMahan claim, then this category will be much narrower than it first appears. Perhaps no number of pinches or headaches can ever warrant defence by lethal force, but a sufficient number of moderate harms, such as a broken arm, can. If so, the distinction might be sound, but it's not particularly useful for thinking about harming in war.

A more plausible suggestion is that the distinction between vital and lesser interests tracks not those interests that can warrant lethal defence and those that can't, but those interests that can warrant lethal defence only when aggregated. This aggregation can be intrapersonal—if I keep breaking the same person's arm, and killing me is the only way to stop me, I think that eventually she may kill me to stop me. But it can also be interpersonal, as in the multiple-person broken arm scenario described above, without violating any of the reductivist's commitments. And what aggregation will allow is not only the use of increased force against an attacker, but an increase in the amount of collateral harm one may risk to innocent people—especially when those people are also endangered and thus also beneficiaries of the defence (I return to this below). Of particular importance for our purposes here is the fact that aggressive action at the level of states will always threaten the interests of multiple people—and usually a great many people. Thus, even when it is only lesser interests that are directly threatened, this does not entail that lethal force cannot be a proportionate defence of those interests.

AGGREGATION AND POLITICAL AGGRESSION

Imagine that I take it upon myself to lock you in your house for an indefinite period, perhaps the rest of your life. I force you to practise a particular religion—let's call it Trolleyology. I make you dress in army camouflage, read only the collected works of Frances Kamm, spend hours enacting moral dilemmas using a toy train set, and start every day with a rousing rendition of what I like to call The Trolley Anthem. I credibly threaten to kill you if you try to force me out of the house or otherwise resist the imposition of my regime.

What might you do to try to stop me doing this? Well, I should think that you may certainly kill me. And you may do so even though you realize that should you submit to the Trolleyology regime, we could rub along together quite nicely. I think you may also kill me even if I believe that in treating you this way, I am acting permissibly. The important question for our purposes here, however, is whether you may try to kill me if doing so is likely to inflict collateral harm on your next-door neighbour, who is wholly innocent in all of this. I think you would be permitted to inflict some collateral harm upon her, although probably not lethal harm. But the amount of harm you may inflict is surely sensitive to how many people are trapped in the Trolleyology house with you. What if your wife and child are imprisoned in the house as well? What if you've got two or three children, and perhaps a couple of grandchildren? At some point, it's going to become proportionate to start inflicting even lethal collateral harms as part of a bid to prevent the unjust, forcible imposition of this regime upon you and your family.

If we grant this, I think we start to see how an individualist can account for the defence of sovereignty as a just cause for war, even when that war will involve collateral harms. The wrong of violating sovereignty is, on a reductivist view, reducible to the wrong of violating autonomy. Individuals have an interest in controlling their own lives, which is summarized in the value we place on autonomy, and is partly manifested by being able to influence the sort of political regime under which one lives. And given the number of people whose autonomy is threatened by an aggressive war, it's possible that the victim state might be justified in inflicting quite substantial collateral damage to defend its members' autonomy. But there's no special moral work being done here by the notion of the collective: it's just a question of numbers.

I think it's also worth saying something about the sorts of conditions that might follow a political invasion to see how limited the force of the Conditional Force Argument is. We can imagine three possible scenarios. In the first, conditions in the victim state will be better than they were prior to the invasion. In the second, conditions will stay the same after the invasion as they were before the invasion. In the third, conditions will be worse after the invasion, but there will still be direct threats only to lesser interests.

What does reductivism say about cases in which conditions improve in the victim state as a result of the invasion? First, only the right sort of improvement is going to count. Even if, prior to the Trolleyology invasion, your family enjoyed a terrible diet, took limited exercise, and spent all day watching rubbish on TV, this doesn't affect whether you may resist the imposition of Trolleyology. Perhaps things would be better for you, in many respects, if you accepted Trolleyology into your life. But this just doesn't matter for whether or not you may forcibly resist my regime, because the whole point of autonomy is choosing for oneself even if one chooses poorly. So too with political autonomy: it is the choosing that matters, perhaps even more than what one chooses.

But it's possible that the value of autonomy does, at some point, give way to the value of justice. I can't interfere in your home simply because your wife does most of the domestic chores, even if this is unjust. But if your wife and daughters suffer systemic and serious injustice, there might come a point at which I may interfere if this will prevent such injustice. Resisting this interference would be impermissible. But of course, the problem for proponents of the Conditional Force Argument is that built into the permissibility of such interference is the assumption that doing so is necessary and proportionate. In other words, this is now looking like a justified humanitarian intervention. The Conditional Force Argument is supposed to show that reductivism cannot permit resisting unjust political invasions, such as those aimed at annexing land for the good of the invader. That reductivism might prohibit defence against a justified humanitarian intervention doesn't support the Conditional Force Argument.

We might reply that an invasion might not aim at these improvements. Improvements in the victim state could come about merely as a foreseen side-effect of an unjust political invasion. But unless we put a lot of weight on the right intention criterion of *jus ad bellum*—and I've argued elsewhere that we ought not to do this[23]—an invasion that brings about humanitarian benefits sufficient to make resistance impermissible is not unjust.

In the second scenario, the victim state suffers some kind of political coup, but the new government threatens no important interests. We might understand the coup as effecting a kind of change of management that has no real impact upon the citizens—that makes little difference to their everyday lives. It's this scenario that shows us why the implications of Rodin's argument are theoretically radical. Rodin's view suggests that resisting this invasion is impermissible, but many people think that states may resist political aggression irrespective of what the

[23] In 'Judging Armed Humanitarian Intervention', (Don E. Schied (ed.), The Ethics of Armed Humanitarian Intervention (Cambridge: CUP, 2014), 93–110), I argue that it's a mistake to focus on the intentions of interveners in cases of humanitarian intervention. What matters is whether there exists a sound justification for intervention.

aggressors plan to do in the victim state (although it does perhaps matter whether the victim state is sufficiently morally valuable to be worth defending).[24]

However, as I'll argue below, this *is* only a theoretically radical implication: it has limited practical relevance because few invasions are like this. Moreover, even in this kind of invasion, the autonomy rights of the members of the victim state are still violated and given the number of people threatened, it can be proportionate to foreseeably bring about some harms, including lethal harms, to protect these rights. The question is how much harm it is proportionate to bring about. I think that the best result that Rodin is going to get is that, contrary to popular belief, it would be disproportionate to resist this kind of invasion if one foresees that resulting conflict will cause significant and widespread harm. Of course, wars often *do* cause such harms, and thus resistance might be impermissible in some cases.

But I don't think this shows that reductivism is false or inconsistent, or that it cannot permit resistance against political aggression in general. It doesn't show that reductivism is false or inconsistent because reductivism isn't meant to be offering an alternative way of endorsing all the causes for war that are endorsed by a traditional collectivist view. As a revisionist account of the ethics of war, reductivism may well restrict causes for war compared to a more traditional account. But nothing in the Conditional Force Argument shows that reductivism cannot ever sanction defence against political aggression. On the contrary, I think that reductivism will permit resisting political aggression when this can be done either by endangering only a limited number of vital interests, or when the aggression is expected to make conditions worse in the victim state, in addition to violating the autonomy rights of individual citizens. And, as I'll outline below, I think that political aggression usually makes things considerably worse in the victim state, which is why the Conditional Force Argument is very limited in scope.

BEYOND AGGREGATION

I argued above that aggregation can be part of a reductivist explanation of the proportionality of a war that aims to defend political interests. But it seems to me that numbers are significant when it comes to political rights not merely for straightforward aggregative reasons, but because the increasing numbers

[24] I think that some undemocratic regimes can lack a right of defence against a political invasion by a sufficiently just regime, although an undemocratic regime may permissibly fight to protect its citizens from more serious harm (e.g. a genocidal invasion). When the state has no or little value for individuals, it could be disproportionate for them to resist if there's no violating of their individual interests in their current regime, and acquiescing imposes no other significant costs upon them.

produce a step-change in what threatens each individual.[25] If you damage my car and prevent me from voting, this won't really make any difference to the sort of country I live in. But imagine that measures are taken before a UK election to ensure that anyone living outside London is unable to vote. This would do much more than frustrate each individual non-Londoner's right to vote—it would not be simply a case of iterating the same harm of vote prevention across many individuals. Rather, the increasing numbers would effect a change in the *sort* of harm being perpetrated against each of those individuals, because it would change the UK from a legitimate democratic state to an illegitimate dictatorship. States coercively impose legal frameworks upon their citizens. A government that is elected only by Londoners, but then attempts to rule over the whole of the UK, will be imposing this framework illegally, unjustly coercing individuals to adhere to it. This is a much more serious wronging of each individual citizen than the wrong of preventing any one individual from voting, and it is this sort of wronging that is threatened by a political invasion.

Moreover, there are unlikely to be many political invasions in which things stay the same in the victim state. One cannot (at least in a previously democratic state) stage a coup, back this coup with threats of violence should anyone resist, and yet change little about the way of life within that state. The coercive background means that the scenario we imagined above, where the government is generally benign and very little changes in the victim state as a result of the invasion, bears no relation to how things are going to be in a state that is subjected to political aggression backed by conditional threats to life and limb. The new government is not benign—rather, it threatens to quash legitimate and reasonable dissent with violence. And things are therefore very different in the UK, because now the securities that guarantee the citizens' current way of life are gone. Instead, they live in a country where laws are illegally enforced upon them, backed by the threat of unjust violence if they don't comply. This is true even if the laws are by and large the same laws that were in place prior to the invasion.

Existing under this kind of regime is likely to be pretty grim. And it's grim even if people do not resist, because living under the threat of these sorts of reprisals is to live in general conditions of fear and mistrust of the sort that usually accompany states that are prepared to violently put down dissenters. For people used to living in liberal democracies, it's probably easy to underestimate the importance of the kinds of protection that have vanished in the state described. But having legally protected recourse in the event of unjust treatment by the government and its agents is a substantial good, as is not living in a

25 Thanks to Jimmy Lenman for helpful discussion of this point.

state of perpetual oppression and fear. When a sufficient number of people are at risk of losing such goods, it can be permissible to engage in proportionate lethal defence of that good. And, given what I argued in section 5.3, lethal defence can be proportionate even when one foresees that it will cause an aggressor to escalate a situation, since mediated harms are heavily discounted in proportionality calculations.

5.4.2 *Collateral Harms*

Indeed, I think that not living in this kind of oppressive state is a sufficiently substantial good that individuals living under such conditions could use lethal force to avoid it, and risk harm to innocent people whilst defending themselves. Kamm has recently argued that women living in Afghanistan under the Taliban had just cause to kill the men who imprisoned them in their own homes on pain of attack, rape, or death.[26] This is perhaps about as close as we can get to an individual equivalent of conditional force at the national level, where resisting the aggressive regime results in war.

This isn't to say that living in an illegitimate dictatorship is the same as being imprisoned in one's home. Being confined to one's home is clearly a much greater imposition on one's autonomy than living in an oppressive state that directly threatens political rights, but that isn't, for example, randomly arresting, torturing, or killing people. But, as I've argued, lesser harms can aggregate across individuals until it becomes proportionate to use lethal force against those who are inflicting them. Whilst the harm to each individual might be less serious when we're dealing with political state aggression rather than imprisoning a woman in her home, the *number* of individuals who are harmed is of course far, far greater in the state case. And as the number of people at risk of harm increases, so too does the amount of collateral harm it's proportionate to risk.

This might be especially so when those who are exposed to the risk of collateral harm are also potential beneficiaries of the defensive action. Consider *Rock*:

> *Rock*: Attacker is going to break the arm of each member of a group of ten people, including Victim. Victim can disable Attacker by throwing a small rock at him. Depending which way he throws it, the rock will hit Attacker and then roll to where it will also break the leg of an innocent person who is not one of the ten, or it will hit Attacker and then roll to

[26] Kamm, 'Self-Defence, Resistance and Suicide: The Taliban Women', 83.

where it will break the leg of one of the ten whom Attacker has threatened (but there's no way to know which one of the ten).

Victim would not be permitted to break someone's leg as a collateral harm of avoiding a broken arm to only himself. But I think he may break a leg as a collateral harm of defending ten people against having their arms broken. I also think that Victim ought to throw the rock in such a way that it will break the leg of the person who is initially threatened by Attacker. If there are collateral costs to the defence of the ten, it seems fairest that these costs befall those who stand to benefit from the defence (even though whoever gets the broken leg ends up worse off overall than if there had been no defence at all). Whilst a defensive war will expose the victim state's citizens to harm, it is those citizens who also stand to gain from the repelling of the aggression. This isn't to say that, if Victim may only throw the rock in such a way that it harms the innocent person who is not part of the threatened group, he may not do this. But it seems preferable to direct it so that it harms someone who had a chance of benefiting from the defence rather than someone who had no chance of benefiting from the defence.

We can explain this by thinking about the necessity principle that governs defensive harming, according to which defence is permissible only if is the least harmful means of averting a threat. On my account of the necessity principle, the *least harmful means* is a moralized notion. For example, consider *Choice*:

Choice: Attacker is going to break Victim's leg because he hates Victim. Victim can avert this by either (a) breaking Attacker's leg, avoiding all harm to himself, or (b) breaking Attacker's arm, at the cost of also breaking his own wrist.

As I argued in Chapter 4, most people do not think that Victim violates the necessity condition if he chooses (a) and breaks Attacker's leg. Even though a broken wrist is objectively less harmful than a broken leg, (a) still counts as the least harmful means available because Victim can weight breaking his own wrist more heavily than breaking Attacker's leg. When determining the least harmful means, harms to (culpable) attackers are heavily discounted compared to harms to Victim. It is plausible to think that collateral harms to potential beneficiaries are also discounted relative to harms to innocent non-beneficiaries. Thus, harming a non-beneficiary rather than a potential beneficiary can violate the necessity principle of self-defence even when each would bear the same harm, since the moralized least harmful means interpretation of necessity requires us to harm the potential beneficiary.

If this is correct, it will have implications for the methods of warfare that an individualist account permits the members of the victim state to employ during their defensive war. It may be that members of the defending state are required to choose tactics that expose their own state's non-combatants to harm rather than tactics that expose innocent non-combatants in the aggressor state to harm (assuming that each method enjoys a similar prospect of success), since it is their own non-combatants who stand to benefit from the defence. This conclusion contrasts with, for example, Tom Hurka's claim that states may favour the lives of their own citizens over the lives of 'enemy' non-combatants.[27] But it seems to me correct. Once one rejects any kind of collective responsibility on the part of citizens of the aggressor state—as the individualist must—innocent people within that state seem to be innocent indirect threats. It would be wrong to shift the costs of defending even other innocent people onto them if the costs could be borne by the beneficiaries of the defensive action.

5.5 Proportionality and a Reasonable Prospect of Success

In the previous chapter, our focus was on harms that had no prospect of averting a threat, and we considered the permissibility of inflicting harm in cases in which the agent knows that it will not avert the threat. In this section, our focus is on what I will call *potentially defensive harms*. A harm is potentially defensive if it has some prospect of averting or mitigating a threat. If it turns out that it does not avert the threat, then it is not a defensive harm on my account. But when we're deciding whether we may inflict a harm, we should treat harms that have some prospect of averting a threat differently to harms that have no prospect of averting a threat.

The *ad bellum* conditions of war are generally taken to include a requirement that the war have a reasonable prospect of success. This requirement holds that one is not permitted to fight even an otherwise just war if one has only a slim chance of victory. Suzanne Uniacke argues that the success requirement poses a particular problem for those who hold reductive individualist views of war. In brief, Uniacke's claim is that there is no requirement of a reasonable prospect of success in self-defence. One may use force against an attacker even if one is unlikely to avert or mitigate the threat she poses. As a result, the *ad bellum* success condition cannot be explained by thinking about what individuals are permitted to do to each other.[28] At best, the reductivist

[27] Thomas Hurka, 'Proportionality in the Morality of War', *Philosophy and Public Affairs*, Vol. 33, No. 1 (2005), 34–66.

[28] Suzanne Uniacke, 'Self-Defence, Just War and a Reasonable Prospect of Success', in Frowe and Lang (eds.), *How We Fight*, 62–74.

view will be incomplete as an account of *jus as bellum*. At worst, this disparity gives us reason to be generally sceptical of the feasibility of a reductivist account of *jus ad bellum*.

5.5.1 *The Subsuming Account*

Jeff McMahan has tried to deal with this problem by denying that there is an independent *ad bellum* success condition. He claims that, 'the plausible element in the requirement of "reasonable hope of success" is subsumed by the proportionality requirement.'[29] Proportionality is, of course, a familiar feature of individual defence, and thus prima facie less worrying for the reductivist.

Thomas Hurka holds a similar view. Hurka argues that if a war has no prospect of achieving its just cause, '[t]his fact, which makes it violate the reasonable hope of success condition, surely also makes it disproportionate, since its destructiveness now serves no purpose whatever. The same is true if the war has only some small probability of achieving relevant goods, since then its expected harm is excessive compared to its expected good. If it takes account of probabilities in this way, as on any plausible view it must, the *ad bellum* proportionality condition incorporates hope-of-success considerations.'[30]

I think it is a mistake on McMahan and Hurka's parts to try to subsume the success condition under proportionality in this way. In this section, I draw attention to some problems with this approach.

THE EXPECTED VALUE PROBLEM

The subsuming view holds that proportionality varies in line with variations in the likelihood of success. The same amount of force, aimed at averting the same severity of threat, could be proportionate in one case, where it has an 80 per cent chance of success, but disproportionate in another, where it has only a 40 per cent chance of success. Consider the following cases:

First Timer: Attacker tries to break Alice's leg. It's his first time trying to break a leg, so he's a bit nervous. Alice has an 80 per cent chance of fending him off by breaking his leg first.

Old Timer: Determined Attacker tries to break Beth's leg. He's so fond of breaking legs that even if Beth breaks his leg first, there's only a 40 per cent chance that this will fend him off.

[29] Jeff McMahan, 'Just Cause for War', *Ethics and International Affairs*, Vol. 19 (2005), 5.

[30] Hurka, 'Proportionality and the Morality of War', 37.

The subsuming view entails that Alice and Beth, who face threats of identical harm, could find that Alice has defensive rights against her attacker, while Beth does not. Since Beth's attacker is much more committed, and less likely to be deterred by a broken leg, breaking his leg could be disproportionate, even though Alice may break her more nervous attacker's leg to avoid exactly the same harm as faces Beth. Notice that Beth's defence is not futile—she is not inflicting harm that is certain to be pointless. It is merely less likely to succeed. It seems to me implausible that Beth's defence can be disproportionate but Alice's proportionate, if each is breaking a leg to try to avert a broken leg.

As I indicated in the earlier discussion of mediated harms, an attacker can sometimes make it impermissible for a victim to defend herself by attacking her in circumstances where she has only disproportionate means at her defence. When I try to flick your ear at a time when you can prevent me from doing so only by shooting me, I make it impermissible for you to defend yourself because you have only disproportionate means at your disposal. But there's a difference between granting this possibility, where you lack proportionate means, and thinking that I can make the available means disproportionate simply by an act of my own will (and not by altering the magnitude of harm I threaten to inflict). Yet this seems to be an upshot of the subsuming view. Determined Attacker can make Beth's defence disproportionate just by strengthening his resolve to break her leg. The subsuming view also suggests that Beth's defence would be disproportionate even if it succeeds. If proportionality is based on a calculation about expected value, and if a 40 per cent chance is not sufficient to make breaking the attacker's leg proportionate, the expected value of her defence will still have been disproportionate even if it does in fact avert the threat.[31]

A proponent of the subsuming view might reply that when it comes to *liable* attackers, any prospect of success suffices to make force proportionate.[32] It's only when we think about harms to non-liable people that the lack of a reasonable prospect of success can make force disproportionate. But I don't think this will work if we're viewing the prospect of success as a component of proportionality, on pain of circularity. As I outlined in Chapter 4, proportionality is internal to liability. Attackers aren't just 'liable' in some empty way: rather, they are liable *to something*—to a specific amount of harm. What determines the amount of harm is proportionality. So an attacker must already be *liable to a proportionate amount*

[31] Things get more worrying still once we think about liability. If one can't be liable to a disproportionate harm, and Beth goes to break her attacker's leg even though it has only a 40 per cent chance of success and is thus disproportionate, it looks like Determined Attacker is not liable to a broken leg, which raises all the problems we covered in Chapter 4.

[32] Thanks to Seth Lazar for this idea.

of harm before we can identify him as someone for whom prospect of success considerations can't make force disproportionate. But if success considerations are part of proportionality, as the subsuming view holds, this means we've already taken success considerations into account when deciding how much harm the attacker is liable to. It's only if success is independent of proportionality that we can determine that an attacker is liable to a certain amount of defensive harm irrespective of how likely that harm is to succeed.

As I outlined in Chapter 4, I think that Determined Attacker is liable to both defensive harms—that is, harms that avert the threat he poses—and 'failed' harms that Beth inflicts in the course of trying to defend herself. As I argue in section 5.5.2, we should judge the proportionality of such harms by asking whether they would be a proportionate means of averting a threat if they succeeded in averting that threat.

THE ESCALATION PROBLEM

The subsuming view also has worrying implications in the following sort of case. Imagine that if I use force of level seven, it has a 50 per cent chance of success of averting a threat. Let's say that's disproportionate. But if I use force of level nine, it has a 90 per cent chance of success with regards to that same aim, which on the subsuming view counts towards making the force proportionate. Obviously, we can tinker with the exact formula for deciding how much success counts towards proportionality, and thus permissibility. But the general upshot must be that by using more force, I can sometimes achieve proportionate means to an end even if *less harmful* means aimed at that *same end* were thought to be disproportionate.

There is something troubling, then, about the way in which the subsuming view understands the relationship between proportionality, success, and the amount of force to be employed. Perhaps McMahan and Hurka have viewed these considerations of force and success as somehow independent of one another. One might reason as follows: if using force of level seven has a 40 per cent chance of success, it's disproportionate for averting a given threat. It would seem sensible to then think that if force of level seven is disproportionate for averting that threat, then any amount of force that exceeds level seven is certainly disproportionate as a means to the same end. But this forgets that in many cases, as one increases the force to be used, one will *thereby* increase the chance of success. Force of level nine might have a 90 per cent chance of success. This must feed back into the proportionality calculation. And thus, until one reaches the point of a 100 per cent chance of success, one can argue for an escalation of force, as long as increasing the amount of force increases one's chances of success.

Of course, the subsuming view allows that proportionality can be sensitive to factors other than the likelihood of success. For example, proportionality will also be sensitive to the magnitude of the threatened harm. We might try to overcome the escalation problem by arguing this consideration will impose 'absolute' limits on what can become proportionate force. So, perhaps it never becomes proportionate to break both your legs to stop you from slapping me, no matter how effective breaking your legs will be, because the threatened harm of a slap is very much outweighed by two broken legs. There is thus a constraint on how much harm I am allowed to inflict, even if more harm improves my chances of successfully averting the threat.

But then the subsuming view must allow that the role played by the likelihood of success is limited by thoughts about what is proportionate even if the harm has a 100 per cent probability of success. This suggests another proportionality constraint that is independent of, and insensitive to, the likelihood of success. Once we concede this, the claim that proportionality incorporates the success condition looks false. As I will argue, meeting the reasonable prospect of success requirement entails meeting the proportionality requirement, but the two conditions are nonetheless distinct.

5.5.2 *Proportionality, Necessity, and Success*

I think we should begin by noticing that Hurka is mistaken when he suggests that a war that has no prospect of success is unjust because it is disproportionate. As I argued in Chapter 4, a harm that cannot avert a threat cannot be a defensive harm.[33] Consequently, wars that have no prospect of success are unjust not because they are disproportionate, but because they cannot be defensive. They therefore fail the *ad bellum* equivalent of the necessity condition—namely, that war is a last resort for securing the just cause. If war cannot secure the just cause, it cannot be a last resort for securing it. And, of course, the proportionality requirement governs *means*: it tells us whether a use of force is a proportionate means of achieving a good. But before a use of force can be a *proportionate* means, it must first *be* a means. Thus, harms that fail to be a means are neither proportionate nor disproportionate. We can sensibly ask questions about their proportionality only when we counterfactually suppose that they were a means—that is, that they did succeed in securing the intended good.[34] This is because it is only on the assumption that force is

[33] Given the collateral harms of war, I'll assume here that the defence of honour that might make it permissible to inflict otherwise unnecessary harm in response to an interpersonal attack will not suffice to make a non-defensive war permissible. (This is not, though, to grant a disparity between war and self-defence, since collateral harms could similarly make the use of force impermissible between individuals. It's just that collateral harms are not typically a feature of interpersonal defence, but are almost inevitably a feature of war.)

[34] I think we can include partial success—where one mitigates but does not fully avert a threat—as a success, since there is still in such cases some good that can be weighed against the harm done.

successful that we can compare the good achieved with the harm inflicted—that is, do a proportionality calculation. When there is no good achieved, the harm fails as a means and cannot be either proportionate or disproportionate.

It's not only when a use of force has no prospect of success that it's a mistake to describe it as disproportionate rather than unnecessary. Merely potentially defensive harms—harms that had some prospect of averting a threat but failed to do so—are also unnecessary. Again, when we ask whether a given harm will achieve a given end—how likely it is to succeed –we're asking how likely it is to be a *means*. Say that a use of force of level seven has a 50 per cent chance of achieving a goal. Say that force of level seven is proportionate to the goal (i.e. if we achieve the goal, the good that results will warrant the harm inflicted). We employ the force, but it does not achieve the goal. In such a case, the force we have used is neither disproportionate nor proportionate. It too has simply failed to be a means altogether, which precludes judgements about whether it was a proportionate means. As in the case of force that had no prospect of success, the only sensible way to ask whether the force was proportionate is to counterfactually suppose that it did succeed, and weigh the inflicted harm against the intended good.

So, the likelihood of success is not relevant to proportionality. Proportionality is about judging uses of force on the assumption that they achieve a particular good. In determining the proportionality of potentially defensive force, then, we should focus on the harm to be averted and the force used to avert it. If a level of force, *if successful in averting the threat*, would be a proportionate means of averting that threat, it is proportionate even if the chance of success is low. For example, if inflicting a broken wrist is a proportionate means of successfully averting a broken wrist, it remains so even if the probability of its averting the broken wrist is low. If a broken leg is disproportionate as a means of averting a broken wrist, then it remains so even if it is very likely to avert the broken wrist.

Similarly, when we ask whether a war would be *ad bellum* proportionate, we are asking, 'Would war, fought with the means at our disposal, be a proportionate way of securing the just cause?' That is, we build an *assumption* of success—of securing the just cause—into our calculation. The calculation cannot, therefore, also be sensitive to the *probability* of success.[35]

Of course, we still want to say something about the permissibility of inflicting a serious harm that has only a slim chance of averting a proportionate threat. But this is precisely why we have a success condition that entails, but is distinct from,

[35] McMahan himself implies this relationship when he says, for example, 'If the expected good would outweigh the unintended harm to civilians, the act is proportionate' (*Killing in War*, 20). The 'would' here surely means '*if achieved*'.

the proportionality condition. When we are considering inflicting such harm, we are considering whether it is permissible *to risk that the inflicted harm will not be a means of pursuing a proportionate good.* That is, we must have already decided that the end, if achieved, is proportionate to the harm we will inflict. We are not, therefore, doing a proportionality calculation when we assess whether a use of force meets the requirement of having a reasonable prospect of success.

5.5.3 *Accounting for the Success Condition*

I suggest that the requirement of a reasonable prospect of success is a lesser-evil constraint on the infliction of proportionate harms. Unlike our proportionality calculations, lesser-evil justifications take probabilities into account. We have to weigh the (expected) cost of doing nothing against the (expected) cost of acting. I think that when a person is morally responsible for an unjust threat of harm, she is liable to harm that has only a slim prospect of success (and such harm is therefore proportionate). This is because she is liable to both defensive harms and harms that her victim inflicts in the course of trying to defend herself. But, as I argue below, inflicting that harm can nonetheless be rendered all-things-considered impermissible if it risks collateral harms to innocent (i.e. non-liable) people.

It is concerns about harm to innocent people that explain why the honour-based justification for harming that I explored in Chapter 4 won't suffice to justify inflicting harms that have a low probability of success. The honour-based justification will not obtain in cases where one is risking collateral harm to innocent people, since collateral harms to innocent people must not only be proportionate but also the lesser evil. As I will argue, it is collateral harms to innocent people that motivate the success condition, and this applies equally to individual defence and war.

There are two obvious explanations of why we might want to include a success requirement in our account of *jus ad bellum*. The first is that we probably think it wrong for a state to order its armed forces to fight a war that will very likely end in defeat, with all the loss of life and injury that defeat will entail. According to this explanation, then, the requirement is motivated by a concern that soldiers' lives ought not to be risked in probably futile endeavours.

The second obvious explanation invokes the more general harm that war inevitably generates, particularly the collateral harm inflicted on the civilian population of both warring states.[36] According to this explanation, wars that

[36] We could extend this concern to the combatants of the other state, depending on what we think about the moral status of unjust combatants. If we think them innocent or fully excused, harms to them could also count against the war. And, even if we think they're morally responsible for threatening, and thus (on my view) liable to be killed, we could still think that there are general moral reasons not to cause (likely) gratuitous harm.

are unlikely to succeed are unjust because they will inevitably inflict harm upon non-combatants (who are here assumed to be innocent), and it's wrong to inflict such harms unless one is reasonably confident of achieving the just cause.

These two explanations are not mutually exclusive. But the second explanation has the advantage that it can explain why a war must not be fought even if a state's armed forces volunteer to fight. If the combatants are not being sent to slaughter, but are choosing to fight rather than surrender, the first explanation of the success requirement will no longer have any force. But even if a state's combatants volunteer to risk their own lives, they cannot thereby make it permissible to endanger the lives of others. Wars that fail the success condition will still be unjust even if combatants volunteer to fight them.

It seems to me that something like this second explanation is the most promising basis of a reductivist account of the success requirement, and that the reductivist should explain the existence of the success requirement in roughly the following way.

An individual using force against an attacker must have some prospect of success for her force to have a chance of counting as defence. We judge the proportionality of this potential defence by comparing the threatened harm with the force to be employed to avert that harm, asking whether, if successful, the defensive harm she inflicts would be a proportionate means of averting the threatened harm. Since attackers are liable to both defensive harms and harms that their victims inflict in the course of trying to defend themselves, an attacker is not wronged by the infliction of merely potentially defensive harm.

But things become more complicated once we raise the possibility of collateral harm to innocent people. As I outlined in Chapter 2, the constraints on harming innocent indirect threats and bystanders are sufficiently stringent that they can be overridden only by harms that meet both a proportionality standard and a lesser-evil standard. It's *proportionate* to kill an innocent indirect threat or a bystander to save just two other innocent people's lives. But the lesser-evil standard, although it entails proportionality, is more stringent than proportionality. And I suggest that unlike proportionality, lesser evil is sensitive to probability. Thus, lesser evil is satisfied—and collateral harms become *permissible*—only when one has a reasonable prospect of achieving a proportionate good that significantly outweighs the harm inflicted on the non-liable person. One may divert a trolley from where it will likely kill ten to where it will likely kill one, but one may not divert a trolley from where it will likely kill two to where it will likely kill one. The standard is set even higher in cases where one intentionally (rather than just foreseeably) harms an innocent person.

This means that if an innocent person stands to be incidentally harmed by one's defence, one's defence must meet both the requirements of proportionality and lesser evil, and thus one must consider whether one's defence is likely to succeed. Consider a revised version of Alice and Beth's predicaments:

Collateral First Timer: In the course of breaking Attacker's leg, Alice will break Passer-By's wrist as a side-effect. Alice's defence has an 80 per cent chance of fending off Attacker.

Collateral Old Timer: In the course of breaking Determined Attacker's leg, Beth will break Passer-By's wrist as a side-effect. Beth's defence has a 40 per cent chance of fending off Determined Attacker.

I think it is proportionate to break an innocent person's wrist as a side-effect of fending off a broken leg.[37] It must be, if Alice is permitted to proceed (which I think she is). On my account, this means that it is also proportionate for Beth to break Passer-By's wrist, since, if Beth's defensive action succeeds, she will have achieved a good sufficient to outweigh breaking Passer-By's wrist. But Beth's action might fail the lesser-evil standard, since there is only a 40 per cent chance that the harm she inflicts on Passer-By will be a side-effect of a means of averting a proportionate harm to Beth. Depending on where we set our reasonableness standard, we might think that a 40 per cent chance of achieving a proportionate good is not enough to satisfy the lesser-evil constraint. If so, Beth's use of force does not become disproportionate. But it does become *unjustified*, because there are constraints on harming innocent people in self-defence that hold even when one would inflict only proportionate force.[38]

I suggested earlier that it's an objection to the subsuming account that Beth's defence against Determined Attacker could be deemed disproportionate even if it succeeds. It might now be objected that the same is true of the lesser evil standard that I have proposed here. Even if Beth goes ahead and uses force, breaking

[37] Those who disagree can alter the relevant harms as they see fit, e.g. a broken wrist in the course of fending off a lethal threat.

[38] In *Killing in War*, McMahan develops a distinction between narrow proportionality and wide proportionality. Narrow proportionality governs harms inflicted on those who are potentially liable to those harms (roughly, those morally responsible for unjust threats, such as Murderer). Wide proportionality governs harms inflicted on those who are not potentially liable to any harm (for McMahan, innocent threats and bystanders, such as Passer-By). I think it's a mistake to call these different considerations two forms of proportionality. I think that narrow proportionality is Proper Proportionality (and I think that McMahan is mistaken to think that this kind of proportionality can be sensitive to considerations of the likelihood of success, as I have discussed here). I think that wide proportionality is basically a lesser-evil justification, and is probably largely akin to what most people (including me) mean by a lesser-evil justification. I don't see, really, why McMahan wants to call this a kind of proportionality. It can't be sensitive to necessity in the same way he says that narrow proportionality is. Collateral harms can be unavoidable, but they are not a means, and it's

Passer-By's wrist, her doing so will be unjustified even if she is successful. But this seems to me correct, because it captures the fact that the objection to Beth's using force is not that her defence is disproportionate, but that it wrongly risked harming a non-liable person. This is true even if it succeeds and the broken wrist is proportionate collateral harm for averting a broken leg: to have wrongly risked harm to a person is a wrong independent of whether or not the harm befalls them, or whether the harm turns out to have been a side-effect of successful defence. The problem with the subsuming account is that it suggests that Beth wrongs *her attacker* even if she inflicts only necessary and successful harm equivalent to the harm that the attacker would otherwise inflict on her, because if her chance of success is low the harm is deemed disproportionate and an attacker cannot be liable to disproportionate harm. What I have suggested does not imply that Beth in *Collateral Old Timer* wrongs her attacker, but only that even successful defence remains unjustified if it unjustifiably endangered a non-liable person.

So, wars must have a reasonable prospect of success—that is, satisfy a lesser-evil justification—because of the collateral damage that they inflict. Wars that have no prospect of success inflict unnecessary harm, and are impermissible because they fail the condition of last resort. Wars that have only an unreasonable prospect of success are impermissible not because they are disproportionate, but because it is unjustified to inflict even proportionate collateral harms in pursuit of a goal that one is unlikely to achieve.

The greater the disparity between the harm and the good, the lower the reasonableness threshold is set. That is, if Beth will only painfully scratch Passer-By's finger if she uses force to avoid a broken leg, she may proceed even if there is only a very low probability of success of achieving the proportionate good. But if she must break Passer-By's wrist, there must be a higher probability of success of achieving the proportionate good. But, as I have argued, this is not because it is disproportionate to proceed with an insufficient probability of success, but because proceeding fails the distinct lesser-evil constraint that is the success requirement.

5.6 An Essentially Political Requirement?

Uniacke denies that this kind of collateral damage-based account, which is so amenable to the reductivist, can explain the success requirement. Such an

the least harmful means that we are interested in when we talk about necessity. (Of course, not all the harms inflicted on the non-liable are going to be collateral harms, but some will be.) And if what I say here is right, 'wide proportionality', or lesser-evil justification, is sensitive to likelihood of success in a way that narrow proportionality isn't.

explanation misses the 'deeper significance' of that requirement, which stems from the requirement that wars be declared by a legitimate authority:

> This latter condition is not simply a matter of procedural legitimacy. On the contrary, it stems from the view that the right to wage war is grounded in the duty of a political authority to protect the community. This is part of its wider duty to act for the good of the community for whose welfare it is responsible, a duty on which its authority depends and on the basis of which it has a right to commit the nation to war. We can note here that if indeed the right of a political authority to resort to war is based on its duty to protect the community, then under the combined conditions of *jus ad bellum* a political authority would also have a duty to resort to war.[39] Personal self-defence, on the other hand, is discretionary: individuals have a right but no equivalent duty to defend themselves against unjust attack.[40]

The first part of this argument, then, holds that if one waged a war that lacked a reasonable prospect of success, one would not be acting for the good of one's people. Thus, one would not be a legitimate authority, and therefore one's war would be unjust. The second part holds that once all the *ad bellum* conditions are met, states have a duty to fight their war. But individuals have no similar duty to engage in self-defence. Self-defence is morally optional.

Uniacke further argues that war cannot be reduced to self-defence because political authorities are 'commanding or committing' their citizens to expose themselves to harm, and to 'engage in or to support widespread acts of killing and destruction'.[41] State leaders can make it the case that everyone in the country is at war, and this exposes all the citizens to moral and physical risks. This too shows that the legitimacy of political leaders is an essential component of a just war: only if they are acting on behalf of the community, and for the good of that community, can their war be just. We cannot capture this essentially political dimension of war by pointing to self-defence.

5.6.1 Legitimate Authority

There are two things that Uniacke's legitimate authority-based account of the success condition could be aiming at. One is a historically accurate description of why traditional just war theory came to include a success condition. The other is a philosophical demonstration that this is the correct ground of the success condition, and that the individualist cannot make sense of it.

If Uniacke is trying to support the former, historical claim, her account seems patently false. Uniacke claims that '[w]ithin Just War Doctrine, this insight [that

[39] See Suzanne Uniacke, 'Self-Defence and Just War', in Dieter Janssen and Michael Quante (eds.), *Gerechte Kriege* (Paderborn: Mentis-Verlag, 2002), 64–78 (citation in original).

[40] Uniacke, 'Self-Defence, Just War, and a Reasonable Prospect of Success', 71–2.

[41] Uniacke, 'Self-Defence, Just War, and a Reasonable Prospect of Success', 72.

political leaders act on behalf of others for whom they are responsible] is closely associated with the view that the legitimacy of political leaders, including their authority to declare war, depends on their acting for the good of the community'.[42] But historically, just war theorists have concerned themselves with who has the power to command, not with who is a legitimate leader in virtue of acting in their country's best interests. Traditional just war theory has accepted that brutal dictators can be legitimate authorities for the purposes of declaring war, despite the fact that such dictators can hardly claim to have any moral or political legitimacy in virtue of protecting their citizens' interests.

Of course, we might say that the wars of dictators are unjust. But I doubt that traditional just war doctrine would say that they are unjust because they are against the *aggressor* state's interests: that, for example, Saddam Hussein's invasion of Kuwait was unjust because it was against the Iraqi people's interests and therefore Hussein was not a legitimate authority. Uniacke's account is therefore unpromising as an attempt to capture the historical origins of the success condition.

This point reminds us that the traditional role of the legitimate authority condition in *jus ad bellum* is that of determining whether a use of force counts as war *at all*. It is included in the *ad bellum* criteria because in order to judge whether something is a just war, one must first know whether it is a war. But legitimate authority does not itself help us to determine whether a war is just or unjust. If one is not a legitimate authority one is traditionally deemed not to be fighting a war at all, rather than fighting a war that is necessarily unjust. We can thus describe the legitimate authority condition as a conceptual constraint on whether or not one is at war. That one *is* a legitimate authority, and thus at war, still leaves it entirely open whether one's war is just.

Since the condition of legitimate authority is not, in this respect, indicative of justice, it is hard to see how it could underpin the success condition, lending it an essentially political dimension in the way that Uniacke envisages. After all, meeting the success condition *is* supposed to be indicative of the justness of one's war. How could a conceptual constraint such as the legitimate authority requirement, which has no moral content for the purposes of *jus ad bellum*, be the best explanation of a moral constraint like the success condition? If Uniacke is aiming at the philosophically best account of the success condition, I think a legitimate authority-based account is again going to come up short.

More generally, I don't think the picture Uniacke paints of a legitimate authority as an authority that acts in the interests of its people is particularly inimical to

[42] Uniacke, 'Self-Defence, Just War and a Reasonable Prospect of Success', 73.

the reductivist. What are worrying from a reductivist perspective are the conclusions Uniacke draws for the nature of a defensive war. Uniacke claims that political authorities have an essentially political *duty* to protect their citizens that shows that defensive war is not to be understood as a discretionary right of self-defence. But this does not follow from the claim that to be a legitimate authority is to act in the interests of one's citizens. Why not characterize the duty of political leaders as a duty to allow individual citizens to defend themselves against unjust harm? The individual citizens have a right to employ such defence (or to pay others to defend them), and their political leaders should not prevent this (and should indeed assist this), just as I ought not to interfere with, but rather assist, an individual engaged in legitimate defence in the domestic realm.[43]

On this picture, it's not the case that states have a duty to wage war, such that waging war cannot be a collective exercise of (discretionary) self-defence. Rather, political leaders have a duty to comply with their citizens' preferences when doing so will be to allow those citizens to justifiably exercise their rights. But they need not comply with these preferences when war is unlikely to succeed, because then the citizens are not justified in exercising their rights to self-defence, because their doing so will unjustifiably inflict collateral harm.

What of the idea that states commit or command their citizens to fight, and thereby expose them to moral and physical risks? Uniacke suggests that this upshot of declaring war reveals an essentially political dimension of war that cannot be captured by the reductivist. But this argument begs the question against the reductivist view. Reductive individualists do not typically think that a state *can* commit its citizens to fight wars, if this means the state's taking the decision to fight out of the hands of those individual citizens. Rather, people like McMahan and myself hold that combatants themselves are responsible for deciding whether to fight, and that they should take that decision after serious and careful reflection about the justness of the war. Citizens can be attacked if, and because, they decide to fight in an unjust war, not because their political leaders have declared an unjust war. This is a central tenet of the reductive individualist view. To think that the mere declaration of war by political leaders makes it morally permissible for enemy combatants to attack citizens of that state is to assume the truth of the collectivist view. And, of course, when a state is engaged in a just war, the reductive individualist thinks that *nobody* in the state becomes liable to attack in virtue of fighting that war.

[43] It's not just rights of self-defence in play, remember—citizens also have duties of other-defence that could explain why states may, for example, conscript people who elect not to exercise their own rights of self-defence. Cheyney Ryan has an interesting discussion of this in 'Self-Defense and the Obligations to Kill and Die', *Ethics and International Affairs*, Vol. 18, No. 1 (2004), 69–73. But I will not explore this further here.

Uniacke might reply that even on the reductivist view, a state's declaring war exposes its non-combatants to the risk of being collaterally harmed, irrespective of whether those non-combatants contribute to the war effort. It also exposes non-combatants on the other side to such risks (and let's assume that at least some of the non-combatants on the unjust side are innocent). But this again is simply a question of lesser evil, easily mimicked on the individual level. If the good that can be achieved by exposing the non-combatants to (risks of) collateral harm is sufficient to outweigh that (risk of) harm, then it may be permissible to wage war (assuming that other criteria are satisfied). If, however, the war has no reasonable prospect of achieving its just cause, then it will fail to be just. There's nothing essentially political about this: as described in section 5.5.3, it is wrong for an individual to use force that is unlikely to avert even a proportionate a threat to herself if doing so exposes bystanders to harm.

5.7 Summary

Reductivist individualists still have a lot of work to do when it comes to explaining central features of *jus ad bellum*. But I do think that the challenges discussed here—that only by granting inherent value to the state can it be proportionate to defend against political aggression, and that reductivism can't explain the success condition—fail.

I have argued that whilst Rodin is correct to think that we bear responsibility for mediated harms, he's mistaken to think that any discount attached to such harms is undone by a duty of care to co-citizens. I have argued for a revised version of the Defence Account of mediated harms, according to which foreseen but unintended mediated harms are heavily discounted in an agent's proportionality calculation. I suggested that the limit to the cost an agent ought to bear rather than trigger mediated harms is roughly that which an agent ought to bear in order to rescue others from harm.

I rejected the claim that lesser interests cannot warrant lethal defence. I argued that the distinction between lesser interests and vital interests tracks those goods that warrant lethal defence only when sufficiently aggregated and those goods that warrant lethal defence without aggregation. Since political aggression threatens serious harm to many individuals, it can be proportionate to use lethal force to avert political aggression. Moreover, it can be proportionate to risk lethal collateral harm to innocent people in the course of averting harm to the lesser interests of a sufficient number of people. However, there is moral reason to distribute the collateral costs of defence amongst potential beneficiaries of that defence. This claim could have significant implications for the methods of warfare that can be permitted by an individualist account of the ethics of war.

In sections 5.5 and 5.6, I considered the relationship between *ad bellum* proportionality and the requirement that a war have a reasonable prospect of success. I rejected McMahan and Hurka's claim that the success requirement can be incorporated into the proportionality requirement. The proportionality requirement governs means of achieving ends. Harms that fail to achieve a good, such as averting a threat, fail to be means and are therefore neither proportionate nor disproportionate. I argued that proportionality requires us to judge whether a level of force, *if successful in averting the threat*, would be a proportionate means of averting that threat. Proportionality is not sensitive to the likelihood of success. The requirement that war have a likelihood of success is a lesser-evil constraint motivated by concerns about collateral harms to innocent people. Collateral harms must pass not only a proportionality test, but also a lesser-evil test. Thus, the requirement that wars have a reasonable prospect of success cannot be subsumed under the proportionality requirement.

Uniacke is therefore right that the *ad bellum* conditions ought to include a success requirement, and that reductivists need to be able to account for this requirement. But, contra Uniacke, I think there is reason to be optimistic that individualism can meet this challenge. The case for seeing the success requirement as essentially political, and stemming from the notion of legitimate authority, strikes me as less than compelling. The view that I have defended, which grounds the success requirement in concerns about collateral harm, seems a more natural way to understand the wrongness of waging a war that lacks a reasonable prospect of success. If this is correct, the success condition is motivated by thoughts about harms to individuals in a way that is amenable to the individualist view.

6

Non-combatant Liability

I have argued for a distinction between direct and indirect threats. A direct threat is someone who will inflict harm upon you. An indirect threat is someone who endangers you in some other way, for example by blocking an escape route that you need to take, or making some other causal contribution to what threatens you. I have argued that being a cause of a direct threat is particularly morally significant. The account of self-defence that I have defended holds that indirect threats can render themselves liable to defensive force only if they are morally responsible for posing an unjust threat—that is, if they have reasonable opportunities to avoid posing that threat and they intentionally fail to avail themselves of those opportunities. If I am right that the rules governing permissible killing between individuals largely determine the rules governing killing in war, my account will have significant implications for the liability of non-combatants on the unjust side of a war. This in turn will have implications for the permissibility of attacking such non-combatants.

In this chapter and Chapter 7, I examine these implications. Drawing on the account of moral responsibility developed in Chapter 3, I will argue that if a non-combatant has a reasonable opportunity to avoid posing an unjust threat and intentionally fails to take that opportunity, she is liable to defensive killing. Much of the argumentative work for this claim—that those who are morally responsible for indirect unjust threats are liable to defensive killing—has been done already. My focus in this chapter is therefore on defending the plausibility of extending this argument to non-combatants.

Of course, there may be some countries in which the cost (or the perceived cost) to a non-combatant of refusing to contribute to an unjust war is so high that we think that she lacks a reasonable opportunity to avoid posing a threat. But there are a great many countries in which this is not the case. In the United States, Canada, and in most European countries, the penalties for a non-combatant who fails to contribute to a war effort are not severe.[1] Indeed, such contributions are often

[1] Some conscientious objectors who refused to contribute to the British war effort in the First

wholly voluntary. I am primarily interested in the liability of non-combatants in countries like these. Most people think that even these non-combatants are not liable to defensive killing, even if they voluntarily and knowingly contribute to an unjust war.

I defend the claim that non-combatants who are morally responsible for threatening as part of an unjust war are liable to be killed by looking at recent attempts to resist this view. I begin with David Rodin's argument that the contributions that non-combatants make lie too far down the causal chain to render their authors liable.[2] I then tackle Jeff McMahan's claim that it is a combination of factors that together show that non-combatants are not typically liable to defensive killing. Both McMahan and Cécile Fabre argue that non-combatant contributions are causally insufficient to ground liability to defensive killing.[3] I argue that, contra McMahan and Fabre, killing non-combatants is not disproportionate. I also argue for a distinction between the exploitative killings I explored in Chapter 2 and what I call *merely opportunistic* killings. A person is killed merely opportunistically if she is killed in a way that uses her to avert a threat for which she is responsible. I argue that non-combatants can be liable to merely opportunistic killing. I also reject McMahan's claim that the uncertain effectiveness of such killings can show that non-combatants are not liable to them. I also consider Fabre's argument that non-combatants are not morally responsible for their contributions.

I find that none of these arguments successfully undermines the idea that non-combatants can be liable to defensive killing. I conclude that the generally accepted ground of the principle of non-combatant immunity—that non-combatants have done nothing to render themselves liable to intentional killing—is false.

World War were disenfranchised for five years after the war. The treatment was most severe for those who had been conscripted to fight and who were either (a) redirected to non-combat roles that they refused to perform, or (b) refused conscientious objector status, and subsequently refused to carry out orders. A small number of these were court-martialled and sentenced to death, although the sentences were not carried out. But this applied only to people who were being called up to join the army—participation in other parts of the war effort was voluntary. This is also true of the Second World War, when joining e.g. the Land Army or working in a munitions factory was voluntary (hence the 'Women of Britain: Come into the factories!' campaign: workers were enticed, rather than compelled, to contribute). And when there is no conscription, of course, most if not all contributions are voluntary.

[2] David Rodin, 'The Moral Inequality of Soldiers: Why *jus in bello* Asymmetry is Half Right', in D. Rodin and H. Shue (eds.), *Just and Unjust Warriors* (Oxford: OUP, 2008).

[3] McMahan, *Killing in War*, 225; Cécile Fabre, 'Guns, Food and Liability to Attack in War', *Ethics*, Vol. 120 (October 2009), 36–63.

6.1 The Principle of Non-combatant Immunity

The principle of non-combatant immunity is one of the linchpins of just war theory. The principle holds, roughly, that it is impermissible to intentionally target non-combatants in war. The traditional defence of this principle is that, unlike combatants, non-combatants have done nothing to render themselves liable to attack. Whereas combatants threaten, and are thus legitimate targets for combatants on the other side, non-combatants do not threaten. They are thus innocent in the original sense of the word: they are 'not harming'.[4]

But this view has become increasingly difficult to defend. After all, we can think of lots of ways in which non-combatants contribute to their country's war effort. They make political contributions, such as voting for the war, writing pro-war articles or books, attending pro-war rallies, and so on. They make material contributions by producing weapons, equipment, and food. The Women's Land Army made this sort of contribution to the Second World War, taking over agricultural production to enable Britain to fight the war despite the blockade of its waters by German U-boats. The Women's Timber Corps provided wood essential to the war effort. Non-combatants also make technological contributions to war, perhaps by designing or testing weapons and machinery for military use. They can also make what we can call strategic contributions, for example by settling land (a persistent feature of the Israeli–Palestinian conflict). And, of course, the war is financed by taxes paid by combatants and non-combatants alike.

It is hard to deny that these myriad activities make a significant—indeed essential —contribution to a country's ability to fight a successful war. Indeed, both the Land Army and the Timber Corps were recently honoured with medals for their contributions to the war. In the face of such clear acknowledgement that non-combatants can be integral parts of a war machine, it is hard to credit the idea that they are nonetheless not part of the threat that their country poses: that they are 'not harming'. But current international law prohibits the intentional targeting of, for example, a person working in a factory making the guns and bombs that will kill enemy combatants, or sewing parachutes that enable troops to land behind enemy lines. The UK *Manual on the Law of Armed Conflict*, for example, stipulates that such people are civilians, and do not count as playing a 'direct part' in the war.

[4] See Jeff McMahan, 'The Moral Equality of Combatants', *Journal of Political Philosophy*, Vol. 14, No. 4 (2006), 377–93, at 380 for a useful discussion of material innocence and moral innocence.

Only combatants are permitted to take a direct part in hostilities. It follows that they may be attacked. Civilians may not take a direct part in hostilities and, for so long as they refrain from doing so, are protected from attack. Taking a direct part in hostilities is more narrowly construed than simply making a contribution to the war effort. Thus working in a munitions factory or otherwise supplying or supporting the war effort does not justify the targeting of civilians so doing. However, munitions factories are legitimate military targets and civilians working there, though not themselves legitimate targets, are at risk if those targets are attacked. Such incidental damage is controlled by the principle of proportionality.[5]

Setting aside the pragmatic reasons for why we might want to endorse this view as a matter of policy, I think it is clearly mistaken as a picture of liability to defensive harm. The use of the phrase 'hostilities' to try to distinguish parts of the war, such that one might contribute to a 'war effort' without playing a part in the 'hostilities' seems wholly artificial. If being directly involved in the hostilities means firing weapons on the front line, then most combatants will not be involved in the hostilities either. And if we broaden the meaning of 'hostilities' to include the military activities behind the front line that provide intelligence, training, and supplies, such that we cover all combatants, it seems arbitrary to exclude the non-combatants playing comparable roles.

Of course, this is not a new observation. Many just war theorists have pointed out that there doesn't seem to be any principled—or morally significant—difference between the contributions of combatants compared to those of non-combatants.[6] And yet the distinction between combatants and non-combatants is supposed to give rise to an important moral difference in how members of these two groups may be treated. If the distinction between combatants and non-combatants is not underpinned by a distinction between harming and not harming, what are our grounds for insisting upon this different treatment?

Several contemporary writers have tried to answer this question. Given the aforementioned difficulties with maintaining the traditional 'not harming' grounds of the principle of non-combatant immunity, these writers have focused their efforts on showing not that non-combatants don't contribute to wars, but that they are not liable to be killed even if they contribute. In what follows, I argue that we should not adopt the solutions that these writers have offered.

[5] *The Manual of the Law of Armed Conflict* (London: MOD, 2004), 2.6.3.

[6] See, in particular, Larry May, 'Killing Naked Soldiers: Distinguishing between Combatants and Noncombatants', *Ethics and International Affairs*, Vol. 19, No. 3, (2005), 39–53. In ch. 7 of *The Ethics of War and Peace: An Introduction* (London: Routledge, 2011), I discuss in some detail the ways in which just war theorists have tried (and failed) to identify a causal distinction between combatants and non-combatants.

6.2 Intervening Agency

6.2.1 *Causal Proximity and Liability*

David Rodin's suggested ground for non-combatant immunity relies upon the idea that causal proximity is relevant to liability. Whilst non-combatants do threaten, the threats they pose are not causally proximate to deaths of enemy soldiers.[7] Rodin suggests that it is a necessary condition of liability to defensive force that one be currently engaged in an unjust attack. Of course, it isn't clear how we ought to cash out this idea of being 'currently engaged' in an attack. Rodin cites and dismisses various attempts at specifying a temporal measure of this condition. In their place, he argues for a *principle of intervening agency* to identify agents who are liable to defensive force.

This principle holds that if two or more agents create an unjust threat between them, and both meet a threshold of minimal moral responsibility, only the agent whose action came last in the causal chain counts as engaged in an unjust attack. Rodin further argues that only this agent—the proximate cause—is a permissible target of defence. Rodin offers two examples to illustrate this principle.

Naughty Minister: Criminal has been released from prison as a result of financial cuts in the prison system. The cuts are a direct result of fraudulent mismanagement of the finances by Minister, who acted in the full knowledge that his actions would endanger the public. Criminal is trying to kill Victim, who can save his life either by killing Criminal, or by lethally trampling over Minister.

[7] David Rodin, 'The Moral Inequality of Soldiers', 52. Rodin's view has echoes of Robert Fullinwider's claim that killing non-combatants is ruled out because such killings cannot be justified by the Principle of Self-Defence ('War and Innocence', *Philosophy and Public Affairs*, Vol. 5, No. 1 (Autumn 1975), 90–7). Fullinwider does not develop the intervening agency line, but rather stipulates that self-defence permits the killing only of direct threats. Clearly, I think this is wrong, as I have argued at length in Chapters 1–3. Larry Alexander offers a rebuttal of Fullinwider's view ('Self-Defence and the Killing of Non-Combatants: A Reply to Fullinwider', *Philosophy and Public Affairs*, Vol. 5, No. 4 (Summer 1976), 408–15) in which he suggests that, 'Although causal remoteness is relevant to the questions of whether a threat exists and whether a person is a necessary or sufficient cause of it, it is irrelevant to the right of self-defence once the threat, the necessary or sufficient causal relation, and the lack of superior alternatives to remove the threat are posited' (413). Alexander considers the possibility that Fullinwider might think intervening agency relevant, and rejects this argument on the grounds that 'only the likelihood of harm, not the number of choices required to bring it about, is directly relevant' (414). Alexander's alternative view of permissible defence, however, seems alarmingly permissive (even to me).

Provocation: Villain culpably provokes Attacker into attacking Victim. Victim can save his life either by killing Attacker, or by lethally trampling over Villain.

Rodin argues that it would be impermissible for Victim to save himself by killing either Minister or Villain in these cases. He acknowledges that Minister and Villain bear perhaps greater moral responsibility for the unjust threat to Victim's life than do the intervening agents in each case. But neither Minister nor Villain is currently engaged in an unjust attack, their engagement in the threat to Victim's life having been 'superseded' by that of the intervening agent. This intervening action transfers liability from the causally remote agents, Minister and Villain, to the causally proximate agents, Attacker and Criminal.

Rodin thinks that it is these sorts of cases that should inform our understanding of the relationship between combatants and non-combatants. Non-combatants are causally remote threats, and combatants are causally proximate threats. Since both combatants and non-combatants meet the threshold of minimal responsibility, it follows that non-combatants are not liable to attack in war, even if we grant that non-combatants can bear greater moral responsibility for a war than do combatants. Non-combatants are not currently engaged in attacks, as required for liability, because the combatants intervene further down the causal line. Intervening agency thus gives us a principled way of sustaining non-combatant immunity in war, even if we grant the role of non-combatants in initiating and sustaining war.

I think that many people would endorse arguments of the sort described above, thinking that by enlisting in the armed forces combatants 'take on' liability to harm in a way that protects their country's civilians. But I think that Rodin's argument is nonetheless mistaken. For a start, it isn't clear that this view will capture all combatants in the liability net. A combatant who loads the bullets into a gun whilst his comrade does the firing will not be liable to be killed on Rodin's account. Both combatants seem like legitimate targets (and certainly, if Rodin is defending the distinction between combatants and non-combatants, he will want to have (at the very least) frontline combatants on the liable side of the distinction).

More generally, I don't think Rodin's principle can be sustained as an account of liability to defensive force; indeed, I think that it is undermined by Rodin's own earlier work. In *War and Self-Defense*, Rodin offers a critique of Alan Gewirth's view of moral responsibility. Gewirth argues that moral responsibility attaches to the proximate cause of a threat, because intervening agency rids those further back in the causal chain of responsibility for the threat. In effect, he says about responsibility what Rodin says about liability. But Rodin argues that we can see that Gewirth's principle is false by thinking about cases like Cheyney Ryan's *Coercion.*

Coercion: The German army capture a town. Nazi forces Mayor to shoot Citizen, on pain of Nazi shooting a much greater number of citizens.

Rodin points out that Gewirth's principle generates the result that Mayor's intervening agency supplants Nazi's responsibility for the killing. This is clearly wrong: as Rodin says, moral responsibility is not exclusive, but can be shared by a number of people.[8] Mayor may take on some responsibility for the killing, but his doing so does not free Nazi of *his* responsibility. Both are morally responsible for the killing of Citizen.

But what also seems clear, and what Rodin overlooks, is that the same is true of these characters' liability to defensive harm. If Citizen has a gun with which he can lethally defend himself, both Nazi and Mayor seem like potentially legitimate targets. Indeed, if killing either would save Citizen's life, it would be morally preferable for Citizen to shoot Nazi, even though Mayor clearly meets Rodin's threshold of minimal agency, and it is his action that is most proximate to the threat to Citizen's life. As I argued in Chapter 5, Nazi's greater moral responsibility means that harms to him count for less than harms to Mayor in Citizen's deliberations concerning the least harmful means of defence. Killing Mayor would violate the necessity principle, if killing Nazi would also save Citizen's life. Cases like this suggest that Rodin's principle concerning killing in war is defeated by the very objection that he levels at Gewirth's account of self-defence: why think of liability as an exclusive attribute, rather than a plastic, shareable attribute?

Rodin also himself commits himself to the idea that it's the currency of the threat (and not whether one's contribution is current) that matters for liability in his discussion of *Goading.*

Goading: Villain hates Victim. He thus deliberately goads Victim into attacking him in order that he may then kill Victim on grounds of self-defence.

Rodin argues that Villain cannot invoke a right of self-defence against Victim.[9] Why not? Well, Rodin says, because Villain is at fault for the creation of the threatening situation to which he now responds. If, as Rodin claims, Villain is not permitted to defend himself against Victim, this suggests that Villain is liable to

[8] Rodin, *War and Self-Defense*, 63. [9] Rodin, *War and Self-Defense*, 79.

the harm that Victim will inflict. But then what matters for liability is not whether one is currently engaged in an unjust attack. Rather, what matters for liability is whether the threatening situation *to which one contributes* is current.[10] What makes Nazi in *Coercion* a legitimate target is his prior contribution to the threat currently facing Citizen. Thus, the claim that causal proximity is key to liability is false. With respect to non-combatants, then, our focus in determining liability should not be their causal proximity to a current threat, but their responsibility for that threat.

We might try to rescue a version of Rodin's idea by arguing that an intervening agent can voluntarily take on liability to defensive killing. This is another pretty popular idea with respect to the relationship between combatants and non-combatants. We talk of combatants 'assuming risks' on behalf of their country's non-combatants: by donning a uniform, a person effectively invites enemy combatants to target them instead of the non-combatants.[11] But I don't know how plausible this idea is. It would be very odd for those posing an unjust threat to get to decide amongst themselves who is liable to be killed to avert that threat, making it impermissible for their victim to aim defensive force at some group members rather than others. Liability to defensive harm doesn't seem like something we get to allocate by agreement.

Of course, we might nonetheless think that there are pragmatic reasons for combatants to agree amongst themselves not to target non-combatants. Just combatants probably do not want their own non-combatants killed, and might thus agree not to kill non-combatants on the unjust side. But such an agreement, even if it were binding on the just combatants, would not eradicate non-combatant liability on the unjust side of the war. They would still have forfeited their rights against attack. Such an agreement would be nothing more than an agreement not to inflict the harms to which those non-combatants are liable. As I say, we don't get to choose by agreement who is liable to defensive harm.

So, intervening agency, even combined with consent on the part of the intervening agent, doesn't give us a plausible way to sustain non-combatant immunity. That non-combatant contributions are causally remote does not show that they cannot render their authors liable to defensive killing. Indeed, parts of Rodin's

[10] Recall the case of the cabin boy in *Dudley v. Stephens* in Chapter 1. The reason why the men were not permitted to kill and eat the cabin boy, even if, as in Kaufman's variation, he had previously threatened their lives, was that he had not contributed to the threat *currently* facing them.

[11] Noam Zohar, for example, argues that '[i]t is soldiers, rather than the civilians, who are subsumed under the collective identity. Civilians too are members of the nation, but their identity as individuals is paramount, whereas those who wear the national uniform are rightly indentified as embodying the nation's agency. It is this that distinguishes soldiers and warrants their treatment under the war ethic . . .' ('Innocence and Complex Threats', 739).

own work seem to suggest that causally remote agents *are* liable to defensive killings if they are morally responsible for contributing to a current unjust threat.

6.2.2 *Shared Intention*

In a more recent paper, Rodin suggests that we can bolster his claims about intervening agency with thoughts about shared intention. He acknowledges that there are some cases in which intervening agency does not supersede the liability of those further down the causal chain. But, he says, we are tempted to make this claim only in cases where,

> there is a strong 'unity of intent' between the responsible party and the threatening party. Either they are cases of criminal conspiracy, as in the hit-man case [where a mafia boss hires an assassin to do his killing for him], or they are cases of institutionalized chain of command, as in the case of military organizations (clearly, commanding officers and rear serving combatants may be liable to attack, thought they may personally pose a direct threat to no one). Most civilians clearly do not possess an analogous kind of 'unity of intent' with the military who conduct operations, and this may form part of the resolution of this puzzle.[12]

We can of course agree with Rodin that members of the armed forces generally have robustly shared intentions. But there are at least two problems with the work that he tries to make this fact do.

The first is that unless he thinks that we can properly attribute responsibility (and liability) to the members of a group only when there is a level of shared intention akin to that which exists in the military or an organized criminal gang (which is implausible), the fact that intentions amongst members of the military are *more* robustly shared than intentions amongst munitions workers won't show that the munitions workers' intentions aren't *sufficiently* shared to ground liability. Other than stipulating that the unity of intention must be the unity manifested by military hierarchies, there is no reason to single out members of the armed forces as the only people with sufficiently linked wills to ground liability for each other's direct threats.

Besides, I think Rodin is wrong to insist that 'most' non-combatants don't share in equal measure the threatening intentions of their combatants—many civilians exhibit a steely resolve to support their country's war effort in any way they can, including the material and psychological support of their combatants. Why is someone who spends her evenings knitting clothes and blankets to keep frontline combatants warm (and often alive) so that they can continue to fight

[12] David Rodin, 'Morality and Law in War', in Hew Strachan and Sibylle Scheipers (eds.), *The Changing Character of War* (Oxford: OUP, 2011), 446–5, at 449.

not sharing in the intentions of her country's armed forces? Rodin seems to be inadvertently endorsing a further possible ground of non-combatant liability—that they share the lethal intentions of their combatants—rather than giving us a reason to restrict liability to members of the armed forces and a few high-level government officials.[13]

The second problem is that Rodin is mistaken to claim that causally remote actions can ground liability *only* when there is also shared intention of the order manifested by the military or organized criminal gangs. Imagine that you tell me that you're going to kill Victim, but that you've lost your gun. You nag me to lend you my gun. I eventually give in—not because I in any way share your intention to kill Victim, but just because I'm sick of your nagging. Do I escape liability to defensive harm, simply because I contributed to the threat to Victim's life out of irritation with you rather than any heartfelt desire to see Victim dead? That seems unlikely. Provided that I know what you're going to do with the gun, my liability is no different than it would be if you and I had meticulously planned Victim's death together.

Cases like *Coercion* are also hard to capture under the proposed notion of shared intention. We surely think that the remotely threatening agent in this case—Nazi—is liable to defensive killing. Yet we would be hard-pushed to describe Mayor, whom Nazi coerces into killing Citizen on pain of the death of many more people, as having a unity of intention with Nazi. They are certainly not together engaged in a criminal conspiracy akin to that of the mafia boss and his hired assassin, or part of an organization akin to the military. Moreover, we are unlikely to think that it is a unity with Citizen's intention that explains Nazi's liability to be killed. Nazi's liability does not arise from his sharing Mayor's intention of killing Citizen, but from his having instigated the killing. If the remotely threatening agents in these two cases are liable to defensive harm, Rodin is incorrect to think that we are tempted to ascribe liability to remote causes only when we have 'a strong "unity of intent"'.[14] Knowledge, even absent intention, can be sufficient to ground liability (recall Selfish Pedestrian from Chapter 3, who has no intention to help Murderer kill Victim, but whose foresight that she will block Victim's escape suffices to render her liable to defensive killing).

[13] An interesting question is whether shared intention in the *absence* of a causal contribution could ground liability. If I have agreed to kill Victim if your prior attempt fails (but I give you no assistance in your attempt on his life), would I render myself liable to defensive harm? These sorts of questions fall under the scope of complicitous liability. See Christopher Kutz, 'The Difference Uniforms Make: Collective Violence in Criminal Law and War', *Philosophy and Public Affairs*, Vol. 33, No. 2 (2005), 148–80, and Saba Bazargan, 'Complicitous Liability in War', *Philosophical Studies*, Vol. 165 (2013), 177–95.

[14] Rodin, 'Morality and Law in War', 449.

On my account, intervening agency plays an indirect role in liability. It can determine whether someone poses a direct threat or an indirect threat, and this can influence how much cost that person ought to bear rather than pose that threat. This in turn influences whether she is morally responsible for posing the threat, and thus whether threatening renders her liable to defensive harm. But our discussion in Chapter 3 suggested that people are required to bear very high costs rather turn themselves into threats, especially when they will be indirect causes of harm. The fact that, for example, Driver in *Drive-By* will be only indirectly endangering Victim's life, and that it's Terrorist who will be doing the killing, doesn't exempt Driver from moral responsibility or liability. Since non-combatants knowingly turn themselves into threats—and into causes—when they produce equipment for their country's war effort, the mere fact that these are indirect threats just isn't sufficient to show that the non-combatants cannot be liable to defensive harm.

6.3 McMahan's Account of Non-combatant Liability

McMahan's account of permissible defence holds that being morally responsible for an unjust threat that someone else poses can be sufficient to make a person liable to defensive killing, assuming that killing them will avert or mitigate the threat. Non-combatants can thus render themselves liable to be killed, on McMahan's view.

But, mindful of the implications of undoing non-combatant immunity, McMahan outlines several reasons why it will nonetheless usually be impermissible to kill non-combatants. He suggests that, ultimately, the lack of non-combatant liability results from the combined force of a range of factors: that killing non-combatants is disproportionate because the non-combatants typically have 'only a low degree' of responsibility for the unjust war, that killing non-combatants generally makes use of them rather than directly averting a threat, and that such indirect killings are of only uncertain effectiveness.[15] And, even when these conditions are not met, and the non-combatants really are liable to be killed, killing them will still be impermissible because even otherwise liable non-combatants are hard to attack without causing collateral harm to non-liable people. In this section, I examine McMahan's reasons against non-combatant liability. In Chapter 7 I consider the relationship between liability and permissibility.

[15] McMahan, *Killing in War*, 213.

6.3.1 Responsibility and Proportionality

McMahan's model of proportionality is sensitive not only to the usual features of the gravity of the threatened harm and the force needed to avert it, but also the moral responsibility of the person posing the threat. McMahan argues that since non-combatants are typically only 'weakly responsible' for the threats posed by their country in war, using lethal force against them would be disproportionate. Since one can be liable only to proportionate harm, non-combatants are not liable to defensive killing. I find the idea that proportionality is sensitive to moral responsibility quite puzzling, especially in light of what McMahan says about the permissibility of killing even fully excused threats in self-defence. For example, McMahan thinks it permissible to kill Resident in *Breakdown*:

> *Breakdown*: Victim's car breaks down in a remote area. He knocks on the door of an isolated farm to ask to use the phone. Unbeknown to him, there's been a series of gruesome murders in the local area. Warnings have been issued to local residents to be wary of strangers. When Resident opens the door, she thinks Victim is the violent murderer come to kill her and tries to shoot him.[16]

McMahan thinks that Victim may permissibly defend himself against Resident even if she is fully excused and thus has only a low degree of moral responsibility for the threat that she poses. He also thinks it permissible for Victim to kill the 'cautious driver', who, despite her meticulous care of her car and careful driving, faultlessly loses control of her car and lethally hurtles towards Victim. Given the apparent permissibility of killing these weakly morally responsible characters, it's hard to see why non-combatants who are weakly morally responsible for an unjust threat are off limits. In addition, McMahan argues that variations in moral responsibility amongst combatants are largely irrelevant if the harm to be averted is sufficiently great.[17] If it is proportionate to kill weakly responsible combatants because of the magnitude of the harm to be averted, it is surely proportionate to kill weakly responsible non-combatants to avert that same harm.

COMBATANTS AND NON-COMBATANTS

It seems to me that this aspect of McMahan's proportionality calculation—the degree of moral responsibility—is being used in two distinct ways in McMahan's work. With respect to unjust combatants, the condition is interpreted as referring

[16] Based on a case in McMahan, 'The Basis of Moral Liability to Defensive Killing', 387.

[17] McMahan, *Killing in War*, 197. See also Seth Lazar, 'The Responsibility Dilemma for *Killing in War*: A Review Essay', *Philosophy and Public Affairs*, Vol. 38, No. 2 (2010), 180–213.

to the extent to which the combatant is morally responsible for posing a threat—whether he is culpable, negligent, or excusably ignorant, and so on. And we are told that, given the sufficient gravity of the harm, it doesn't matter very much which category of responsibility the combatant falls into provided that he passes a threshold of minimal responsibility. When dealing with combatants, then, variations of responsibility are dwarfed by the enormity of the harm they are helping to perpetrate, making practically all combatants fair game.

But with respect to non-combatants, the responsibility aspect of the proportionality condition seems to refer to the part of the threat for which the non-combatant is causally responsible, i.e. it concerns whether the non-combatant makes enough of a causal contribution to render killing her proportionate (irrespective of whether she makes it culpably, ignorantly, and so on). For example, when McMahan says that non-combatants are only weakly morally responsible for threats they pose, he supports this claim not by invoking ignorance on the part of the non-combatants, but by emphasizing the causal triviality of the contributions they make:

> In some unjust wars, many civilians do bear some responsibility but the degree to which most of them are responsible is very slight ... They may pay their taxes, vote or even campaign for particular political candidates (sometimes on the basis of general sympathy with their overall positions on matters of policy but seldom because of the advocacy of war), participate in the culture from which the country's political leaders have emerged, fail to protest their country's unjust war, perhaps because they correctly believe that to do so would be ineffective, or perhaps because they approve of the war, and so on; but none of these things, nor even all of them together, is ordinarily sufficient for the forfeiture of a person's right not to be attacked and killed. Military attack exceeds what a person may ordinarily be liable to on the basis of these comparatively trivial sources of responsibility.[18]

The defence of the claim that non-combatants lack sufficient moral responsibility focuses not, for example, on their excusable ignorance with respect to what they do, but rather on the causal triviality of what they do. What makes killing non-combatants disproportionate, then, is not that proportionality is sensitive to moral responsibility, but rather that it is sensitive to causal contributions.

Of course, we might think that facts about causal contribution are indeed relevant to determining proportionality and thus liability. This could explain why McMahan thinks it permissible to kill the weakly responsible threats in the cases of self-defence described in section 6.3.1. The causal contribution of the threatening person in these cases is very significant. They are going to singlehandedly kill

[18] McMahan, *Killing in War*, 225.

an innocent person. In contrast, non-combatants typically make only small contributions to their country's unjust war. Each voter, for example, bears only a tiny degree of causal responsibility for the threat posed by their warmongering leader. Each munitions worker contributes only a relatively small number of weapons (or perhaps only parts of weapons). Even if McMahan's presentation of this argument conflates small causal contributions with minimal moral responsibility, he might nonetheless be right that these contributions are just too insignificant to render their authors liable.

6.3.2 *Causal Thresholds and Proportionality*

Cécile Fabre advances a similar view. Fabre argues that any kind of liability-based account of defensive killing must look at what non-combatants do as individuals, not merely invoke the results of group endeavours.[19] And, in order to be liable, those individual contributions must pass a threshold of causal significance. Fabre argues that most non-combatant contributions will fall below this threshold: she suggests that even if the overall output of a munitions factory constitutes a significant contribution to the war, making pieces of guns is not enough to render an individual liable to be killed.

But it seems to me wrongheaded to understand liability as subject to this sort of casual threshold. Consider the following case, *Hit*.

> *Hit*: Mafia Boss wants to take Victim out, but he cannot afford to hire Assassin, who is extremely skilled and thus extremely expensive. Mafia Boss has a whip-round amongst all the members of his mob, none of whom really like Victim. Everyone coughs up a few pounds for the assassination fund.

Each member of the mob plays only a small role in hiring Assassin. Their contribution is slight—a few pounds out of Assassin's hefty price. But if killing a member of the mob is a means of saving Victim's life, I do not think that such a killing would be ruled out on grounds of being disproportionate. Rather, I think that Victim would be permitted to kill any individual member of the mob (or even all of them), and that his target would not be permitted to defend himself. That each mobster makes only a small contribution cannot protect him from liability to defensive harm.

I think the same is true of those making weapons in munitions factories. Stipulating the existence of a causal threshold that protects non-combatants from liability just doesn't fit with our wider intuitions about liability to defensive harm.

[19] Fabre, 'Guns, Food and Liability to Attack in War', 61.

And this idea of a threshold commits Fabre to pronouncing differences in liability in cases that should strike us as morally similar. For example, imagine that a factory owner can run his factory in one of two ways. He can have a standard assembly line, in which 200 workers each fit a particular component of every gun. Or he can train each worker to make an entire gun from scratch. Either way, he ends up with 200 guns at the end of each day. Let's assume that Fabre's threshold lies somewhere between making pieces of guns and making complete guns (we may need to vary the example in accordance with our intuitions about where the threshold lies, but this detail need not concern us here). The workers on the assembly line model don't pass the causal threshold with respect to any particular weapon, whereas those working in tandem to produce complete weapons do.[20] Fabre's account suggests therefore that whilst the workers in the first set-up are not liable to be killed, the workers in the second are so liable. But this difference in liability hardly seems plausible. What matters, surely, is that they are contributing weapons for the unjust side of the war. It is this fact that grounds the liability of those making entire guns from scratch. If they were not sending their weapons to the war effort, or if they were not on the unjust side of the war, their contributions would not render them liable. And since those making pieces of guns are also contributing weapons for the unjust side of the war, those workers must be similarly liable.

More generally, we have reason to be sceptical of a view that entails that merely spreading the causal load for an unjust threat dissolves liability for that threat. This is pretty unattractive as a moral principle. Fabre suggests that whilst making pieces of guns does not meet the causal threshold for liability, 'taking overall responsibility for negotiating and drafting sales contracts between one's factory and the army might'.[21] But what if 'overall responsibility' for the contracts is shared by a team of people, rather than a single person? Does the liability that attached to the solitary contractor evaporate once we spread the load? I suspect that it does not, but rather attaches to all those who contribute. Those who conspire or collude in the creation of unjust threats cannot rid each other of liability simply by working as part of a team. And if it is not disproportionate (and thus impermissible) for Victim to use force against individual members of the mob in *Hit*, I do not think it disproportionate (and thus impermissible) for just combatants to use lethal force against individual workers who contribute to the unjust lethal threats they face.

[20] We can vary what the workers produce depending on where we think the threshold lies (maybe they make a tank a week, or a plane a year).

[21] Fabre, 'Guns, Food and Liability to Attack in War', 61.

Fabre is right that an individual's liability to defensive harm is determined by her individual contribution to an unjust threat. But she is wrong to focus on the extent to which an individual contributes to the threat rather than on the magnitude of the threat to which she contributes. We do not care, for the purposes of liability, how much money each member of the mob gives in *Hit*—about the extent of their contribution to the assassination fund. All we care about is the fact that they gave money *to fund a lethal threat*. And because they funded a lethal threat, they are liable to lethal defence. Proportionality is about the harm one helps bring about—the threat that faces a victim partly as a result of one's behaviour. If it is proportionate to kill members of the mob in *Hit*—which it must be if killing them is permissible—there seems to be no reason why it is disproportionate to kill non-combatants who make pieces of guns.

So, McMahan is wrong to think that causal triviality undermines proportionality, and both he and Fabre are wrong to think that it undermines liability. Given the significance of what non-combatants knowingly contribute *to*—the mass slaughter and maiming of innocent people—even a small contribution to that project is sufficient to render a person liable to lethal defence.

6.3.3 Necessity and Indirect Killing

What about the necessity condition? Does this undermine non-combatant liability, at least for those who, like McMahan, believe that liability has an internal necessity condition, such that a person can be liable only to the least harmful means of averting a threat? McMahan describes necessity as 'perhaps the most important' of the considerations that might afford non-combatants protection:

> Even when there are civilians in a society who bear a significant degree of responsibility for an unjust war ... they cannot be liable to attack unless attacking them can make an effective contribution to the achievement of a just cause ... unless they are themselves the immediate source of a threat, killing them cannot be directly effective as a means of averting a wrongful threat in the way that killing in [individual] self-defense is.... But the contributions that civilians make to the threats their state poses in war often lie in the past and can no longer be prevented.... In general, therefore, the only way that killing civilians can serve as a means of averting an unjust threat is indirectly, through affecting the action of others.[22]

We should be clear about what precisely McMahan is claiming in the case of, for example, non-combatants who have voted a warmongering politician into power. Is the objection to their being liable to harm based on the fact that their contributions lie 'in the past and can no longer be prevented'? As I have argued, it's

[22] McMahan, *Killing in War*, 225.

the currency of the threat that matters for liability. Given this, that a *contribution* lies in the past is no barrier to liability. As long as there is an aggressive war, the threat to which the voters contributed is still current. The work of showing that the contributing non-combatants are not liable must be done instead by the stipulation that nothing can now be done to the non-combatants to mitigate or avert the threats to which they have contributed. In this case, they will not be liable to harm on either an internalist or proportionate means account of liability. But as McMahan points out, even those non-combatants whose contributions lie in the past can sometimes be usefully killed. One might, for example, kill them in order to frighten the enemy state into submission. McMahan thinks that it is possible that non-combatants could be liable to this kind of killing. However, he also seems to think that such killings require a higher burden of justification than other defensive killings, partly because they are opportunistic, and partly because their effectiveness is uncertain.

I agree with McMahan that such killings can be permissible when they involve a person who is liable to defensive harm. But this is because whilst it is especially bad to kill an innocent person in a way that exploits her or makes use of her, this badness does not obtain in the case of a person who has rendered herself liable to defensive harm. When one uses a bystander to avert a threat, one is purely profiting from their presence. But in a case where one harmfully uses a person to avert a threat for which she is morally responsible, one is not using her purely to profit from her presence, but rather to prevent her past actions from making one worse off. If I use your body to shield myself against a lethal projectile that you have remotely fired towards to me, I don't derive a benefit from you, but rather use you to maintain the status quo by averting the impending harm of your threatening action. The same is true when one uses the killing of a person to scare others, as in *Mob*.

Mob: Victim is being chased by an angry racist mob who are trying to kill him. They corner him in a dead-end street. One of the mob throws a knife to the ringleader, who advances menacingly towards Victim. Unbeknown to the mob, Victim has a concealed gun. But he also has terrible eyesight: his short-distance vision is just awful. He cannot hope to accurately aim at the ringleader at such close range. His only hope of saving his life is to shoot the guy who threw the ringleader the knife, who is standing further away. When the rest of the mob realize that he has a gun and he's not afraid to use it, they will be scared off.

Victim is defending himself against a threat for which the knife-thrower bears moral responsibility. It does not seem impermissible for Victim to kill the knife-thrower if this is the only way in which he can save himself. That he will, in some sense, be *using* the knife-thrower (or rather, using the *killing* of the knife-thrower) as a means of scaring others into ceasing to pose an unjust threat doesn't make the action wrong, given what the knife-thrower has done.

We might call such killings 'merely opportunistic' to distinguish them from the objectionable exploitative killing of a bystander. Such merely opportunistic harming lacks the moral repugnance that attaches to the exploitative harming of bystanders to make oneself better off than one would have been in their absence. If this analysis is correct, there is no higher burden of justification to be met when one is killing a person merely opportunistically. So, whilst this supports McMahan's claim that non-combatants can be liable to opportunistic harm, it undermines any implication that such killings are especially difficult to justify even when they are aimed at those who are morally responsible for unjust threats.

We should, furthermore, be realistic about how many non-combatants will evade liability on these grounds. It might be true of some non-combatants that their only contributions to the unjust war lie in the past and that nothing—not even opportunistic harming—will avert or mitigate the threats to which they contributed. But in the case of a non-combatant who is currently contributing to the war effort—perhaps by making the sorts of contributions described at the start of this chapter—killing her will prevent her from so contributing. It is therefore an effective, eliminative means of averting the threat that she poses.

So, even if McMahan's internalist account of liability to defensive harm were correct, thoughts about necessity would provide protection to only a limited group of non-combatants.[23] And, I think that McMahan's internalist account of liability is false. In Chapter 4, I defended a new account of liability to defensive harm that I called the proportionate means account. On this account, a non-combatant is liable not only to the least harmful means of averting a threat, but also to any proportionate means of averting a threat. If this account is correct, non-combatants will be liable to an even greater range of harms than on McMahan's account, since they will be liable to harms that are a means of averting threats even if those means are not the most efficient way of averting those threats.

[23] Honour-based justifications for harming of the sort I explored in Chapter 4 won't have much traction in war, since (a) they obtain against only culpable aggressors and many non-combatants, whilst morally responsible, won't be culpable threats, and (b) collateral harms make it impermissible to inflict honour-defending harms. Finally, even when a non-combatant can be attacked without also causing collateral harms, honour-based justifications don't justify inflicting very serious or lethal harms, which are typically the only harms that combatants are able to inflict.

A further relevant debate, of course, is that which I raised in Chapter 4 concerning narrow liability and broad liability. We need to know the purposes for which a person can be liable to harm: whether she may be harmed to avert only the particular threat for which she is responsible, or any proportionate unjust threat. If a non-combatant can be harmed only to avert the particular threat for which she is responsible, this will limit her liability compared to the broad account. I return to this issue in Chapter 7.

6.3.4 Uncertain Effectiveness

Finally, McMahan thinks that it's problematic that killing non-combatants opportunistically—for example, to frighten other people in their state into pressuring their government to end the war—relies upon a causal chain that will have variable effectiveness. This argument speaks to both the internalist and proportionate means accounts of liability, since it relies upon uncertainty about whether killing a person will be a means of averting a threat or not. If killing some non-combatants will not cause other people to bring about the end of the war, then such killings won't avert threats and will not, on my account, be defensive. However, as I argued in Chapter 4, it seems plausible that one can render oneself liable to harms that one's victim inflicts in the course of trying to defend herself against unjust threats. If such harms fail, it doesn't follow that one was not liable to them. I doubt that McMahan wants to endorse a general position that harms that fail to avert unjust threats are impermissible or wrong those who are morally responsible for the threats. If I am right about that, the fact that the opportunistic harming of non-combatants is not certain or even likely to succeed cannot show that the non-combatants are not liable to such harm.

6.3.5 Combined Force

Of course, McMahan's claim is that it's the combined force of these factors that serves to preclude liability from attaching to most or many non-combatants. And there is of course something attractive about the claim that it would be wrong to attack non-combatants because there was some chance—however slight—that doing so could stop their country's unjust war. But the problem is that none of the factors seem terribly persuasive independently of each other, and so their combined force is unlikely to be very persuasive either.[24] If the merely opportunistic killing of liable people doesn't demand a higher justificatory burden than eliminative killing

[24] Compare McMahan's claim that just causes for war are only those things that do themselves warrant maiming and harming. He argues that combining lesser causes that do not themselves warrant maiming and harming cannot give rise to a justification for war. See Jeff McMahan, 'Just Cause for War', *Ethics and International Affairs*, Vol. 19, No. 3 (2005), 1–21.

of liable people, the fact that killing non-combatants must be opportunistic to be useful doesn't lend any weight to the claim that such killings are impermissible. If the fact that harming a liable person only has some moderate chance of averting the threats for which she is responsible doesn't generally show that she is not liable to be harmed, the fact that non-combatant killings have only some prospect of halting the war won't show that they're not liable to be killed by just combatants who are trying to defend themselves. Absent these factors, all we're left with is a lack of liability in cases in which there's nothing that can be done to a non-combatant to avert a threat for which she is responsible. But ruling out these kinds of killings isn't much of a victory for non-combatant immunity. Such killings would be pointless and thus have no attraction for just combatants trying to win a just war.

This leaves only McMahan's observation that it will very often be impossible to harm a liable non-combatant without also harming innocent non-combatants. I will call this the Isolation Problem. In Chapter 7, I will argue that this, along with the difficulty of identifying liable non-combatants, generates substantial non-combatant immunity. But it does not undermine non-combatant *liability*: immunity reflects that it is all-things-considered impermissible for just combatants to attack non-combatants, but it does not show that the non-combatants are not liable to attack.

6.4 Ignorance

A third strategy for showing that non-combatants are not liable to defensive killing is familiar from debates about the moral equality of combatants. People frequently invoke the ignorance of combatants regarding the justness of their war in order to undermine the idea that combatants might be morally responsible for participating in unjust wars. Fabre similarly argues that non-combatants are not liable to defensive killing even if they contribute to an unjust war. It is simply too hard for non-combatants to know that they pose unjust threats, which means that they cannot be made liable by posing those threats.

Fabre argues that, 'even if civilians who provide unjust combatants with the material resources which they need are unjustifiably contributing to wrongful killing, they are not, on the whole liable to attack'.[25] Fabre claims that one can become liable to be killed only if one is morally responsible for an unjust threat, something she and I agree on. If one is unavoidably ignorant of either the fact that one poses a threat, or the fact that the threat is unjust, Fabre believes that this negates moral responsibility.[26] Thus, non-combatants who are unavoidably

[25] Fabre, 'Guns, Food and Liability to Attack in War', 56.

[26] Fabre, 'Guns, Food and Liability to Attack in War', 58. I argue in section 6.4.1 that only ignorance that one poses a threat at all seems to preclude liability (as in the *Light Switch* case in

ignorant of the fact that they pose an unjust threat are not morally responsible for doing so, and are not liable to be killed.

6.4.1 The Mixed Character of War

So are non-combatants unavoidably ignorant? Yes, says Fabre. She defends this claim by emphasizing the mixed character of war. Wars often have both just and unjust phases. For example, what began as a war of aggression might become a partial war of defence if the opposing army is breaching the rules of *jus in bello*. Non-combatants who contribute to the just threats posed by combatants during these just phases of a war do not act wrongly, on Fabre's view, and are not liable to be killed.[27] Because of this mixed character of the war, a non-combatant on even the *ad bellum* unjust side of a war cannot know whether the equipment she makes will be used for good or for ill: for the just or the unjust ends of the war. She therefore cannot know whether she is contributing to an unjust threat, and her unavoidable ignorance protects her from liability to defensive killing.

Fabre acknowledges an obvious objection to this line of argument that finds its roots in the distinction between doing and allowing. This distinction gives rise to a presumption of erring on the side of not causing unjust harm, even if one will allow unjust harm as a result. If it is more important to not inflict unjust harm than it is to rescue people from unjust harm, or to perpetrate just harm, it is morally incumbent upon non-combatants to not contribute to what might be an unjust threat, even at the risk of failing to rescue or failing to contribute to a just threat. But Fabre argues that this objection 'has bite' only at the beginning of a war.[28] As the war goes on, the more likely it is to acquire additional, just ends like thwarting retaliatory killings. As the chances of contributing to a just threat improve, the presumption against contributing becomes correspondingly weak. And, Fabre argues, even if non-combatants do unjustifiably contribute to unjust threats—'[e]ven if (as I suggested in Sec. IV) running the risk of wrongfully harming someone (as civilians would do by contributing to an unjust war) is morally worse than running the risk of not helping someone thwart an unjust threat', they are still not liable to defensive killing.[29]

Chapter 3). Being ignorant that a threat that one knowingly poses is unjust does not (as in *Hologram* in Chapter 3 and *Breakdown* in Chapter 4).

[27] It isn't obvious to me that this is true. Providing support for one part of a war can facilitate the fighting of another part of that war. If, as I argue in section 6.4.1, the onus is on agents to not contribute to unjust harm even at the risk of failing to prevent unjust harm, Fabre's argument will not undermine the liability of non-combatants facilitating the just parts of an unjust war.

[28] Fabre, 'Guns, Food and Liability to Attack in War', 60.

[29] Fabre, 'Guns, Food and Liability to Attack in War', 60.

> [I]f *individuals'* rational and moral agency is decisive for their liability, then there should be some fit between the costs which agents, as individuals, are liable to incur for acting wrongfully, and their degree of moral responsibility for their actions. To deem them liable to be killed merely in virtue of knowingly taking the risk of wrongfully contributing to unjust lethal threats, given (a) that there is a strong chance that they will in fact either contribute to just threats or not contribute to any threat ... and (b) that they cannot know either way how their contribution will be used, does not pass the fittingness test.[30]

Fabre is not denying that that there is a duty to avoid wrongfully harming people, and that this outweighs the duty to help people. Indeed, she explicitly endorses this duty.[31] But she says that choosing wrongly under the epistemic constraints described cannot render a person liable to be killed. The degree of moral responsibility that attaches to non-combatants who choose to contribute is too low to render them liable to lethal harm.

But this reply fails to hit its target. Fabre is meant to be tackling the objection that when non-combatants lack information about the justness of their war, they ought to err on the side of caution by not contributing to that war. This objection suggests that those who do not so err render themselves liable to be killed. Fabre's response is that even those who choose to contribute will lack moral responsibility for contributing and so will not be liable. But her explanation of *why* they lack moral responsibility as laid out in (a) and (b) above seems to amount to little more than the claim that the non-combatants cannot know whether they will be contributing to an unjust threat. And surely the presumption that if a non-combatant doesn't know how her contribution to the war will be used then she ought not to contribute cannot be undermined by pointing to the fact that she doesn't know how her contribution will be used. The presumption is designed to guide agents in the face of precisely the sorts of epistemic constraints to which Fabre draws attention. It cannot be defeated by invoking those same constraints.

Perhaps, however, the presumption is sensitive to probabilities. If there is, as Fabre suggests, a strong chance that one might contribute to a just threat (or no threat at all), perhaps the presumption against causing unjust harm is overcome. It might well be permissible to take a very small risk of unjustly harming someone in order to save someone from an unjust harm.

There are at least two problems with using this response to defend Fabre's argument. First, if, as Fabre herself says, what we are talking about is how to treat non-combatants who *unjustifiably* contribute to unjust threats—who wrongly choose to contribute when they ought to refrain from contributing—invoking

30 Fabre, 'Guns, Food and Liability to Attack in War', 60.

31 Fabre, 'Guns, Food and Liability to Attack in War', 55.

probabilities doesn't help. That their contributing is unjustifiable means that the chance of contributing to unjust harm is not sufficiently small to make contributing permissible. And the reason why it is not permissible is precisely that the presumption against causing harm, even at the cost of failing to save, wins out in such a case. Moreover, as I argued in Chapter 3, when one is knowingly turning oneself into a threat, the threshold for a reasonable belief that the threat one poses is just is very high indeed. Below that threshold, one takes the sort of moral risk that Otsuka describes. And, as he argues, 'it is not unfair that if the person one endangers happens to be innocent, one is by virtue of engaging in such dangerous activity stripped of one's moral immunity from being killed'.[32]

6.5 Risks of Threatening, and Risks That One's Threat Is Unjust

When one *knows* that one is harming or contributing to a project that aims at harming, one can be liable to harm even if one is unsure about whether the threats to which one contributes are unjust. This is not a claim about shared intention—as I argued in Chapter 3 and in section 6.2.2, there can be liability in cases where a contributor to a lethal threat does not share a direct threat's lethal intent. Lending you my gun out of irritation, rather than because I want to see Victim dead, doesn't exempt me from liability.[33] Rather, the claim is that there's a morally relevant difference between risking that one will pose a threat, and risking that the threat that one knowingly poses is unjust. When it comes to a risk that one will pose a threat, there's a degree of risk that one can permissibly take without rendering oneself to defensive harm should it turn out that the risk eventuates in harm. Neighbour in *Light Switch* is not liable to harm because she reasonably believes that her actions do not pose a threat.

Things are different when a person knows that she poses a threat. The relevant reasonable belief in these cases is the belief that one lacks a reasonable opportunity to avoid posing this threat. The standard for reasonableness is very high in these cases, especially when one is intentionally turning oneself into a threat (and not merely allowing oneself to threaten). One must be responding to very good evidence if one is to evade moral responsibility for posing a threat in these circumstances.

[32] Michael Otsuka, 'Killing the Innocent in Self-Defense', *Philosophy and Public Affairs*, Vol. 23, No. 1 (1994), 74–94, at 91.

[33] Nor is it a claim that illicitly invokes collective responsibility. That an individual knowingly contributes to a project that aims at harming is a fact about *her*, and about what she, individually, is doing.

Non-combatants who knowingly contribute to the unjust side of a war *know* that they are contributing to threats. That's the point of the war effort. The risk that they take concerns not posing a threat, but rather the justness of the threats to which they knowingly contribute. Given this, their ignorance about the justness of the threats that they knowingly cause themselves to pose isn't sufficient to undermine their liability to defensive harm.

Recall Dignitary in *Hologram*. I argued that Dignitary counts as morally responsible for an unjust threat to Victim unless she has very good evidence that Victim intends to unjustly, non-defensively kill her, and that she therefore has no alternative to threatening Victim that is not unreasonably costly. I suggested that the same is true of Driver in *Mistaken Drive-By*. Even though he threatens only indirectly, he is a cause of what endangers Victim: the direct threat to Victim's life is causally downstream of Driver's actions. Both Dignitary and Driver know that they are threatening, but they believe that there is some chance that the harm they inflict will be just. Many non-combatants who knowingly contribute to their country's war effort are in this position.

Do non-combatants who contribute or have contributed to unjust wars fought by the sorts of countries in which we are interested here—the USA, Canada, Israel, and most European countries—typically have a reasonable belief that they lack a reasonable opportunity to avoid posing a threat? I think the answer to this question is no. To meet the reasonable belief standard that applies when one intentionally turns oneself into a cause of a threat, the non-combatants would need very good evidence that to do otherwise would be unreasonably costly for them, imposing costs beyond those which they are required to bear rather than endanger the people whom they are helping to harm. Unreasonable costs could include that if the war is not fought, those whom they are helping to harm will inflict serious and widespread unjust harms on innocent people. If a non-combatant has very good evidence that this is the case, then she might not be morally responsible for contributing to the war and therefore not liable to be killed.

But, I contend, many non-combatants do not have very good evidence that this is the case. Some non-combatants will believe that their war is unjust, and that they are not preventing widespread wrongdoing by engaging in it, but contribute to it nonetheless. Some will believe that they are preventing widespread wrongdoing, but on the basis of insufficient evidence. Many will not have thought much about the justness of the war at all. A consequence of the widespread acceptance of the principle of non-combatant immunity is that it undermines the moral pressure on non-combatants to think about the justness of their country's war, just as the putative independence of *jus in bello* from *jus ad bellum* discourages combatants from thinking about whether their war is just.

In addition, as with Driver in *Mistaken Drive-By*, even if a non-combatant does have sufficient evidence that she lacks a reasonable opportunity to avoid posing a threat, her belief might nonetheless turn out to be mistaken. If she is in fact contributing to unjust threats, it might be permissible for those whom she has unjustly endangered to use defensive force against her to avert the threat she poses, even though she is innocent. Our duty not to intentionally turn ourselves into causes of unjust harm requires us to bear serious costs to prevent those harms befalling our victims. (However, as I argue in Chapter 7, it's unlikely that such harming will be all-things-considered permissible in the case of non-combatants, since it will require that killing the non-combatant achieves sufficient good to outweigh the morally weighted collateral harm inflicted in killing her.)

If we are to resist the conclusion that non-combatants are morally responsible for the contributions they make to the war, we will have to show that they do not know that the activities in which they are engaged are dangerous. This might afford protection to some non-combatants, who are non-culpably ignorant of the fact that their actions contribute to lethal threats to innocent people. But it's not going to help those who know that they are making contributions to the war effort: those producing military equipment, designing or testing weapons, building military vehicles, or supplying other materials (including food and medical supplies) used to facilitate the military campaign. I suggest that these people also engage in a form of moral risk-taking when they knowingly contribute to the war effort, since in intentionally causing themselves to threaten, they take the gamble that those whom they threaten may be innocent, and that the harms they knowingly help inflict are therefore unjust.

Overall, then, the circumstances that Fabre describes—of contributing to an *ad bellum* unjust war that has acquired some *in bello* just causes—don't support her claim that non-combatants lack sufficient moral responsibility to be liable to defensive killing. When an enterprise is morally mixed and one cannot know whether one will be contributing to the right parts, one must prioritize not harming the innocent over aiding the innocent. Non-combatants who opt to contribute to wars without knowing whether they will be contributing to just or unjust threats cannot plead ignorance in order to escape liability.

6.6 Summary

I have considered a variety of attempts from contemporary authors to resist what seems to be a clear implication of liability-based accounts of defensive killing: that those who responsibly pose indirect threats are liable to be killed. Together these arguments represent the most common defences of the idea that non-combatants are not liable to be killed: the causal remoteness of the threats non-combatants pose, the comparative triviality of those threats, and the conditions of ignorance under which they are made. I suggested that none of these arguments is successful in showing that non-combatants retain immunity from defensive killing. I think, on the contrary, that non-combatants are often liable to such killings, and that this conclusion follows naturally for those who think that moral responsibility for an unjust threat renders a person liable to defensive harm. We ought to reject the idea that the Principle of Non-Combatant Immunity picks out any morally significant feature of non-combatants, and with it the idea that it is always morally impermissible for just combatants to attack non-combatants on the unjust side of the war.

This is in part because non-combatants knowingly turn themselves into threats by contributing to their country's war effort. When one knowingly poses a threat, one cannot escape liability simply because one is unsure or mistaken about the justness of the threat that one poses. Rather, a person who intentionally threatens escapes liability only if she has very good evidence that she lacks a reasonable opportunity to avoid posing that threat, or if it turns out that the threat she poses is not unjust. Most non-combatants who contribute to the unjust side of a war do not have very good evidence that they lack a reasonable opportunity to do otherwise, and thus can be liable to defensive harm in virtue of their contributions to unjust threats.

7

Non-combatant Immunity

I argued in Chapter 6 that non-combatants who responsibly contribute to unjust lethal threats in war render themselves liable to lethal defensive harm. But, as I have emphasized throughout, liability is distinct from all-things-considered permissibility. A person who is morally liable to harm may still enjoy moral immunity from harm, by which I mean that harming her—even if only to the extent that she is liable—would be all-things-considered impermissible.

In the first part of this chapter, I return to the rival accounts of narrow liability and broad liability that I introduced in Chapter 4, and explore the range of purposes for which a person who is morally responsible for an unjust threat may be harmed. I argue for the narrow view of liability, suggesting that a person can be liable only to harms that are a means of averting the particular threat(s) for which she is responsible. I suggest that harming a person to avert a threat for which she is not responsible makes exploitative use of her, and that a person who is liable to defensive harm is not thereby liable to exploitative harms. However, it can nonetheless be all-things-considered permissible to exploitatively harm a person who is liable to defensive harms, if the alternative is that serious harm befalls a wholly non-liable person.

I then explore the reasons why even a liable non-combatant might enjoy moral immunity from attack. I suggest, that contrary to what we might expect, the requirement that defensive force be necessary for averting or mitigating a threat provides only limited protection to non-combatants, even when combined with the narrow view of liability. This is because the macro-threats of an aggressive war make even a narrow view of liability fairly permissive when it comes to killing in war.

I argue that two main considerations prohibit attacking non-combatants. The first is what I call the identification problem—the difficulty of knowing which non-combatants have responsibly contributed to their country's unjust war. The second is the restriction on collaterally harming innocent people.

7.1 Broad Liability and Narrow Liability

7.1.1 Eliminative Harming and Exploitative Harming

In Chapter 4, I introduced the rival accounts of narrow liability and broad liability using *Alley*:

> *Alley*: Roof Shooter is shooting at Victim from the roof of a building, maliciously trying to kill him. In an independent (but simultaneous) attack, Better Shooter is shooting through a basement window at Victim. Victim can hide from Roof Shooter's bullets, but not from Better Shooter's. However, he can shoot Roof Shooter, and Roof Shooter's body will then fall from the roof and block Better Shooter's line of fire, saving Victim's life.[1]

According to the broad account of liability, once a person is liable to a defensive harm, she may be proportionately harmed to avert any unjust threat, not just the particular threat for which she is responsible. If this account is correct, Roof Shooter is liable to harm that averts the threat that Better Shooter poses.

The narrow account of liability, in contrast, holds that a person can be liable only to defensive harm that averts the particular threat for which she is responsible. If this account is correct, Roof Shooter is not liable to be harmed to avert Better Shooter's threat.

In my version of *Alley*, Roof Shooter poses a genuine threat to Victim. But in McMahan's original version, Roof Shooter is a merely apparent threat because Victim has had an opportunity to replace her bullets with blanks. Call this version *Apparent Alley*. Whilst Apparent Roof Shooter believes that she is threatening Victim's life, Victim knows that she poses no threat at all. McMahan wonders whether, in this case, Apparent Roof Shooter's culpable attempt would be sufficient to ground liability to defensive harm, such that Victim may kill her to avert the genuine threat posed by Better Shooter. And, despite sharing the intuition that killing Apparent Roof Shooter could be permissible, McMahan ultimately thinks that it is a mistake to sanction such a killing, since doing so will cast the net of liability implausibly wide.

> If [Victim's] choice is between killing Apparent [Roof Shooter] and allowing himself to be killed by [Better Shooter], it does not strike me as wrong to think that he would be justified in sacrificing Apparent [Roof Shooter] to save himself. It would be another matter, of

[1] I've adapted this from a set of cases in McMahan, 'Self-Defense and Culpability', *Law and Philosophy*, Vol. 24 (2005), 751–74, at 757.

course, for [Victim] to shield himself from [Better Shooter's] fire by killing a passerby who was telling outrageous lies to his wife on the cell phone. A principled line must be drawn between Apparent [Roof Shooter's] culpability and that of the mendacious husband. But I do not know where to draw it.[2]

The focus of McMahan's concern is thus somewhat different from our focus here. McMahan is wondering whether a mere attempt, absent the posing of an actual threat, could render a person liable to be killed by Victim. McMahan's reason for rejecting liability in such a case is that once we jettison the requirement that a person be morally responsible for an actual threat, we have no principled way of demarcating the relevant sources of responsibility. Any sort of responsible wrongdoing—such as lying to one's wife—could be a ground of liability to harm. Of course, killing a person because he is lying to his wife would be disproportionate. But McMahan is surely correct that this isn't the right sort of answer: the problem isn't that killing the husband is disproportionate to his wrongdoing, but that his wrongdoing is irrelevant to the threat to Victim's life.

In contrast, McMahan thinks that we do have principled grounds for identifying responsibility for posing a genuine threat as the ground of liability to defensive harm because 'if a person has culpably made it the case that either she or someone else must be harmed, then other things being equal (and subject to relevant restrictions such as proportionality) it is permissible as a matter of justice to ensure that she rather than anyone else is harmed'.[3]

But if this is the explanation of why posing a threat is an appropriate ground of liability, then it looks like McMahan must also think that killing Roof Shooter is impermissible in my version of *Alley*, when she poses a genuine threat. Roof Shooter has not made it the case that either she or Victim must be harmed, because Victim has ways to evade Roof Shooter's attack without harming her. It is *Better* Shooter who has made it the case that someone must be harmed—Roof Shooter merely provides by her presence a way for Victim to ensure that it is not Victim who is harmed.

McMahan's reluctance to endorse killing Apparent Roof Shooter comes, as I have described, from a kind of slippery slope concern. Once we grant that people who make no causal contribution to a threat can be liable to defensive harm, we have no way to restrict the relevant sources of responsibility that could ground such liability. The principled justification of fairly distributing an unavoidable harm to those who are responsible for it no longer applies. If it is to avoid the charge of arbitrariness, the expansion to mere attempters (but not to the lying husband) must be captured by some other moral principle.

[2] McMahan, 'Self-Defense and Culpability', 765.
[3] McMahan, 'Self-Defense and Culpability', 764.

The only plausible candidates for that role seem to be Apparent Roof Shooter's willingness to harm Victim or her intending to harm Victim. But McMahan is unpersuaded: 'what if Apparent [Roof Shooter] had made her attempt yesterday and now just happens to be passing through the alley at the right moment to be used as [Victim's] shield? Or what if the basis of her culpability is a similar attempt she made a year ago against a wholly different person? And so on.'[4] In such cases, it would still be true that Apparent Roof Shooter had been willing, or intending, to kill an innocent person. But there's something worrying about the idea that a person might be liable to defensive killing merely on the basis that she was willing or intending to perform an unjust killing at some point in the past.

I agree with McMahan that in *Apparent Alley*, Apparent Roof Shooter is not liable to be killed. Apparent Roof Shooter gets lucky in this case, since Victim knows that he does not pose a threat. The case is thus different to *Apparent Murderer* from Chapter 3:

Apparent Murderer: Enemy hates Victim and wants to kill him. He points what he mistakenly believes to be a loaded gun at Victim. Victim, thinking that the gun is loaded, believes that only by killing Enemy can he save his life.

In *Apparent Murderer*, Enemy culpably causes Victim to believe that killing Enemy is necessary to avert a threat that Enemy poses. I argued that responsibility for this kind of belief grounds liability to harm that Victim inflicts in the course of defending himself (although, on my view, harm directed at Enemy would not properly be described as defensive).

However, I suspect that responsibility for this sort of belief can ground only narrow liability—that is, Victim may harm Enemy only in ways that he thinks necessary to avert the particular threat he believes Enemy poses. This is because Enemy's liability comes from his moral responsibility for Victim's belief that he must kill Enemy to avert a threat to himself. But it's hard to see how Enemy could be morally responsible for making Victim think that he must kill Enemy to avert a threat posed by somebody *else*. In *Apparent Alley*, for example, Roof Shooter is not morally responsible for Victim's belief he can kill her to avert a threat from Better Shooter in any way that could ground liability to harm. Victim's belief is triggered simply by Roof Shooter's presence, not by her responsible behaviour. This is also true in *Alley*, where Roof Shooter poses a genuine threat.

In *Alley*, Victim knows that he can avoid any threat from Roof Shooter without harming her. Even though Roof Shooter poses a genuine threat, she will manage

[4] McMahan, 'Self-Defense and Culpability', 764.

only an attempt on Victim's life, just as Apparent Roof Shooter will manage only an attempt in McMahan's case. Nonetheless, I think Victim may treat Roof Shooter and Apparent Roof Shooter differently, and I suspect that the proportionate means account of liability does a better job than internalism of explaining why this is so.

An illuminating way of approaching this case is to ask whether it would be permissible for Victim to defend himself against Better Shooter in a way that unavoidably kills Roof Shooter as a side-effect. Would Victim be permitted to, say, throw a grenade at Better Shooter even if the ensuing explosion would also kill Roof Shooter? I think that the answer to this question is clearly 'yes'. Victim cannot be required to refrain from defending his life because his defence will harm someone else who culpably and lethally threatens him. But one may not, ordinarily, kill a non-liable person as a side-effect of saving one's own life. If so, the fact that Victim may kill Roof Shooter as a side-effect of saving his own life suggests that Roof Shooter is indeed liable to be killed.[5]

The internalist account of liability cannot explain this. Killing Roof Shooter is not a *necessary* means of averting the threat for which she is responsible. Victim has another, less harmful way to evade this threat, because he can hide from her bullets. Given this, the internalist account of liability that McMahan endorses cannot permit Victim to kill Roof Shooter in the side-effect case. This seems like a mistake to me. The proportionate means account of liability that I proposed in Chapter 4, however, can explain the permissibility of killing Roof Shooter as a side-effect. Roof Shooter is liable to harms that are a proportionate means of averting the threat that she poses. Killing her, even as a side-effect of throwing a grenade at someone else, is a proportionate means of stopping Roof Shooter from posing a threat to Victim. She is thus liable to such harms, since they avert the threat that she poses to Victim.

In order to know whether Roof Shooter's liability to defensive harm permits Victim to use her body in order to block Better Shooter's bullet, we need to know whether her liability to proportionate means of averting a threat also includes liability to be usefully harmed. Usually, when a person poses a threat,

[5] McMahan has suggested that non-combatants might sometimes render themselves liable to measures short of lethal attack, including being harmed as a side-effect. I don't think that this is true when they contribute to lethal threats because, as I have argued, I think that those who contribute to lethal threats are liable to lethal defence. But even if it were true with respect to non-combatants, it wouldn't work here because there are no relevant circumstances that could make Roof Shooter liable to be incidentally, but not intentionally, killed. If she's liable to be incidentally killed, it's because she's morally responsible for an unjust lethal threat. The only thing preventing McMahan from saying that she's liable to be intentionally, eliminatively killed is that such a killing isn't necessary, not any sort of mitigating factors about Roof Shooter's responsibility.

it is eliminative killing that is required to avert that threat. But as we saw in Chapter 6's discussion of the useful killing of non-combatants, it can sometimes be possible to opportunistically kill a person to avert a threat for which she is responsible. I suggested that when one opportunistically kills a person to avert threats for which she is responsible, such killings lack the feature that typically makes them so objectionable—namely, that one is using the person to make oneself better off. The exploitative aspect of these killings doesn't seem to obtain when one uses her only to prevent her earlier actions from making one worse off. But if Victim kills Roof Shooter in order to have her body block Better Shooter's bullets, he is using her to prevent *Better Shooter's* actions from making Victim worse off. He is therefore using Roof Shooter to make himself better off than he would have been in Roof Shooter's absence. Such use of Roof Shooter is exploitative by my lights.

So, I do not think that Roof Shooter is liable to be usefully killed. Does this mean that Roof Shooter is not liable to be killed at all in *Alley*? No. If Victim kills her, it's a proportionate means of averting a threat that Roof Shooter poses, and she's therefore liable to be defensively killed on even a narrow account of liability. (Again, internalists will not be able to make this move, since killing Roof Shooter is not necessary for averting the threat she poses.) What is at issue is whether the fact that Victim would be killing her in order to make use of her makes the killing all-things-considered impermissible. And I don't think it does. Victim faces a situation in which either a wholly non-liable person (Victim) will be non-defensively killed, or a person who is liable to eliminative, incidental, or merely opportunistic killing, but not to exploitative killing, will be killed. If Better Shooter succeeds in killing Victim, he very seriously wrongs him, since Victim is liable to no harm at all. But when a person is liable to be eliminatively killed, exploitatively killing her does not greatly wrong her. It wrongs her somewhat, but not enough to make it impermissible for Victim to kill her to avoid a much greater wrong to himself. The disparity between the morally weighted harm that Victim faces and the morally weighted harm that Roof Shooter faces is sufficiently great that killing Roof Shooter can meet a lesser-evil justification.

Note, then, that this argument will permit usefully harming a person only when she is *already* liable to harm that is a proportionate means of averting a threat, which is true only while she herself poses a threat. Imagine that Roof Shooter poses a genuine threat to Victim, but fails in her attempt to kill him and then gives up on her attempt—that is, she ceases to pose a threat. Then, 12 months later, Better Shooter tries to kill Victim and Roof Shooter is situated in such a way that Victim can use Roof Shooter's body to block Better Shooter's bullets. Killing Roof Shooter in this case will not be permitted by my account because, unlike in *Alley*, the *killing* of Roof Shooter will not also be a means of averting a threat. Roof Shooter herself poses no threat, and so killing her can't be a means of averting a threat—only Roof Shooter *herself* can be the means. Thus, if he kills her exploitatively, Victim will not be only mildly wronging her, inflicting a somewhat worse harm than that to which she is liable. Rather, he will be violating Roof Shooter's right not to be killed along with her right not to be used. Here, what Victim will do to Roof Shooter will be *worse* that what Better Shooter will do to Victim. Thus, there's no justification for doing it and it's impermissible.

7.1.2 Non-combatants and the Threats of War

This debate has implications for liability in war. However, as I will argue, these implications are not as significant at we might think. It's true that conventional accounts of killing in war hold that enemy combatants may be targeted at any time for any military purpose. But the claim of the narrow account is not that a just combatant may kill only to avert threats to herself, such that she may not kill a combatant without first establishing that he plans to kill her. Rather, a just combatant may kill an unjust combatant to prevent his posing any proportionate unjust threat to other people. Doing so still harms the unjust combatant only to avert the particular threats for which he is responsible. Since nearly all combatants pose threats of some sort (or plan to do so during the course of the war) and these usually are lethal threats, the narrow account will not generally constrain the killing of unjust combatants.

It might seem that the distinction is more important for non-combatants, if what I have said about non-combatant liability in Chapter 6 is true. The broad account will permit one to kill an otherwise liable non-combatant to avert any proportionate threat, whereas the narrow account will limit this to the averting of threats for which the non-combatant is responsible. But one of the characteristics of a war is that the specific micro-threats posed in combat are simply a means of bringing about the larger ends of the war. So, when unjust combatants fight, their offensives promote the macro-threat that justified the waging of a defensive war in the first place. A munitions worker who makes guns does not simply enable unjust combatants to endanger the lives of particular just combatants during a number of specific offensives. She also, in doing so, helps the unjust combatants further the unjust macro-threats that are the ends of their country's aggressive war. *These* threats are still current even when her own contributions to those threats lie in the past, and any particular offensives to which she contributed are over.

Once we take the broader threats of an unjust war into account, even a narrow account of liability is going to find people liable to be harmed for a wider range of purposes than we might expect. Consider the following case:

Munitions: At the beginning of the war, Worker worked in a factory making guns for the unjust side. Two years later, she has retired and no longer works in the factory. Just Combatant is trapped behind enemy lines. Whilst being pursued by enemy combatants, he grabs Worker to use as a human shield to save his own life.

Even if Worker did not make the particular guns that the enemy are using to threaten Just Combatant, the fact that she has made some guns that have been used to further the unjust war means that she has previously contributed to the on-going macro-threat of aggression. Even though killing her can't eliminate those previous contributions, this doesn't show that she's not liable to harms that frustrate the pursuit of the unjust war. Recall from Chapter 6 McMahan's claim that it is the importance of defeating the aggressive war that partly explains why even weakly responsible unjust combatants may be killed. If so, defeating the aggressive war should be no less important when it comes to the permissibility of harming liable non-combatants.

7.2 The Identification Problem

So why might a non-combatant who is liable to be killed nonetheless enjoy moral immunity from harm? I suggest that one reason for such immunity is the difficulty of knowing which non-combatants are liable to harm. When it comes to combatants, their locations and uniforms mark them out as belonging to their country's armed forces. Once we know that a person is a member of their country's armed forces, it seems that we can be confident that they contribute to their country's war effort. But there's no reliable way of identifying non-combatants who have responsibility contributed to unjust threats.

Seth Lazar argues that we cannot, in fact, have such confidence when it comes to identifying combatants who contribute to the war effort.[6] Lazar argues that, for example, many combatants never fire their weapons in combat. But Lazar operates with a much narrower conception of what it is to pose a threat than I do: he talks of those who 'play only a facilitating role', citing military mechanics and engineers as examples of people who do not, therefore, contribute much to the war effort. Lazar's arguments might be problematic for someone who endorses

[6] Lazar, 'The Responsibility Dilemma for Killing in War', 198.

a causal threshold for liability, or thinks that proportionality is about how much one contributes to a threat, not the magnitude of the threat to which one contributes. But I've argued that these positions are incorrect. Even if a soldier does not fire his weapon in a particular attack (or any attack), it does not follow that he makes no contribution to his country's war effort. A soldier's mere presence in a particular location can be a contribution to his country's war effort: setting up camp in a particular place can, for example, force the enemy to circumvent that camp through much more inhospitable or otherwise dangerous territory.

Moreover, since joining the military is an expression of one's willingness to pose a threat to enemy combatants, I think unjust combatants can be liable to be killed on grounds similar to those that render Enemy liable in *Apparent Murderer*. As I have argued, Enemy is liable to be killed even though he poses no threat at all, since his responsibility for Victim's belief that he poses a threat renders him liable to harm that Victim inflicts in the course of trying to defend himself. Unjust combatants pointing loaded guns at just combatants seem to me to render themselves similarly liable, even if they do not intend to fire those guns.[7]

But even if we know that, for example, 40 per cent of the population voted for a clearly war-mongering leader who is now pursuing an aggressive war, we have no way of knowing which particular individuals voted for that leader. Elections are anonymous. The identification problem will apply to various types of non-combatant contribution. In many cases, the efforts required to identify liable non-combatants will simply outweigh, in terms of military efficiency, any benefits that harming them might afford the just combatants. In the absence of uniforms or other identifiable symbols of the sort worn by combatants, ignorance about which non-combatants are liable to harm will result in its often being impermissible to inflict harm upon them.

7.3 The Isolation Problem

However, I think that it is restrictions on collateral damage that are likely to be the source of non-combatants' most significant moral protection from attack, making it impermissible to attack even those people whom one knows to be liable to defensive harm. The reasons for this are twofold. First, unlike combatants,

[7] Again, Lazar disagrees because he thinks that this argument only works insofar as the unjust combatants are culpable (or, I suppose, morally responsible) for making the just combatants believe that they pose a threat ('The Responsibility Dilemma for Killing in War', 192). I think they are so responsible, but I'll have to leave the issue of combatant responsibility for another day.

non-combatants are going to be living amongst other people, including people who are innocent with respect to the unjust war being waged by their country (all children, for example, will be so innocent on my view, since even those who contribute to the war effort will lack moral responsibility for doing so). It will often—perhaps usually—be very hard to target a non-combatant without causing collateral harm.

Second, the permissibility of collateral harm is determined by weighing the good that an attack achieves against the collateral harm caused. And, in order to be permissible, collateral harms must not only be proportionate to the good achieved, but also meet a lesser-evil standard. As I argued in Chapter 5, lesser-evil standards are sensitive to the prospect of success. This sets the bar for permissibility very high. Even if a particular non-combatant is liable to be killed in virtue of responsibly contributing to unjust lethal threats, it does not follow that killing her is likely achieve a sufficiently significant good to make it permissible to inflict the collateral harm that killing her will entail. Even when killing a responsible non-combatant is certain to achieve some good, it will normally be only a very small amount of good, and therefore it's still unlikely to be sufficient to meet a lesser-evil standard. Whilst this does not undermine the claim that the responsible non-combatant is liable to be killed, it will render it impermissible to attack her when doing so will cause even moderate harm to innocent people.

7.4 Summary

I have argued that we ought to favour the narrow account of liability to harm. Drawing on the distinction between merely opportunistic and exploitative harms that I outlined in Chapter 6, I argued that harming a person to avert a threat for which someone else is responsible, as Victim would do in *Alley*, exploits her. Even those who are liable to defensive harms are not thereby liable to exploitative harms. But, I also argued that exploitatively killing a person who is liable to defensive killing can be justified as a lesser evil. I also argued that adopting the narrow account of liability does not entail an especially restrictive view of the range of purposes for which a non-combatant may be harmed. However, the combined difficulties of identifying liable non-combatants and attacking them without causing collateral harm provides non-combatants with fairly widespread immunity from attack. But this immunity is based upon contingent features of the situation of a typical non-combatant. It is not grounded in any deep moral principle about the innocence—either material or moral—of non-combatants.

8

Implications and Objections

None of the strategies canvassed in Chapter 6 provides adequate support for the claim that non-combatants are not liable to be killed in war even if they knowingly contribute to the their country's war and that war is unjust. We ought to reject the idea that the Principle of Non-Combatant Immunity picks out any morally significant feature of non-combatants compared with combatants, and with it the idea that it is always morally impermissible for just combatants to attack non-combatants on the unjust side of the war. It may *often* be impermissible, but this impermissibility, when it arises, does not rest on features of the non-combatants themselves, but on contingent features about the difficulty of identifying liable non-combatants and harming them without causing collateral harm.

In this chapter, I anticipate what I'm sure is only a small sample of the objections likely to be raised against the argument I have put forward and the conclusions that I have drawn. I first consider and reject Noam Zohar's argument that reductivist individualist views like mine are effectively endorsing terrorism. I then consider the objection that my view would sanction the attacking of neutral medics assisting combatants on both sides of a conflict (I call this the Red Cross Objection, but here 'the Red Cross' really serves as a placeholder for anyone performing the kind of role under discussion). I argue that whilst this is an upshot of my view, it is not a reason to reject my view. I then consider an objection from Frances Kamm concerning the permissibility of a just combatant's killing any number of non-combatants to save his own life. Finally, I explore whether paying one's taxes might ground liability to harm.

8.1 Terrorism

Noam Zohar argues that, at first glance, what he calls extended accounts of self-defence (ESDs) look promising as accounts of the rules of war. ESDs are those accounts of self-defence like mine that permit the killing of innocent threats. Zohar claims that such accounts can explain why just combatants may kill unjust combatants, even though those unjust combatants do not act wrongly in fighting for their country.

Zohar's take on the moral equality of combatants—and on why this thesis is morally worrying—is somewhat idiosyncratic. The direction of most people's concern has been to show why it is that unjust combatants may kill just combatants: why those engaged in legitimate defence can be permissibly attacked by an unjustly invading force. Zohar approaches the problem in reverse. For him, what needs explaining is why just combatants have rights of defence against this unjust, invading force that is made of up what he takes to be morally innocent people. And he thinks that Judith Thomson's account of self-defence can explain these rights because, as I outlined in Chapter 2, Thomson does not require fault or even moral responsibility on the part of threat in order to deem that threat a legitimate defensive target.

Despite this apparent advantage of ESDs, Zohar argues that such accounts cannot support a second key tenet of the war ethic, namely a permission to kill even non-attacking members of the armed forces. Zohar claims that in order to cover all the permissible wartime targets, an account of self-defence would have to extend the range of legitimate targets to include soldiers not engaged in combat roles. But then the difficulty is that an ESD cannot restrict the range of legitimate targets to combatants alone. An account of self-defence that permits killing innocent threats—that does not require culpability or even agency in its targets of defence—will inadvertently render innocent non-combatants legitimate targets too.

> Under ESD, once killing in 'self-defence' has been permitted against the innocent and extended to enemy soldiers in general, a plausible case can be made for extending it to civilians as well ... We require a moral argument [for the wrongness of terrorism], but if ESD is correct, applying to innocent obstructors and hence to non-attacking soldiers, it seems to follow that siege and terrorism can in principle be justified by the same token. Since ESD allows killing innocent people insofar as they passively contribute to the threat against us, it can often plausibly apply to noncombatants as well—perhaps to the entire enemy population. If, then, we are to justify the war ethic in such a way that precludes terrorism and preserves noncombatant immunity, it cannot be by means of endorsing ESD.[1]

So, Zohar takes extended accounts of self-defence to be the most promising basis of a reductive individualist view of war, since these accounts can explain the permission to kill innocent unjust combatants. But they nonetheless fail as

[1] Zohar, 'Innocence and Complex Threats', 748.

comprehensive explanations of the rules of war. We should therefore reject the reductivist individualist view.

8.1.1 Combatant Equality

I think that Zohar is mistaken to claim that Thomson's account of self-defence supports the moral equality of combatants. Thomson argues that one may kill an innocent person in self-defence if, *and only if*, she will otherwise violate your right not to be killed, or some other comparable right. By virtue of violating your right not to be killed, the innocent threat loses her own right not to be killed. She thus has no right of counter-defence against you. It is therefore impossible, on Thomson's account of self-defence, to have mutual permissions of defence: in her view, defensive rights are necessarily asymmetric. So, if just combatant A is permitted to kill unjust combatant B even though B is an innocent threat, it must be because B will violate A's rights. But if this is true, B has no right not to be killed by A that he can lethally defend. So Thomson's view cannot support the moral equality of combatants.

But whilst this removes what Zohar identifies as the virtue of Thomson's account of self-defence, it doesn't undermine the plausibility of thinking that the rules of interpersonal morality underpin the rules of war. A proponent of an ESD need not accept Zohar's claim that many or all unjust combatants are morally innocent, and that a battle is thus best understood as two groups of innocent threats trying to kill each other. My account of self-defence also fails to support the mutual permission to kill between opposing combatants. On my view, a person may engage in self-defence only to avoid the infliction of harms that she has a right not to bear. But I share McMahan's view that the vast majority of combatants on the unjust side of a war are morally responsible for unjust threats, and are thus liable to defensive harms at the hands of just combatants. Its rejection of the moral equality thesis is, I think, one of the most plausible and attractive tenets of reductivist individualism.

8.1.2 Non-combatant Immunity

However, I think that the second strand of Zohar's argument is partly correct. As I have argued, those of us who think that the range of legitimate targets in self-defence extends to those who indirectly threaten cannot hold that only combatants are liable to attack in war. Lots of non-combatants will count as indirect threats in virtue of making the sorts of contribution that I detailed in Chapter 6. A person's contribution may be indirect, but this fact alone cannot grant her immunity when she is morally responsible for the threat that she poses. Notice, though, that Zohar himself says that 'condemnation of "terrorism" rightly emphasizes the killing of the innocent, for it is focused not on attacks against culpable civilians (such as the oft-mentioned prowar journalist or cabinet member) but on ordinary, random civilians'.[2] If this is indeed what marks out terrorism (or is at least what is to be condemned about terrorism), then my view does not endorse terrorism, or at least does not endorse what is typically wrongful about terrorism. *Innocent* indirect threats are not legitimate targets of defensive force. Killing randomly is also not sanctioned by my account, which discriminates between the liable and the non-liable. But my view does hold that non-combatants who are morally responsible for posing unjust, indirect threats are liable to proportionate defensive harm.

One might reply that terrorism is marked out not merely by its attacking of innocent non-combatants per se, but by the fact that the killings are terroristic—that is, intended to terrorize others. Such killings seem to make use of their victims in a particularly objectionable way. Samuel Scheffler, for example, argues that it is the multiple using of its victims to scare others that renders terrorism a particularly egregious violation of Kantian principles.[3]

I have argued that non-combatants can render themselves liable to be killed, and in Chapters 6 and 7 I indicated that those people who are liable to be defensively killed may be killed in ways that make use of them to avert threats for which they are responsible. I suggested that killing a person to avert a threat for which she is responsible is merely opportunistic, not exploitative. If Victim kills the person who throws the ringleader the knife in *Mob*, for example, he certainly uses the killing to scare other people. But he does not exploit the person he kills, nor does he wrong him in any other way.

If so, it does seem to me that non-combatants could, in principle, render themselves liable to killings of this sort. If this would be the only, or perhaps just the most efficient way, of saving the lives of innocent people on the just side of the war, it certainly isn't obvious that there is something intrinsically wrong with this kind of action compared to other forms of defence. Whether or not such a killing is an act of terrorism is unclear to me—the notion of terrorism has become so contested that even if we count such a killing as terrorism, I'm not sure what normative force attaches to that label. As I say, the killing does not strike me as impermissible, so if it is terroristic, this seems to be an argument that terrorism is not always wrong. That they might sometimes endorse terroristic killings will not, therefore, show that reductivism or extended accounts of self-defence are incorrect.

2 Zohar, 'Innocence and Complex Threats', 735.

3 Samuel Scheffler, 'Is Terrorism Morally Distinctive?', *Journal of Political Philosophy*, Vol. 14, No. 1 (2006), 1–17.

8.2 The Red Cross Objection

The Red Cross provide medical care to both just and unjust combatants alike, returning many of them to the battlefield where they continue to fight and kill. This means, in effect, that the medics of the Red Cross contribute to the unjust threats posed by unjust combatants in war. They presumably realize that they do so: they know that at least some of the unjust combatants whom they heal will be sent back to the front to fight. And members of the Red Cross act voluntarily—nobody is coerced into joining this sort of organization. It looks, then, as if Red Cross medics (and those performing similar roles in war) are morally responsible for unjust indirect lethal threats, and, according to my account, are therefore liable to defensive killing by just combatants. But, it has been suggested, this surely proves that my view is absurd, and quite possibly evil.[4]

I do not think that this conclusion is absurd (or evil). Consider *Rescue*:

> *Rescue*: Attacker breaks into Victim's house, and kills Victim's family. As he is trying to strangle Victim, Victim hits Attacker over the head, rendering him unconscious. Victim calls the emergency services, who dispatch both the police and an ambulance. The ambulance arrives first. Paramedic immediately starts trying to revive Attacker.

Assume that Victim correctly believes that if Paramedic revives Attacker, Attacker will continue in his attempt to murder Victim. Victim hastily tells Paramedic this. Now imagine that Paramedic replies, 'Oh yes. I assumed as much. But if I don't revive him now, he'll die.' Victim, in terror, asks whether Paramedic will restrain Attacker before waking him up, or help Victim to fend Attacker off once he resumes his attack. 'Oh no', replies Paramedic. 'I couldn't possibly do that. You see, I'm *neutral*. And, what's more, I swore an oath in medical school to do no harm. So, whilst you have my sympathy, I'm afraid you're on your own. And I'd grab something heavy if I were you, because I'm about to wake him up.'

Nobody would think Paramedic's response morally permissible. If she cannot (or will not) restrain Attacker, she may not wake him up if she knows that he will then try to kill Victim. If Paramedic has indeed sworn to do no harm, she must refrain from contributing to the unjust threat that Attacker will pose. The prohibition on causing harm trumps the prohibition on allowing harm. And the prohibition on causing unjust harm—which is what Attacker will inflict on Victim—certainly trumps rescuing someone from just harm, which is what Victim has inflicted upon Attacker. Paramedic's proclaimed neutrality, and her

[4] Thanks to Jimmy Lenman for the objection. Thanks to Rob Hopkins for the evaluation.

Hippocratic Oath, simply have no purchase in a case like this. If Paramedic tries to revive Attacker, I think that Victim may forcibly prevent her from doing so. By knowingly contributing to an unjust threat to his life, she renders herself liable to defensive force.

If I'm right that Paramedic may not treat Attacker because Attacker will then try to kill Victim, why is it absurd to think that the Red Cross may not treat unjust combatants who will then try to kill just combatants? Take two of the popular explanations of why the Red Cross are not liable to be killed. The first is that doctors have a duty to aid, and doing one's moral duty cannot render one liable to be killed.[5] The second is that the Red Cross provide only welfare support, not military support, and that this kind of support does not count as contributing to the war effort.[6] But these explanations pertain no less to Paramedic in *Rescue*, and they do not manage to exempt her from liability to defensive harm. I think that both these explanations fail to show that members of the Red Cross are not liable to be killed. As Fabre argues, doctors have at best a prima facie duty to heal the sick that is defeated by the duty not to cause unjust harm. One cannot, by promising, exempt oneself from the ordinary moral duties that apply to people in general, which include a duty,

> not to contribute to a wrongdoing unless one has a justification for doing so. The Hippocratic Oath arguably aims at providing just such a justification, but it must show that the doctor's professional obligation to her patient is weightier than her general duty not to enable the latter wrongfully to kill enemy combatants. It is not clear that it is .... Given that wrongfully failing to help is generally thought to be morally preferable to harming wrongfully and, I submit, to significant contributing to the imposition of a wrongful harm, there is a *prima facie* reason for thinking that she should not help him.[7]

Fabre seems to me correct that the Hippocratic Oath, like other professional obligations, does not trump one's general moral obligations in the sorts of case under discussion. This is why the paramedic in *Rescue* cannot invoke her Hippocratic Oath as a justification for reviving Attacker. It is also why a doctor

[5] McMahan makes use of this sort of idea with respect to a tactical bomber who will inflict collateral harms on innocent people ('The Basis of Moral Liability to Defensive Killing', 399). McMahan suggests that, in doing what he ought to do, the bomber forfeits none of his rights against attack, even though he inflicts unjust harms (hence the slogan 'justification defeats liability'). If one thinks that doctors have a duty to aid, one might think that their doing so cannot render them liable to attack. Frances Kamm considers this argument with respect to doctors who treat combatants, suggesting that 'if someone made the threat possible in virtue of carrying out a superior duty, his liability to harm might not increase—for example, if a doctor saves combatants, he makes possible the continuation of the war' (F. M. Kamm, 'Failures of Just War Theory: Terror, Harm, and Justice', *Ethics*, Vol. 114 (July 2004), 650–92, at 689).

[6] See e.g. Michael Walzer, *Just and Unjust Wars* (New York: Basic Books, 1977), 146.

[7] Fabre, 'Guns, Food and Liability to Attack in War', 54–5.

may not, for example, bring a patient with a dangerous communicable disease to a place where she might infect other people, even if that is the only place where her patient can be effectively treated. Her obligation not to expose others to harm outweighs her obligation to treat her patient (and this applies irrespective of whether the others whom she will expose are also her patients). If a doctor may not, in this case, treat a wholly innocent person who has no intention of wronging others in virtue of the fact that treating her will expose others to risks of serious harm, it seems to me pretty plausible that members of the Red Cross may not treat unjust combatants who intend to return to the battlefield to try to unjustly kill just combatants.

8.2.1 *Guns and Food*

What of the argument that welfare contributions, as opposed to military contributions, are not a relevant grounds for determining that a person poses a threat? We might think that there is some kind of intrinsic moral difference between supplying medical resources and supplying weapons: that medicine (or food) just isn't the *right sort of thing*—the right kind of contribution—to count as contributing to a lethal threat. This thought underpins Michael Walzer's claim that there is a morally significant difference between supplying the things that soldiers need as men, and supplying the things they need as soldiers.[8]

But it's not clear what this difference consists in. We might say that the food or medicine doesn't *cause* the threat. But nor does the gun cause the threat: it merely enables or facilitates it. As Fabre has argued, 'although it is true that, strictly speaking, it is the guns as used by combatants which kill, not their specialised rations or wound dressing, it is equally true that combatants are not able to kill if hunger or untreated wounds make it impossible for them to lift their arms and train those guns on the enemy. Generally, meeting combatants' material need for food, shelter, appropriate clothing, and medical care goes a long way toward enabling them to kill in war, even if the resources in question do not in themselves constitute a threat.'[9]

Compare *Gun* with *Food*:

Gun: Hunter knows that when Hooligan gets a new gun, he always tries it out by killing someone. Hooligan comes into Hunter's shop and tries to buy a new gun. If Hunter does not sell him the gun, Hooligan will not kill anyone.

[8] Walzer, *Just and Unjust Wars*, 146.
[9] Fabre, 'Guns, Food and Liability to Attack in War', 43–4.

Food: Grocer knows that when Hooligan eats Weetabix, he always kills someone afterwards. Hooligan comes in and tries to buy some Weetabix. If Grocer does not sell him the Weetabix, Hooligan will be too hungry to kill anyone.

If there is some intrinsic, morally significant difference between supplying food and supplying weapons, Hunter should be prohibited from supplying Hooligan with goods in *Gun*, but Grocer should be permitted to supply Hooligan with goods in *Food*. If supplying this necessary element of Hooligan's attack just isn't the right sort of contribution to matter, it's hard to see why Grocer ought not to give Hooligan the Weetabix. But it strikes me as impermissible for either Grocer or Hunter to sell their goods to Hooligan when they know that the result will be the infliction of unjust lethal harm on some innocent person. If so, pointing to the different nature of food compared to weapons can't be enough to sustain a moral difference between those supplying welfare goods and those supplying military goods.

As I have argued throughout, it is knowledge and foresight that grounds moral responsibility, not malicious or lethal intent. But since we can hold the (lack of) lethal intent constant across these types of contribution, intent cannot explain any alleged difference in the permissibility of each person's making their contribution. It seems to me, therefore, that there is no morally relevant difference between Hunter's and Grocer's positions with respect to the threat posed by Hooligan. I agree with Fabre that the putative distinction between welfare contributions and military contributions lacks moral significance. This distinction will not, therefore, explain the impermissibility of targeting those providing only welfare contributions.

8.2.2 *Neutrality*

What about the neutrality of the Red Cross: the fact that their members assist not only unjust but also just combatants? I suggested above that Paramedic ought *not* to be neutral between Victim and Attacker, because Attacker poses an unjust threat to Victim. Does this mean that the Red Cross ought not to be neutral between just and unjust combatants?

I think that the answer to this question is yes, but that this does not entail that the Red Cross may not assist unjust combatants. I think that it *is* permissible for the Red Cross to assist unjust combatants. But it is permissible if, *and only if*, the just combatants consent to their doing so.

Imagine a variation on *Rescue*, *Dangerous Rescue*:

Dangerous Rescue: Victim and Attacker are both badly injured. Attacker's accomplices are guarding the entrance to Victim's house, and will let Paramedic in only if she agrees to treat both Victim and Attacker.

It might well be in Victim's best interests to consent to Paramedic's treating both of them. And if he does consent, he thereby consents to the threat that she poses to him by treating Attacker. I have argued that a threat of harm is unjust if the target has a right not to bear the harm. And whilst one can come to lack rights by forfeiting them in the way that results in liability to harm, one can also come to lack rights by consenting to be treated in a particular way. When Victim consents to the threatening activities of Paramedic, the threat that Paramedic poses to Victim is not unjust. Therefore, treating Attacker under these circumstances does not render Paramedic liable to defensive killing.

Similarly, when just combatants *consent* to the activities of the Red Cross, they consent to the threats that the medics pose. Thus, the medics do not pose unjust threats in aiding the unjust combatants, and are not liable to defensive killing. But it is the consent, and not their neutrality or status as medics, that gives the Red Cross immunity from intentional attack.

Why would just combatants consent to the Red Cross's assisting unjust combatants? Well, presumably they would do so only if consenting is in their own interests. It would obviously be best for them if the Red Cross assisted only the just combatants. But the Red Cross cannot operate under these conditions, because it is presumably only when they treat both sides that combatants on both sides will refrain from attacking them. So, the just combatants have a choice between having the Red Cross help both sides, and having them help neither side. If they are made better off overall by having the Red Cross help both sides, they could rationally consent to the Red Cross's contributing to the threats posed by unjust combatants.

But we can imagine cases in which the just combatants are not made better off overall by the activities of the Red Cross. Perhaps the just combatants have plenty of medics of their own, and are thus unlikely to derive any great benefit from the presence of the Red Cross. The unjust side, however, might have comparatively few medics, and thus derive substantial benefit from the Red Cross's assistance. Under such circumstances, it seems irrational for the just combatants to agree to the Red Cross's intervention, because this intervention will make them worse off. If they do not consent to the Red Cross's activities, it seems to me that they are wronged by those activities, and that Red Cross medics are liable to attack if they try to help unjust combatants return to the battlefield where they will maim and kill just combatants, and frustrate the achievement of their just cause.

Why doesn't this argument also offer protection to other non-combatants who contribute to an unjust war, such as the munitions workers or scientists? I suggested in Chapter 6 that it might be in the just combatants' interests to agree not to target unjust non-combatants if this will stop their own non-combatants being targeted. But I said that this did not show that the unjust non-combatants were not liable to be killed. Rather, I said that it is an agreement to not inflict the harms to which the non-combatants are liable.

The difference arises because it will never be in the interests of those on the just side of a war to consent to unjust non-combatants posing threats in the first place. Such consent would be wholly irrational, because if the non-combatants do not supply the military with money, food, weapons, clothes, and the like, there can be no war at all (or at least, it will be a very short war). Thus, the unjust non-combatants will always fail the condition—which can be met by the Red Cross—that they pose unjust threats just in case the just combatants consent to their doing so. Any pragmatic agreement that just combatants make to refrain from attacking unjust non-combatants is made under duress, and is not, I contend, morally binding on the just combatants.

8.3 The Unlimited Casualties Objection

Frances Kamm has pressed the following objection against my view.[10] I say that munitions workers on the unjust side of the war are liable to be killed if they contribute to lethal threats. But this suggests that a just combatant is permitted to kill *any number* of munitions workers to save his own life, because if each worker is liable to be killed, killing him must be proportionate. And, I take it, the objection is that this seems bad. Surely a just combatant cannot kill any number of non-combatants to save his own life?

Although part of the force of Kamm's objection comes from the fact that she's hypothesizing the death of non-combatants to save the life of a combatant, we should remember that on the reductivist account that I am defending, the distinction between combatants and non-combatants is not morally significant. If Kamm's case is different from the observation that my account seemingly permits an innocent person to kill an unlimited number of responsible attackers to save her own life—something that is true of pretty much any non-consequentialist account of permissible defence—it must be because she is relying on an assumption that the non-combatants are merely minimally responsible attackers.

McMahan describes a similar problem in *Killing in War*. McMahan imagines that the enemy has unjustly imprisoned ten innocent civilians.[11] He suggests that it seems plausible that each military guard at the prison is liable to be killed

[10] At a seminar on Chapter 6 of this manuscript, Harvard University (May 2010).

[11] McMahan, *Killing in War*, 24. I also consider this case in Helen Frowe, 'Review of Jeff McMahan's *Killing in War*', *Journal of Moral Philosophy*, Vol. 10, No. 1 (2013), 112–15.

during an operation to free the civilians. If so, killing each guard in a bid to free the civilians must be proportionate. But what if (a) the guards are reluctant conscripts (let's assume this makes them only minimally morally responsible), and (b) to free the civilians, we will have to kill 500 guards? McMahan suggests that killing so many guards—especially reluctant conscripts—to free just ten people would in fact be *dis*proportionate. But how can this be? If each guard is liable to be killed, this means that killing him is proportionate. How, then, could increasing the number of liable guards make killing them *dis*proportionate? It doesn't look like this is possible. If killing 500 guards to rescue ten civilians is indeed disproportionate, we must conclude that none of the 500 were liable to be killed in the first place.

This is indeed McMahan's explanation of this puzzle: '[I]f this guard is one of five hundred, killing him would make only a small contribution to the release of the prisoners. The good that can be achieved by killing him alone is therefore insufficient for the harm he would thereby suffer to be narrowly proportionate—that is, proportionate in relation to his potential liability.'[12] Since killing him is disproportionate, the guard is not liable to be killed.

I don't think that invoking either proportionality or necessity solves this problem. I think that proportionality is judged by the magnitude of the threat to which a person contributes. If lethal force is a proportionate response to wrongful imprisonment—and let's assume it is—each guard is liable to lethal force. I don't think we should endorse the idea that committing wrongs as part of a large group can preclude one's being liable to defensive harm.

And, not only is killing each guard a means of averting the threat that he poses, it's also necessary for averting the threat that each poses. As I argued against Statman in Chapter 5, accounts of self-defence don't typically require us to make ourselves better off overall. A defensive harm counts as necessary if it averts the threat that a particular person poses even if other people will then go on to harm me. In Statman's multiple rape case, for example, the fact that three of the five men will carry out the rape even if the victim kills the other two doesn't in any way undermine either the liability of the two to defensive harm or the necessity of killing them in order to avert the threat that they pose.

So, we must find some other explanation of the wrongness of killing all the guards. I think the best explanation, open to both externalists and internalists, is going to be to reject the received wisdom that one may kill any number of responsible attackers to protect a good that ordinarily warrants lethal defence (although it might be interesting to consider how we think we should treat the 500 guards in

[12] McMahan, *Killing in War*, 24.

a case where the ten civilians are to be executed at dawn). Roughly, this explanation will have to hold that there comes a point at which the aggregate value of the lives of the attackers, even responsible attackers—at perhaps at some point even culpable attackers—is such that one cannot bring about their deaths.[13] The claim is not that such people are not liable to be killed, or that killing them is disproportionate. I think that the guards *are* liable to be killed: I think that the claims that I made about the single gang-member—that he would not be permitted to engage in counter-defence against Victim, and that he would have no justified complaint against being killed—apply equally to the prison guards. Killing the guards would not, I think, wrong *them*. If the just combatants attempted a rescue of the unjustly imprisoned civilians, I do not think that the guards would be permitted to engage in lethal counter-defence against them. But there are general moral reasons not to cause massive amounts of harm that apply even when those harms are directed at people who are liable to them. Killing 500 people to rescue ten from imprisonment seems to be a case in which those reasons obtain.

8.4 Taxation

I deny that there is a causal threshold for liability to defensive killing, such that one must make a significant contribution to an unjust threat if one is to be liable to defensive killing. But some people have objected that this means that taxpayers who finance an unjust war will be liable to attack on my view.

Some people have put the objection in the following way:

1. Lots of people pay tax
2. If everyone who pays tax is liable to defensive killing, lots of people will be liable to defensive killing
3. Therefore, taxation cannot be a basis of liability.

As it stands, this is rather unconvincing. Perhaps, though, people might be getting at a slightly different objection, namely that if I think that taxation can be a source of liability, then I can no longer claim to be supporting any kind of discrimination when it comes to killing in war. I'm just advocating what people call 'total war'. Of course, this isn't quite right. I'm explicitly discriminating between those people who are liable to be killed, and those who aren't. But certainly, my argument suggests that the class of those who are liable to be killed is much wider than generally believed—although, even if it includes those paying taxes, this

[13] As Victor Tadros once put it to me: 'At some point, you've got to admit that you're just not *that* important.'

group of people still excludes many people even amongst the working-age adult population. Those who are unemployed, too disabled to work, or very low-paid will not pay tax in many countries. Difficulties with identifying taxpayers and attacking them without collaterally harming non-liable people will still make attacking taxpayers generally impermissible, even if they are liable to attack.

I do not find the idea that taxation might be a source of liability to defensive harm as implausible as most people seem to. We are all familiar with the use of trade sanctions against certain countries. We do not think that companies ought to pour money into Zimbabwe when this money will be siphoned off by a malevolent government and used to perpetrate unjust harms against its people. The existence of these sanctions suggest that we recognize that funding states or groups that are in the business of killing, maiming, and oppressing people is morally wrong. The rise of ethical banking evidences similar concerns. People care about where their money is invested: they think they ought not to be contributing to companies connected to criminal or immoral activity. It is not a huge step to extend this concern to what our own government does with our money.

Of course, what *is* seen as a huge step is the claim that not only is it wrong to financially support the perpetration of unjust lethal harm, but that it is *so* wrong that those who lend this support are liable to be killed as a result. They might be liable to sanctions or fines. But surely they cannot be liable to physical attack.

I am not so sure about that. The members of the mob in *Hit* make only financial contributions to the threat to Victim's life, but it seems to me that they are nonetheless liable to defensive killing. Pointing to the nature of the contribution that one makes through taxation thus seems unlikely to show that taxation cannot ground liability to harm.

Whether paying taxes that contribute to an unjust war is a ground of liability depends upon whether, in paying one's taxes, one counts as intentionally contributing to an endeavour that aims at harming, and whether one has a reasonable opportunity to avoid so contributing. Taxes clearly contribute to a country's war effort. So, I don't think that taxpayers can evade liability by claiming ignorance about the fact that they contribute to threats. But perhaps the condition of having a reasonable opportunity to do otherwise will be more helpful.

8.4.1 Unreasonable Costs?

One argument for why taxation should not ground liability is that our whole infrastructure would collapse if we stopped paying taxes. After all, it's not only wars that are funded by our taxes. Our schools, transport system, and health system are also funded by our taxes. People would die if we stopped funding the

NHS. And so, we might think, we don't have a reasonable opportunity to avoid contributing to our unjust war via our taxes, because the cost of not paying those taxes would be so high.

I used to think that this was a good reply to the taxation question. The harm that would result if a substantial number of people simply stopped paying their taxes would be significant. Given my caveat that moral responsibility attaches only to those contributions to harms that we could reasonably have avoided making, perhaps those people who pay their taxes are exempt from liability on these grounds.

But on closer reflection, I'm not sure that this will suffice. For a start, the kind of scenario painted above—where we stop paying our taxes and society breaks down—is really very unlikely. In most Western democracies—which are the sorts of country in which I am interested here—governments are not likely to continue fighting a war if public resistance is such that, as a result of a refusal to pay taxes, basic services are threatened. Refusal to pay one's taxes not only exempts one from the moral liability to defensive harm that such contributions might ground. It can also help to prevent the infliction of unjust harms.

But even if we grant that serious harms would result from a refusal to pay taxes, it doesn't follow that citizens may choose instead to contribute to unjust wars. Consider a case from Frances Kamm, which we can call *Oops*.

> *Oops:* The government of a country engaged in an unjust war launch a missile towards their enemy's territory. The missile will hit a populated area. Whilst the missile is mid-air, the government suddenly realize that their war is unjust, and that the killings their missile will inflict are therefore unjust. The missile cannot be detonated mid-air. The only way to stop it from hitting the populated area is to redirect it onto their own territory, to where it will cause an equal amount of damage.[14]

Kamm thinks that the government ought to redirect the missile because the 'citizens of a country are liable for having risks and harms imposed on them in order that their country not be unjust.'[15] The costs of correcting the wrongs of a malfunctioning state—such as a state that has been waging an unjust war—should be borne by those who also benefit from and participate in that state.

McMahan puts forth a similar argument as a reply to the idea that if combatants refuse to fight in unjust wars, this will undermine the capabilities of their

[14] F. M. Kamm, 'Failures of Just War Theory: Terror, Harm, and Justice', *Ethics*, Vol. 114 (July 2004), 650–92, at 682.

[15] Kamm, 'Failures of Just War Theory', 682.

country's armed forces. This could hamper the state's ability to fight just defensive wars as well as unjust wars, and so endangers the legitimate interests of the state's citizens. But, McMahan says, this is not a good reason to permit combatants to fight in unjust wars.

> When the malfunctioning of political or military institutions that are fundamentally just results in unjust war, some people will have to suffer the costs of that malfunctioning. Who, as a matter of justice, ought they to be: those who are being unjustly warred against, or those whose institutions have gone off the rails? It seems that when an institution malfunctions in a harmful way, those who designed, direct, participate in, and normally benefit from it are liable to pay the costs. They are responsible for the functioning of the institution by virtue of having established and administered it as a means of furthering their purposes. It would be unjust if they were to impose the costs of its malfunctioning on others.[16]

It seems to me that these thoughts tell against the idea that pointing to how bad things would be for *us* if we were to stop paying our taxes can somehow show that our paying them cannot be a source of liability. In effect, continuing to pay our taxes when our country is engaged in an unjust war unfairly shifts the cost of our state's malfunction onto other people. Certainly, this seems like a *pro tanto* wrong. For it to be nonetheless permissible for individuals to continue to pay their tax, we would have to show that in ceasing to do so we would be allowing *so much* harm to people in our country (and perhaps in other places where we send foreign aid) that the citizens of the country that we are unjustly warring against are obliged to let us cause harm to them rather than allow those harms to come about. The disparity between these two harms would have to be great indeed to support the permissibility of contributing to the unjust war. Combined with the unlikelihood of our suffering these very great harms if we refuse to pay our taxes, I suspect that there are few, if any, wars in which this sort of argument could show that taxation is not a ground of liability.

It doesn't seem to be true that paying others to carry out unjust harms, rather than inflicting them oneself, exempts one from liability. Nor is it true that financial contributions to unjust harm are not the right sort of contributions to ground liability. And it's far from obvious that we can cite the costs to ourselves of not paying our taxes as justification for funding unjust wars. There may be other, better arguments than those I have considered here for the claim that taxation is not a ground of liability. But it does seem to me that the onus is on those who want to deny that knowingly financing unjust wars can ground liability to show why this is the case.

[16] *Killing in War*, 74.

8.5 Summary

Many people will be uncomfortable with the conclusions of this book. They might seem inhumane and pretty far removed from our ordinary conception of the rights and wrongs of war. But we should remember that what drives the reductive individualist project is a concern about unjust harm—harm to innocent people—and there's nothing inhumane about that. Taken seriously, though, this concern requires us to reject the very ingrained notion that the killing of a combatant is in some important way less bad or morally worrying than the killing of a non-combatant. Given our long-standing practice that non-combatants should be shielded from attack, we are not used to pitting the lives of combatants against the lives of non-combatants quite as explicitly as I have done here. We might accept that non-combatants can be collaterally harmed, but we usually do so only because we grant the importance of the mission—of the military objective that helps to win a war. We don't often do so because we grant the importance of the combatants themselves, thinking that they might be allowed to prefer their own survival to that of non-combatants, and, moreover, to kill non-combatants in defence of their own lives. But once we start thinking about the moral liability of individuals to defensive harm, we have to focus not on their status as combatants or non-combatants, but on whether they may be harmed in order to save innocent people from harm. And when one is weighing the lives of those who are acting in legitimate self-defence against those who are, at least in part, morally responsible for the threats against which those people are defending themselves, it is deeply plausible to think that the defenders should be permitted to avoid harm to themselves by harming those who have helped to put their lives at risk.

Bibliography

Larry Alexander, 'Self-Defence and the Killing of Non-Combatants: A Reply to Fullinwider', *Philosophy and Public Affairs*, Vol. 5, No. 4 (Summer 1976), 408–15.

Saba Bazargan, 'Complicitous Liability in War', *Philosophical Studies*, Vol. 165, No. 1 (2013), 177–95.

Nancy Ann Davis, 'Abortion and Self-Defense', *Philosophy and Public Affairs*, Vol. 13, No. 3 (1984), 175–207.

Cécile Fabre, 'Guns, Food and Liability to Attack in War', *Ethics*, Vol. 120 (October 2009), 36–63.

Helen Frowe, 'Non-Combatant Liability in War', in Helen Frowe and Gerald Lang (eds.), *How We Fight: Ethics in War* (Oxford: OUP, 2014), 172–187.

Helen Frowe, 'Judging Armed Humanitarian Intervention', in Don E. Schied (ed.), *The Ethics of Armed Humanitarian Intervention* (Cambridge: CUP, 2014), 93–110.

Helen Frowe, 'Review of Jeff McMahan's *Killing in War*', *Journal of Moral Philosophy*, Vol. 10, No. 1 (2013), 112–15.

Helen Frowe, *The Ethics of War and Peace: An Introduction* (London: Routledge, 2011).

Helen Frowe, 'Killing John to Save Mary: A Defence of the Moral Significance of the Distinction between Doing and Allowing', in Joseph Keim Campbell, Michael O'Rourke, and Harry S. Silverstein (eds.), *Action, Ethics, and Responsibility* (Cambridge, Mass.: The MIT Press, 2010), 47–66.

Helen Frowe, 'Equating Innocent Threats and Bystanders', *Journal of Applied Philosophy*, Vol. 15, No. 4 (2008), 283–4.

Robert Fullinwider, 'War and Innocence', *Philosophy and Public Affairs*, Vol. 5, No. 1 (Autumn 1975), 90–7.

Barbara Herman, *The Practice of Moral Judgement* (Cambridge, Mass.: Harvard University Press, 1993).

Thomas Hurka, 'Proportionality and the Morality of War', *Philosophy and Public Affairs*, Vol. 33, No. 1 (2005), 34–66.

Frances M. Kamm, 'Self-Defence, Resistance and Suicide: The Taliban Women', in Helen Frowe and Gerald Lang (eds.), *How We Fight: Ethics in War* (Oxford: OUP, 2014), 75–86.

Frances M. Kamm, 'Substitution, Subordination and Responsibility: A Reply to Scanlon, McMahan and Rosen', *Philosophy and Phenomenological Research*, Vol. 80, No. 3 (2010), 702–22.

Frances M. Kamm, *Creation and Abortion* (Oxford: OUP, 1993).

Whitely Kaufman, *Justified Killing: The Paradox of Self-Defence* (London: Rowman and Littlefield, 2009).

Whitely Kaufman, 'Torture and the "Distributive Justice" Theory of Self-Defense: An Assessment', *Ethics and International Affairs*, Vol. 22, No. 1 (Spring 2008), 93–115.

Christopher Kutz, 'The Difference Uniforms Make: Collective Violence in Criminal Law and War', *Philosophy and Public Affairs*, Vol. 33, No. 2 (2005), 148–80.

Gerald Lang, 'The Limits of Self-Defence', unpublished manuscript (2007).
Seth Lazar, 'The Moral Importance of Winning', unpublished manuscript (2010).
Seth Lazar, 'The Responsibility Dilemma for Killing in War: A Review Essay', *Philosophy and Public Affairs*, Vol. 38, No. 2 (2010), 180–213.
Jeff McMahan, *Killing in War* (Oxford: OUP, 2009).
Jeff McMahan, 'Killing in War: Reply to Walzer', *Philosophia*, Vol. 34 (2006), 47–51.
Jeff McMahan, 'The Moral Equality of Combatants', *Journal of Political Philosophy*, Vol. 14, No. 4 (2006), 377–93.
Jeff McMahan, 'The Basis of Moral Liability to Defensive Killing', *Philosophical Issues: Normativity*, Vol. 15 (2005), 387–405.
Jeff McMahan, 'Self-Defense and Culpability', *Law and Philosophy*, Vol. 24 (2005), 751–77.
Jeff McMahan, 'Just Cause for War', *Ethics and International Affairs*, Vol. 19, No. 3 (2005), 1–21.
Jeff McMahan, *The Ethics of Killing: Problems at the Margins of Life* (New York: OUP, 2002).
Jeff McMahan, 'What Rights may be Defended by Means of War?' in Seth Lazar and Cécile Fabre, *The Morality of Defensive War* (Oxford: OUP, 2014), 115–56.
Larry May, 'Killing Naked Soldiers: Distinguishing between Combatants and Noncombatants', *Ethics and International Affairs*, Vol. 19, No. 3 (2005), 39–53.
Richard Norman, *Ethics, Killing and War* (Cambridge: CUP, 1995).
Robert Nozick, *Anarchy, State and Utopia* (New York: Basic Books, 1974).
Michael Otsuka, 'Killing the Innocent in Self-Defense', *Philosophy and Public Affairs*, Vol. 23, No. 1 (1994), 74–94.
Jonathan Quong, 'Killing in Self-Defense', *Ethics*, Vol. 119, No. 3 (2009), 507–37.
Jonathan Quong and Joanna Firth, 'Necessity, Moral Liability and Defensive Harm', *Law and Philosophy*, Vol. 31 (2012), 673–701.
David Rodin, 'The Myth of National Self-Defence', in Cécile Fabre and Seth Lazar, *Justifying National Defence* (Oxford: OUP, 2014), 64–84.
David Rodin, 'Morality and Law in War', in Hew Strachan and Sibylle Scheipers (eds.), *The Changing Character of War* (Oxford: OUP, 2011), 446–65.
David Rodin, 'The Moral Inequality of Soldiers: Why *jus in bello* Asymmetry is Half Right', in David Rodin and Henry Shue (eds.), *Just and Unjust Warriors* (Oxford, OUP: 2008), 44–68.
David Rodin, *War and Self-Defense* (New York: OUP, 2002).
Cheyney Ryan, 'Self-Defense and the Obligations to Kill and Die', *Ethics and International Affairs*, Vol. 18, No. 1 (2004), 69–73.
Daniel Statman, 'On the Success Condition for Legitimate Self-Defence', *Ethics*, Vol. 118 (July 2008), 659–86.
Victor Tadros, *The Ends of Harm* (Oxford: OUP, 2010).
Victor Tadros, 'Orwell's Battle with Brittain: Vicarious Liability for Unjust Aggression', unpublished manuscript.
Judith Jarvis Thomson, 'Self-Defense', *Philosophy and Public Affairs*, Vol. 20, No. 4 (1991), 283–310.
Suzanne Uniacke, 'Self-Defence, Just War and a Reasonable Prospect of Success', in Helen Frowe and Gerald Lang (eds.), *How We Fight: Ethics in War* (Oxford: OUP, 2014).

Suzanne Uniacke, *Permissible Killing: The Self-Defence Justification of Homicide* (Cambridge: CUP, 1994).

UK Department of Defence, *The Manual of the Law of Armed Conflict* (London: MOD, 2004).

Peter Vallentyne, 'Defense of Self and Others against Culpable Rights Violators', (unpublished manuscript, 2013, available at time of going to press at <http://www2.bgsu.edu/departments/phil/conferences/selfdefense/>)

Michael Walzer, *Just and Unjust Wars* (New York: Basic Books, 1977).

Noam Zohar, 'Risking and Protecting Lives: Soldiers and Opposing Civilians', in Helen Frowe and Gerald Lang (eds.), *How We Fight: Ethics in War* (Oxford: OUP, 2014), 155–171.

Noam Zohar, 'Innocence and Complex Threats: Upholding the War Ethic and the Condemnation of Terrorism', *Ethics*, Vol. 114 (2004), 734–51.

Noam Zohar, 'Collective War and Individualist Ethics: Against the Conscription of "Self-Defense"', *Political Theory*, Vol. 21, No. 4 (1993), 606–22.

Index

actions 74–5, 96, 114, 134
  see also defensive action
Afghanistan 145
agency 47, 49–50, 53, 68, 74–5, 109–10, 199
  eliminative 70
  intervening 127, 132, 166–72
  minimal 168
  moral 183
  proximate 166–7
  rational 183
  remote 167, 169–70
  see also principles, of intervening agency
agential responsibility 74–5
  see also innocence, agential
aggregation 14, 129, 139–46, 160, 209
  interpersonal 140–1
  intrapersonal 140–1
aggressors 24, 42, 98, 109–10, 115, 117–18, 145
  culpable 12–13, 106–7, 110, 117, 179n24
  less than culpable 104–6, 115
  see also attackers; states; threats
aggression
  averting 160
  genocidal 126
  lesser 129
  political 13–14, 126, 129, 137–45, 160
Alcove (case) 52, 57–61
  see also Subway (cases)
Alexander, L. 166n7
Alley (case) 92–3, 118, 189–94, 197
  see also Apparent Alley
allowing 134
  oneself to threaten 74, 79–80, 84–7, 184
  see also doing and allowing distinction; harms, allowing
Angry Rape (case) 129–31, 133–5, 137–8
Apparent Alley (case) 189–91
Apparent Murderer (case) 85, 191, 196
Attack (case) 75
attacks
  conditional 131
  intentional 206
  on non-combatants 162–87
  unjust 157, 166–8
  see also threats
attackers 30n16, 107, 110, 113–14, 117–20, 145–6, 154
  culpable 1, 90, 106–7, 110, 117–20, 140, 146, 209
  harming 117–18
  innocent 1, 68
  liable 149
  multiple 111
  responsible 207–9
  unjust 97, 103
  see also threats
attempted murder 108
autonomy 141–2, 145
  political 142

Barrier (case) 50
Baseball (case) 36–7, 82
behaviour
  involuntary 3
  voluntary 3
beliefs 11, 74–6, 81–6, 100, 184–6, 191
  see also knowledge; mistakes
Bigger Alcove (case) 61–2
blame 74
bodies 67–9
Bomb (case) 135–6
Breakdown (case) 104, 110, 117, 120, 173
Bridge (case) 24, 30, 32–3, 42, 48, 50, 57–62, 64, 72, 78, 87
Busy Well (case) 68–9
bystanders 6–10, 21–46, 48–54, 56, 66, 68, 70, 125, 128, 131–2, 154, 160, 178–9, 190
  causal account of 7, 25–7, 42–3, 48
  culpable 26–7, 29–30
  definition of 22, 23, 25–6, 28–9, 31, 42–3
  exploiting 53, 64, 70, 179
  and harmful agency 46
  and indirect threats 32–3
  innocent 1, 26, 28, 31, 50, 131–2
  and innocent threats 49, 54
  as non-harmful 46
  and obstructors 24, 42–3
  and onlookers 31–2
  responsible 26–9, 45
  and threats 6–8, 21–30, 37–46, 63
  treated as a means 46
  see also killing, bystanders; Moral Equivalence Thesis

Careful Motorist (case) 82, 173
causes 23–9, 34, 36, 41–5, 74, 78, 80, 82, 86–7, 134, 204
  indirect lethal 7
  proximate 166–9
  remote 167, 171
  see also indirect causes

Choice (case) 146
claims 41
coercion 144, 171, 202
Coercion (case) 168–9, 171
collectivism 2, 123–4, 140–1, 143, 159
combatants 94, 127n10, 154, 159, 164–7, 169, 185, 195, 211–12
  contributions to war 165
  enemy 94, 159, 164, 169, 194–6, 199, 203
  frontline 167, 170
  identifying 195–6
  ignorance of 181
  in bello moral status of 124
  innocent 199–200
  just 15, 17, 124, 169, 181, 187, 194–6, 198–200, 202–7, 209
  liability to harm of 167
  moral equality of 181, 199–200
  and non-combatants 166–7, 169, 173–5, 185, 195–8, 206–7, 213
  moral responsibility of 173–4
  voluntary 154
  unjust 15, 124, 129, 173–4, 181, 194–6, 198–200, 202–6
community 128
compensation 92, 96, 102, 114–16
Conditional Force Argument 13–14, 124–130, 141–3
conscientious objectors 162n1
conscription 163n1
consequentialism 3
consent 1, 169, 205–7
contributions to war 164–5, 174–8, 181–8, 195–9, 204–7, 209–12
  causally remote 169
  material 164–5, 175, 181–2, 186, 194, 204–7
  from medics 202–7
  military 204–5
  past 177–9, 194
  political 164, 174, 196, 209–12
  strategic 164
  technological 164
  unjustifiable 183–4
  welfare 202–5
costs 76–84, 86, 102–5, 116, 132–3, 135–8, 153, 160, 172, 185–6
  of aiding 102
  collateral 146, 160
  lethal 76, 78–9, 82–4, 86
  of a malfunctioning state 212
  reasonable 77–8, 80, 86–7, 185
  of refusing to contribute to an unjust war 162, 210–12
counter-defence 12, 56, 70, 90, 92, 102–3, 107, 117–18, 120, 200, 209
  prohibitions on 115–16
culpability 81, 105, 167, 174, 189–91, 199, 201
  see also attackers, culpable; bystanders, culpable; obstructors, culpable; threats, culpable

Dangerous Rescue (case) 205–6
Davis, N. A. 55–6
Defence (case) 131–2
Defence Account of mediated harms 14, 129–32, 135–7, 160
defensive action 22, 33–6, 38, 44–5, 54, 99–101, 103, 109, 132, 145, 147
  see also actions; harms, defensive
defensive force *passim*
  see also force
Deflection (case) 131–2
Deliberate Trolley (case) 33–4
democracy 15–16, 144
desert 91, 106–7
deterrence 107
dictatorship 144–5, 158
Discovery (case) 34, 63–4, 72
Diversion (case) 50
doing and allowing distinction 11, 67, 79–80, 182–4
Draper, K. 115
Dresden 5
Drive-By (case) 80, 82, 172
Drowning Child (case) 29–30
duress 77–8, 80, 207
Duress (case) 77–8, 86
duties 30, 67–70, 82–4, 103, 135–6, 157, 159
  to act for the good of the community 157
  to aid 102, 203
  to allow citizens to defend themselves against unjust harm 159
  to avoid contributing to an endeavour that aims at unjust killing 84
  of care 128, 130, 138–9, 160
  not to cause unjust harm 203
  not to cause unnecessary harm 117–18, 203
  not to defensively kill 70
  to engage in self-defence 157
  not to harm 102, 105
  humanitarian 104–5
  not to indirectly endanger an innocent person 71
  not to kill 68, 70
  not to non-defensively kill 70–1
  to prevent harm 67
  and privileges 47
  to protect the community 157, 159
  to resort to war 147
  not to wrongfully harm 183

escalation problem 150–1
Existing Shield (case) 65–6
expected value problem 148–50

exploiting 56–8, 60, 71
externalism 12–13, 88–96, 99–103, 105–6, 119, 208
  backwards 12–13, 90, 93–4, 99–102, 105–6, 119
  and luck 95–6
  proportionate means 90, 105–6, 100, 114–20, 178–80, 191–3

Fabre, C. 16, 163, 175–7, 181–4, 186, 203–5
Factory (case) 136–7
facts 7
  moral 7
fallibility 107–8
  see also mistakes
First Timer (case) 148–9, 155
First World War 162–3n1
Firth, J. 12, 88n1, 89–90, 94–7, 99, 101–5
Flagpole (case) 65–6
Food (case) 205
force 97, 102–3, 118, 148, 150–2, 154, 158, 160, 173
  and aggregation 140
  conditional 124–6, 145
  eliminative 46, 54, 64, 89n2
  exploitative 54
  ineffective 97–8
  insufficient 99–102
  lethal 110–11, 117, 125, 127, 131, 139–40, 145, 160, 173, 177, 208
  lethal defensive 48, 76, 78, 85, 177
  levels of 150
  maximum 118
  necessity of using 64, 88n2, 91, 96–102, 104, 111–12
  non-exploitative 46
  and proportionality 64, 78, 92, 110, 127, 145, 149–55
  targets of 93, 167
  unjustified 155
  unlimited 118
  unnecessary 106–7, 111–12, 115–16
forfeiture 3, 12, 23, 56, 72, 79, 81, 83, 85–6, 94–6, 174
  see also rights
Fullinwider, R. 134, 166n7

Gewirth, A. 167–8
Goading (case) 168–9
goods 125, 128, 138, 144–5, 148, 151–2, 160–1, 197, 208
  military 204–5
  proportionate 136, 154–6
  welfare 204–5
Grenade (case) 38–9
guilt 42–3
Gun (case) 204–5

harms 12, 21, 34–5, 53, 67, 69, 73, 77–8, 85–6, 97, 109, 113, 124, 138, 144, 146, 161, 173, 177, 181–5
  allowing 67n37, 182–4, 202–3
  causing 24–5, 67n37, 80, 82, 128n11, 172, 182–4, 202–3, 212
  collateral 14–15, 17, 141, 145–7, 153–7, 159–61, 172, 179n24, 186, 188, 196–8, 203n5, 213
  defensive 11–12, 17, 72–120, 147, 149–50, 153–4, 162, 165–73, 175–7, 188–9, 200, 208
  deserved 91, 106
  eliminative 70, 189–94
  exploitative 9, 188–94, 197
  failed 150
  foreseen 14, 129–32, 137–9, 143, 145, 154, 160
  immunity from 188
  inadvertent 9
  instrumental 106, 119
  intentional 154
  just 185
  lethal 3, 7, 14, 69, 74, 117, 126, 128–9, 141, 160, 179n24, 183, 205
  liability to 3–4, 16–17, 72–120, 153–4, 162, 165–73, 175–8, 181–97
  magnitude of threatened 151
  mediated 14, 127, 129–38, 145, 149, 160
  moderate 140, 145
  morally-weighted 69–70, 117, 193
  necessary 88–9
  non-consensual 1, 21, 46
  non-defensive 9, 80, 107, 136, 151, 179n24, 191
  non-eliminative 67n37
  non-lethal 3
  to non-liable people 149, 153–6
  opportunistic 179–80
  permissibility of 1–2, 4, 6–8, 12, 16–17, 34, 44, 46, 67, 188
  physical 12, 109, 114
  potentially defensive 147–56
  proportionate 12, 113, 132, 153–6, 173, 189
  prospective 77
  saving others from 132
  serious 69–70, 85–6, 99, 109, 113, 125, 133, 152–3, 160, 179n24, 185, 204, 211
  unintended 14, 131, 160
  unjust 11, 16, 23, 70, 72, 83, 98, 114, 129, 159, 182–6, 203n5, 205, 210–11, 213
  unnecessary 89, 106–7, 111–12, 115–17, 156
  see also objectivism; Preventing Harms Account
harming 99–101, 155, 188
  deferred 108, 113–14
  eliminative 189–94
  as an end in itself 106
  exploitative 189–94
  knowingly 82
  impermissibly 89
  as a means 69, 90, 106, 135, 151–2
  refraining from 103–4
  as a side-effect 69, 89n2, 128, 130, 155–6, 191

harming (*Cont.*)
usefully 193
in war 93, 140
Hart, H. L. A. 42
Heavy Bridge (case) 35, 78
Helpless Trolley (case) 35, 40
Herald of Free Enterprise 24n6
Herman, B. 109
Hippocratic Oath 202–3
Hit (case) 175–7, 210
Hohfeld, W. N. 47
Hologram (case) 81–2, 84, 86–7, 182n27, 185
honour 12–13, 90, 101, 105, 109–15, 117–19
and proportionality 110–13
re-asserting 113–14
restoration of 114
House (case) 128
Human Shield (case) 51–3, 56–9, 62–3, 67–8
human shields 8, 37, 44–5, 51–2, 127n10, 195
humanitarian intervention 142
Hurka, T. 14–15, 93n10, 147–8, 150–1, 161
Hussein, S. 158

identification problem 188, 195–6, 198, 210
ignorance 5, 16, 74n3, 75, 82, 108n32, 174, 181–7, 196, 210
impossibility cases 12
indirect causes 36, 45, 74, 80, 84–6, 172
individualism 2, 139, 141, 147, 157–61, 162, 198
see also reductive individualism
ineffective defence 89, 97–8
innocence 8–9, **24–6**, 30, 40, 45, 50, 164, 197
agential 74
material 24–5, 28–9, 197
moral 25, 28, 43, 74, 197, 199
see also threats, innocent
innocents 1, 6, 9–10, 14–15, 37–40, 46–7, 51, 54–5, 69, 72, 79–80, 86, 94, 115, 145, 153–5, 160–1, 174–5, 177–8, 184–6, 188, 191, 197, 199–201, 203n5, 204–5, 207, 213
aiding 186
not harming 186
see also obstructors, innocent; threats, innocent
instrumentalism 88n1
see also internalism; liability
instrumentality 93
see also liability and instrumentality
insufficiency cases 12
insufficient defence 89–90, 99–102
intentionally failing 73, 75–6, 79–80, 82, 85–7, 162
intentions 74–7, 79, 82, 100, 134, 170, 184, 191, 204–5, 210
see also shared intention
interests 158
important 142
lesser 13–14, 125–7, 129–31, 139–41, 160
political 129–30, 143–4
vital 13–14, 125–7, 129–31, 138–40, 143, 160
internalism 11–13, 88–99, 101–6, 110, 114–19, 178–80, 191–3, 208
international law 164
intuitions 3–4, 13, 36, 38, 43–5, 60, 63, 66, 90, 92, 94, 103, 105–6, 108, 112, 115–16, 133, 135, 137, 175–6, 189
Iraq 158
Isolation Problem 181, 196–8, 210
Israeli-Palestinian conflict 164

jus ad bellum 13–15, 124, 142, 147–61, 182, 185–6
jus in bello 124, 182, 185–6
just cause 124–9, 141, 148, 151–2, 154, 160, 177, 180n25, 206
just war theory 15, 123, 164
traditional 2, 157–8
justice 142, 158, 190, 212
justifications 54, 80, 194, 203
for harming 89
honour-based 12–13, 90, 101, 105, 109–15, 117–18, 153, 179n24
Kantian 109–10
lesser evil 9–11, 15, 37, 67, 69–71, 78–9, 82, 84–5, 153–6, 160–1, 193, 197
and liability 203n5
punitive 106–9

Kamm, F. 17, 68–9, 131–2, 136n19, 140–1, 145, 198, 203n5, 207, 211
Kant, I. 109–10, 201
Kaufman, W. 30n16
killing 17, 64–6, 70–1, 80, 86, 97, 100, 113, 157, 171, 191, 194
avoiding 78–9
bystanders 21, 37, 44, 46, 49, 54, 66, 70
combatants 194, 213
defensive 16, 69, 72, 83, 111–12, 177–8, 180, 199–200, 206, 208
direct threats 37, 54
directly 130
eliminative 8, 54, 67, 180–1, 193
exploitative 8, 10, 51, 53–4, 56–7, 163, 178–9, 193–4, 197, 201
indirect 172, 177–80
indirect threats 72
innocents 178, 191, 200–1
innocent obstructors 57–8, 61, 70
innocent threats 21, **46–71**, 198–200
just combatants 199
as a means 51–3, 56, 58–9, 61–3
merely opportunistic 163, 179–81, 201
non-combatants 98, 162–3, 166n7, 172, 174, 180–1, 193, 198, 213

non-defensive 9, 69, 75, 79, 81–2, 86–7, 185, 193
opportunistic 178, 180, 193
Otsuka on 65–6
permissibility of 8, 37–8, 40, 44–5, 53–4, 56, 60–1, 103, 105, 108–11, 115, 162, 178, 181
privilege of 47
refraining from 102, 104, 116
responsibility for 68
retaliatory 182
to scare 178–80, 201
as a side-effect 136–7, 192
targets of 49–50, 167, 194
unjust 9, 81–2, 84, 87, 185, 191, 204
unnecessary 102, 104, 107, 117–18
useful 192–3
in war 15–17, 123, 194–5, 209–12
see also letting die
knowledge 76, 81–2, 84, 102, 171, 183–7, 195–6, 198, 202–3, 205
see also beliefs

Lang, G. 39
last resort 14, 151, 156
Late Rape (case) 108
Lazar, S. 125, 149n32, 195–6
legitimate authority 157–61
letting die 65–7, 71
liability 3, 10–12, 15–17, 72–87, 88–120, 162–87, 206, 212
to attack in war 159, 164–5, 167, 177, 181–7, 206–7, 209–13
backward looking accounts of 12–13, 73, 90, 93–4, 99–102, 105–6, 119
broad account of 17, 92–4, 180, 188–95
and causal proximity 166–70
and causal triviality 175–7, 187, 195–6
complicitous 171n14
to defensive harm 72–120, 153–4, 162, 165–73, 175–8, 181–97, 200–3, 206, 208–13
and desert 91, 106
externalist accounts of 88–96, 99–102, 105–6, 110, 114–15, 118–20, 178–80, 191–3, 208
to honour-defending harms 105
and instrumentality 88n1, 90
internalist accounts of 88–99, 101–6, 110, 114–19, 178–80, 191–3, 208
to be killed 16, 26, 28, 37, 76, 79–80, 83, 85, 91–3, 97–8, 102–6, 162–3, 167, 170–3, 175–7, 181–7, 189, 191–3, 195–6, 201–3, 206–10
and luck 94–6
to merely opportunistic killing 163
narrow account of 17, 92–4, 180, 188–95, 197
and necessity 11–12, 88–120, 177–80
non-combatant 162–87, 194–5, 198, 201–2, 206–7
to non-defensive harms 85, 98, 100, 105, 107–9, 115, 118, 154, 168–9, 180–1, 191–2, 195
and permissibility 188
pluralist accounts of 90, 102–5
and proportionality 118–19, 149–50, 173–5, 207–8
proportionate means account of 13, 90, 105–6, 110, 114–20, 178–80, 191–3
to punitive harm 90, 106–9
to unnecessary harms 115–16, 120
in war 194–5
see also compensation; harms, liability to
Light Switch (case) 74–5, 81–2, 184
Lucky Escape (case) 88, 91, 94, 97–8, 105, 108, 114–18, 120

Mad Wife (case) 134
Mafia (case) 36
Malicious Bridge (case) 25–30, 48, 78
Manual on the Law of Armed Conflict 164–5
maxims 109–10
McMahan, J. 14–16, 24, 26–8, 48, 53–4, 72, 74n3, 82, 83n9, 91, 93n10, 98, 115, 123–4, 139–40, 159, 161, 163, 189–92, 195, 200, 203n5, 207–8, 211–12
on non-combatant liability 172–81
on reasonable prospect of success 148, 150, 152n35, 155n38
means/ends distinction 106, 135, 151–3, 161
medical personnel 17, 198, 202–7
see also Red Cross objection
method 2–6
Meteor (case) 58, 62
Mistaken Bridge (case) 81, 84
Mistaken Drive-By (case) 84, 185–6
mistakes 80–7, 107–8, 186–7
epistemic 81, 83–7, 107–8
moral 81
Mob (case) 178–9, 201
Moral Equivalence Thesis (MET) 6, 21–2, 33, 37, 44–5, 46, 48–51, 53
moral luck 94–6
moral responsibility 1, 10, 15, 23, 26–9, 37, 40, 45, 49–50, **72–87**, 107, 115–16, 162–3, 166, 169–70, 183–9, 193, 195, 199, 211
for a belief 85, 191, 196
and children 197
collectivist view of 123, 147
Gewirth's view of 167–8
and ignorance 181–2
individualist view of 123–4
and knowledge 205
for mediated harms 131–3, 136
minimal 207–8
for participating in an unjust war 181

moral responsibility (*Cont.*)
for posing an unjust threat 73, 81–3, 86, 88–9, 91–6, 102, 104–5, 116, 119, 132, 153, 162, 166–7, 170, 172–82, 184–8, 190, 200–1, 213
and proportionality 173–5
sources of 174, 190
and threats 46–7, 49–50, 72–89, 91–6, 102, 104, 190
for unjust, indirect, lethal threats 202
for a war 167
moral rules 123, 139
morality 13–14, 138–40
interpersonal 124, 139–40, 200
and legality 6
Multiple Bridges (case) 35
Munitions (case) 195

Naughty Minister (case) 166–7
necessity 1, 11–17, 72, 93, 95, 98n19, 100, 102, 105, 111, 114–15, 142, 146, 168, 188, 192, 208
and honour 116–18
and indirect killing 177–80
and liability to defensive harm 88–120, 177–80, 208
and proportionality 118–19, 151–3
and reasonable prospect of success 151–3
see also force, necessary; unnecessary defence
neutrality 205–7
non-combatants 15–17, 91, 98, 127n10, 147, 153–4, 160, 162–198, 200–1
contributions to war 16, 162–5, 174–8, 181–8, 194–6, 198, 200, 203–7
ignorance of 181–4
immunity of 163–7, 169, 172–99, 206, 213
innocence of 164
innocent 129, 137, 147, 160, 181, 199, 201
intentions of 170–1
liability 162–88, 194–5, 198, 201–2, 206–7
moral responsibility of 16, 163, 173–4, 197, 200–1
and the threats of war 194–5
unjust 206–7
see also identification problem; liability, non-combatant
non-instrumentalism 88n1
see also externalism; liability
non-violent resistance 126–8
Norman, R. 34

objectivism 101
obligations 55, 64, 68–70, 85, 102, 136
to give someone medical treatment 203–4
see also duties
obstructors 8, 22, 24–27, 32–6, 43–4, 59
culpable 43, 48
innocent 8, 42, 48, 57–8, 61, 70, 199
villainous 42
Old Timer (case) 148–9, 155
onlookers 7, 31–2
Oops (case) 211
other-defence 1, 137, 140, 159
Otsuka, M. 6–8, 21, 23, 33, 37–40, 44, 46, 48–54, 64–7, 70–1, 81, 184
owning 59–63

pacifism 21
Paralysis (case) 32
Parry, J. 136
permissions 25
agent-relative 8, 54–6
to attack combatants 165
to attack non-combatants 162, 195–8
to break someone's leg 145–6
to contribute to war 184
to use defensive force 21, 47–8, 54, 70, 99, 106, 117, 119, 129–32, 137, 149, 153, 172, 186, 191, 200
to fail to rescue 132–3
to fight a war 147
to harm 34, 37, 41, 44, 68, 92, 94, 108–10, 117, 119, 153, 180, 188, 193–7
to harm bystanders 46
to harm in counter-defence 92, 103, 107
to kill 37–8, 40, 44–5, 47–8, 50, 53, 56, 60–1, 92, 94, 102, 105, 108–11, 113, 115, 117, 162, 177–9, 190–4, 198, 200
to kill bystanders 28, 46, 48–50, 53
to kill combatants 199
to kill innocent threats 46–71, 199
to kill non-combatants 172, 177–9, 198
to pay tax 212
to resist political aggression 126
of states 14, 126
to target non-combatants 164–5
philosophy 4–5
Pinch (case) 127, 129–30, 132–4, 140
Poison (case) 31
political aggression
see aggression
politics 157–61, 164
Preventing Harm Account of mediated harms 131–5
principles 3, 63n31, 176, 190
of intervening agency 166–8
of non-combatant immunity 163–6, 185, 187, 198
of self-defence 166n7
see also combatants, moral equality of; necessity; non-combatants, immunity
Private Trolley (case) 62
privileges 47

property 126
  see also owning; rights
proportionality 1, 10, 13–17, 28–9, 56, 69, 73, 76, **78**, 92, 98, 103, 105, 110–13, 115, 117–19, 125, 127, 137, 139–40, 142–5, 160–1, 172, 179, 190, 192, 194, 196–7, 201, 207–9
  and causal thresholds 175–7, 196
  jus ad bellum 14–15, 124–31, 152, 161
  and killing non-combatants 163, 172, 207
  and reasonable prospect of success 147–56, 161, 197
  and responsibility 173–5, 201, 207–9
  in war 93n10, 165, 179, 207
proportionate means account
  see externalism
Provocation (case) 167
punishment 74, 106–9, 112–13, 128
  corporal 107

Quong, J. 8–9, 12, 54, 56–63, 71, 88n1, 89–90, 94–7, 99, 101–5

Racist Ray Gun (case) 30
rape 99, 106–14, 125–6, 129–30, 133–4, 137–8, 145, 208
Rape (case) 99–102, 106–12, 114, 119, 133
Ray Gun (case) 22, 32, 51–3, 65–8, 71, 79, 83
reasonable prospect of success 14–15, 124, 147–61, 197
  and the legitimate authority condition 157–60
  reductivist account of 154, 156–7
  subsuming view of 148–51, 155–6, 161
reasonableness 73–87, 184–7, 210
Red Cross Objection 198, 202–7
reductive individualism 2, 4, 13, 15–16, 123–5, 139–43, 159, 161, 162, 198–200, 213
  and *jus ad bellum* 124, 147–56
reductivism 13–15, 93, 123, 125–6, 128–9, 140–3, 154, 156–61, 162, 198, 207
Rescue (case) 202–3, 205
rescuing 14, 30, 33n17, 55, 64, 66, 68–9, 71, 132–3, 135–6, 138, 160, 182, 202–3, 208–9
restoration 114
revisionism 2, 15, 143
right intention 142
rights 3, 12, 47–8, 70, 96, 159
  against having force inflicted upon one 118, 169, 203n5
  agency 94–6
  to be aided 102
  autonomy 143
  to commit the nation to war 157
  to compensation 92, 115
  of counter-defence 90, 96, 102–3, 117–18, 120, 200
  to defence 70, 115–16, 130, 149, 157, 159, 166n7, 199–200
  forfeiting 56, 79, 83–7, 96, 102–3, 119, 169, 174, 203n5, 206
  humanitarian 104
  infringements of 56, 70
  not to be killed 23, 48, 56, 70, 79, 81, 84, 94–6, 102–3, 174, 194, 200
  liberty 96
  over our bodies 57
  political 125, 143–5
  property 71
  not to suffer harm 70, 72, 84, 86–7, 91, 102, 200, 206
  not to be used 194
  violations of 8, 23, 47–8, 56, 70, 93n10, 136, 200
  to vote 125, 139, 144, 163n1
  waiving 56
  see also autonomy; owning
risks 84, 157, 159–60, 169, **183–7**, 211
  that one's threat is unjust 184–7
  of threatening 184–7
River (case) 133, 135
Rock (case) 145–6
Rodin, D. 13–14, 16, 24, 47n3, 48, 125–31, 138–40, 142–3, 160, 163, 166–71
rules
  governing killing in war 123, 162
  governing permissible killing 162
  governing resort to war 124
  of interpersonal morality 200
  of self-defence 123
  of war 198–200
Ryan, C. 168

sanctions 210
Scheffler, S. 201
Second World War 5, 124, 163n1, 164
self-defence 1–2, 5–6, 8–9, 19–120, 208, 213
  extended accounts of 198–200
  individual 125, 159
  legitimate targets in 200–1, 213
  personal 157
  and a reasonable prospect of success 147–56, 197
  Thomson's account of 8, 47–8, 199–200
  war and 4, 123–160
self-preservation 54
Selfish Bridge (case) 76–8, 80–1, 171
siege 199
shared intention 170–2, 184
Shields (cases) 38
  Attached 39
  Innocent 39
  Obstructing 38<Index2>
Shootout (case) 38–40

Snappy Bridge (case) 75, 78
sovereignty 13–14, 125–6, 141
Spacious Well (case) 64, 66, 71
Sprinkler (case) 100
states 2, 13–14, 123–8, 137–40, 144, 153–4, 157–60, 177, 210–12
aggressor 126–8, 130, 137–8, 145, 147, 158
malfunctioning 211–12
oppressive 145, 210
victim 127–8, 130, 137–8, 141–3, 146–7
Stationary Shield (case) 64, 66
Statman, D. 12, 90, 109–14, 208
status quo 41
Subway (cases) 52, 57
supererogation 136
Surgery (case) 134

Tadros, V. 9, 67–8, 71, 116n44, 135
Taliban 145
taxation 16–17, 164, 174, 209–12
terrorism 17, 198–202
Thomson, J. 6–8, 23–5, 27, 33, 42–3, 46–9, 52, 54, 70, 199–200
thought experiments 3–5
threats 6–7, 16–17, 21–45, 84, 108–9, 148, 152, 160, 179–80, 195, 199, 204, 206–7
agentially innocent 74
apparent 189
avoiding posing 73–87, 162, 184–6, 194
averting 89, 91–4, **97–102**, 104–6, 110–11, 114, 117–19, 147, 149–52, 154, 160–1, 163, 172–3, 177–81, 186, 188–9, 191–4, 197, 201, 208
avoiding 97
causal contributions to 36–7, 74, 78–9, 82, 86, 162, 174, 185, 190
causally proximate 167–9
causally remote 167, 187
conditional 131, 144
culpable 12, 30, 34, 36, 41, 47, 56, 63, 75, 96, 104, 106–7, 110, 191
currency of 30n16, 168–70, 178
direct 7, 9, 11, 22, 31–2, 36–7, 39–40, 43–5, 46, 54, **63–4**, 72, 74, **77–80**, 82, 84–7, 131, 162, 166n7, 170, 172, 184–5
direct innocent 82
direct lethal 7, 32, 43, 63–4, 78
harming 46
to one's honour 90, 109–15, 117–18
indirect 2, 7, 9–11, 16, 22, 31–2, 34, 36–8, 40, 43–5, 46, 54, 63, 72, 74, 76, **77–80**, 85–6, 147, 162, 172, 185–6, 200–1
indirect lethal 7, 10, 16, 32, 43, 45, 64, 76, 202
innocent 1, 6–11, 21–3, 25, 26n12, 29, 37–40, 42, **46–71**, 79, 81, 84, 147, 198–200
innocent direct threats 37, 40, 72, 75n5
innocent indirect threats 37, 71, 72, 147, 154, 201
just 182–3, 186
justifiable 41–2
lethal 11, 16, 22, 43, 48, 84, 92, 105, 107, 117, 176–7, 183, 186, 188, 191, 194, 197, 203–4, 207
macro- 17, 188, 194–5
magnitude of 78, 149, 151, 173, 177, 196, 208
micro- 194
mitigating 147, 172, 178–9, 188
morally responsible 10–12, 17, 23, 25, 29, 37, 46–7, **72–87**, 105, 174
nondefensive 79
non-moralized account of 40–3
and obstructors 22
permissibility of 43, 77
physical 13, 39n28, 90, 107, 112, 114, 119
serious 110
to a state 123–8
unjust 3–4, 9–12, 16–17, 72–5, 79, 81, 83–6, 88–9, 91–2, 95–6, 102, 105, 110, 115–16, 119, 162, 166–7, 169–70, 172–3, 176–7, 179–89, 194–5, 197, 202–3, 205–7
of war 194–5
wrongful 26–7, 177
see also attackers; bystanders and threats; indirect causes; obstructors
Tracks (case) 29, 31–3
Trolley (case) 23, 33, 60–2
trolley cases 9–10, 37–40, 43, 50, 58
trying 114

Uniacke, S. 15, 40–1, 99–100, 147, 156–61
Unjust Aggression (case) 97–8, 103–4
Unjust Poisoning (case) 98, 104
Unlimited Casualties Objection 205–7
unnecessary defence 12–13, 100, 112
value 55, 126, 128, 143, 160

voluntariness 3–4, 15, 23, 96, 154, 163, 169, 202
Walzer, M. 123n1, 204
wars 2, 4, 13–17, 153
aggressive 178, 182, 194–6
contributions to 162–5
defensive 13–14, 125, 146–7, 159, 182, 194, 212
ends of 182
just 158–9, 181, 212
just side of 207
mixed character of 182–4, 186
phases of 182
Second World 123–4
as *sui generis* 123, 140
total 209
unjust 2, 15, 151, 154, 157–60, 174, 180–2, 185–6, 195, 198, 201, 209, 211–12

unjust side of 162, 176, 185, 187, 195, 198, 200, 207
see also reductivism

Warsaw ghetto uprising 111
welfare 157, 203–4

Wickforss, Å. 89n2
wronging 4, 14, 56–7, 68, 72, 85, 87, 89, 96, 102, 111, 115, 117, 154, 180, 193–4, 201, 204, 206, 209

Zohar, N. 17, 41–2, 47n3, 127n10, 169n12, 198–201